THE AM

For Marjorie and John

THE AMERICAN PRESIDENTS

Heroic Leadership from Kennedy to Clinton

Jon Roper

Edinburgh University Press

© Jon Roper, 2000

Edinburgh University Press Ltd
22 George Square, Edinburgh

Typeset in 11pt Times
by Hewer Text Ltd, Edinburgh, and
printed and bound in Great Britain by
MPG Books Ltd, Bodmin

A CIP Record for this book is
available from the British Library

ISBN 0 7486 1226 2 (paperback)

Contents

Acknowledgements   vii

1. 'The Focus of the Anxious Crowd of the Age'   1
2. Circling the Wagons: The Frontier and American History   16
3. John F. Kennedy: Hero   41
4. Lyndon Johnson: Casualty of War   67
5. Richard Nixon: Heroic Failure   91
6. Gerald Ford and Jimmy Carter: Faith Healers   115
7. Ronald Reagan: Star   136
8. George Bush: Deputy   159
9. Bill Clinton: Survivor   182
10. All-American Heroes?   207

Bibliography   225
Index   237

Acknowledgements

I would like to thank my colleagues in the Department of American Studies at the University of Wales, Swansea, for creating and sustaining an amicable academic environment in which to work. In particular, I am indebted to two valued friends. Phil Melling, for more years than he – or I – may care to remember, has shared with me willingly his creative insights into contemporary American culture and society, and his sense of humour. Bill Ehrhart's equally honest and forthright intelligence has given me many important perspectives on the impact of the Vietnam war upon American political life. The concluding words of one of his books have become the epigraph for this work.

I am grateful to Richard Maidment for his encouragement, and to Spike Molineu at the University of Ohio, John Johnson at the University of Northern Iowa and Bill Atwill at the University of North Carolina, Wilmington, for inviting me to America to discuss there some of the themes that this book explores.

The US Information Agency helped to track down some important references, as did librarians on both sides of the Atlantic, but I owe special thanks to Georgina Murphy at the Connelly Library at LaSalle University, whose professional and prompt replies to requests for source material were much appreciated. I have benefited too from the help I have received from the staff at Edinburgh University Press who have been involved with this project from its commission to its publication, and who have made important contributions to the final result.

The greatest debts are the most personal. So thank you, Caitlin, Aisling and Jack, and thanks – and more – to Nicola.

'Didn't we think we bestrode the world. Didn't we have a lot to learn.'
(W. D. Ehrhart, *Ordinary Lives*)

CHAPTER ONE

'The Focus of the Anxious Crowd of the Age'

INTRODUCTION: THE PRESIDENT AS HERO

On the morning of 24 July 1963, four months before his assassination in Dallas, President John F. Kennedy was at the White House, meeting delegates to the 18th Annual American Legion 'Boys Nation'. Among his audience was Bill Clinton. His handshake with his hero, captured in what is now a famous photograph, resonates with symbolic significance. Kennedy and Clinton, connected in that timeless gesture, encapsulate the two major generational shifts in post-Second World War American politics: JFK, the first president to be born in the twentieth-century, and Bill Clinton, the first of the 'baby-boomers' to be elected chief executive. More than that, the two presidents are joined through the drama of two of the most important events in late twentieth century American political life. If the assassination of JFK shaped the contemporary consciousness, and conscience, of the nation, so too did his legacy in Southeast Asia – America's war in Vietnam. Kennedy, then, inspired by the challenges of cold war confrontation, attempted to define and to personify a style of presidential leadership in an image which his assassination would both crystallise and mythologically confirm in the popular mind: the president as all-American hero.

In 'Superman Comes to the Supermarket', his account of Kennedy's nomination for the presidency in 1960, Norman Mailer observed that

> simply, America was the land where people still believed in heroes: George Washington; Billy the Kid; Lincoln, Jefferson; Mark Twain, Jack London, Hemingway; Joe Louis, Dempsey, Gentleman Jim; America believed in athletes, rum-runners, aviators; even lovers, by the time Valentino died. It was a country which had grown by the leap of one hero past another . . .[1]

Mailer saw JFK's heroic potential. After the Eisenhower years, 'it was a hero America needed, a hero central to his time'. For 'only a hero can capture the secret imagination of a people, and so be good for the vitality of his nation'. Roosevelt, Churchill, Lenin and de Gaulle were heroes; so too Hitler, the 'hero as monster, embodying what had become the monstrous fantasy of a people'. And indeed, 'without . . . a hero the nation turns sluggish'.[2]

For Thomas Carlyle, in his nineteenth-century lecture *On Heroes*, 'in all epochs of the world's history, we shall find the Great Man to have been the indispensable saviour of his epoch; the lightning, without which the fuel never would have burnt'.[3] Kennedy's contemporaries cast him in this mould, connecting the image of the heroic leader with the prevailing national mood. Theodore Sorensen, the principal phrase-maker of the New Frontier, characterised the political and popular culture of the United States as one in which there was 'a craving for superheroes and father figures as strong among many Americans as it is among the citizens of any monarchy'. Moreover, he argued, it was 'the Kennedy Administration, with its high ideals and spirited approach [which] unintentionally raised expectations of the Presidency to a level that facilitated subsequent attempts to monopolise power in the White House'.[4] He is disingenuous in his use of the word 'unintentionally'. For Kennedy and his supporters consciously projected the president in the role of activist and heroic leader. Following his assassination, his political heirs, not least his brother Robert, and his admirers, among them Sorensen himself, carefully preserved and promoted that myth in the popular mind. According to William Manchester, therefore,

> the real Kennedy vanished on November 22nd 1963 . . . What the hero was and what he believed are submerged by the demands of those who mourn him. In myth he becomes what they want him to have been, and anyone who belittles this transformation has an imperfect understanding of how the emotions of an entire nation may be moved.[5]

He was the fourth twentieth-century president to die in office, and the fourth chief executive – after Lincoln, Garfield and McKinley – to be assassinated. During his funeral procession, the first such state event to be televised, a riderless horse led the way, the reversed boots in its stirrups symbolic of a fallen chieftain. Living in the shadow of JFK, his successors, from Lyndon Johnson through to Bill Clinton, would be unable to aspire to the idealised vision of leadership Kennedy-style.

And at the same time, they would have to confront the most complex part of their inheritance: the effect of the war in Vietnam on American politics, culture and society. The aftershocks of Vietnam, indeed, would continue to define the parameters within which their presidential leadership might be framed.

Americans who came of age in the 1930s and early 1940s knew no other president than Franklin Roosevelt (FDR). For many of them he was the model of a presidential hero: the leader who not only had defied the morale-sapping shock of economic depression, but had also been commander-in-chief as the nation faced both the forces of Japanese fanaticism and of German fascism. Following FDR, modern chief executives had to operate in a climate of cultural expectations moulded around the hope for similar inspirational leadership, even though the passing of the twenty-second amendment to the Constitution in 1951 meant that, limited to two terms in office, they would never emulate Roosevelt's tenure on the presidency.

So Roosevelt set a standard of modern presidential leadership. Yet cold war presidents soon acquired a new responsibility, unknown to FDR himself. As the 'leader of the free world', who had the ultimate decision-making power for the nation, and by extension, for the Western Alliance as well, since 1945 the president also has had the authority to make that most apocalyptic of decisions: whether to use nuclear weapons in time of war. Roosevelt himself did not have to make such a choice. Although he ordered the development of the atomic bomb, orchestrated in the Manhattan Project, he died just prior to its first successful testing in New Mexico. President Truman's decision to use the weapon against Japan was made at a time when the United States still had a monopoly on the technical know-how of its construction. But since 1949, when the Soviet Union developed its own nuclear capability, and until the ending of the cold war diffused international tensions, each president faced the possibility of conflict with another superpower possessing similar weaponry. In that sense it mattered crucially to Americans who they elected to be in charge of the nation's nuclear arsenal.

Roosevelt's immediate successors, Harry Truman and Dwight D. Eisenhower, between them clarified and solidified his legacy. The Truman doctrine and its accompanying definitions of America's role in international relations was a talisman, charting the course for cold war America's global strategy of containment. Eisenhower – the authentic and battle-hardened hero – then emerged as the popular leadership choice for the 1950s: the soldier-turned-statesman who would guide the nation through the initial challenges of the nuclear age and superpower confrontation. But as Mailer would write: 'in periods of dull anxiety, one is more likely to look for security than a dramatic confrontation, and Eisenhower could stand as a hero only for that large number of Americans who were most proud of their lack of imagination'.[6] Contrast Kennedy.

On 12 April 1965, in conversation with Arthur Schlesinger jr. the philosopher Isaiah Berlin described JFK.

> He was serious and glowed with a kind of electric energy; and a rather inspiring figure to work for – that I could perceive. And there was this mysterious charismatic quality, certainly . . . He was a natural leader, and absolutely serious, absolutely intent. There was something deeply concentrated and directed, fully under control. If ever there was a man who directed his own life in a conscious way, it was he – it seemed to me he didn't drift or float in any respect at all. Some kind of embodied will, you felt. This was really very impressive.[7]

The more so given that Berlin's opinion was informed by a meeting with the president at a dinner on the day when, it subsequently emerged, Kennedy had first learnt of Soviet nuclear missile installations in Cuba.

In 1965 too, as military intervention in Southeast Asia began to escalate, Alfred de Grazia described the American presidency as 'the focus of the anxious crowd of the age'.[8] During the cold war, confronted by a totalitarian threat, its ideological enemies led by dictators who themselves promoted the myth of heroic leadership – a Stalin or a Mao; a Khrushchev or a Ho Chi Minh – how might democratic America respond? Its own leaders had to be equal to the challenge. In an era of superpower rivalry, and against the background of possible nuclear confrontation, attention was fixed on the possibilities and potential of presidential leadership. As Alexis de Tocqueville had predicted over a century earlier,

> it is chiefly in its foreign relations that the executive finds occasion to exert its skill and its strength. If the existence of the Union were perpetually threatened, if its chief interests were in daily connection with those of other powerful nations, the executive government would assume an increased importance in proportion to the measures expected of it and to those which it would execute.[9]

So it proved.
For Walter Fisher,

presidential heroes need to be romantic figures, but they need to be more than that . . . To be an American hero, . . . one must also be visionary and mythic, a subject for folklore and legend. The American hero evokes the spirit of the American Dream, of the ways people and things are when the spirit of America transcends the moment, and her destiny is manifest. The American hero is the symbolic embodiment of this dream in a single person, most predominantly, in certain presidents.[10]

In these terms, the president as heroic leader must in some way connect a vision of the future with the mythic narratives of America's past. And yet each chief executive also comes to the office burdened with the knowledge that they will be judged against the standards set by those who have gone before. In this sense, Kennedy's image and style moulded the potential of the office for his successors, during the cold war and beyond it.

Kennedy did not simply shape the charismatic dimensions of his office as the cold war entered the televisual age. With a more self-conscious intent than either Roosevelt, Truman or Eisenhower, and through the dramatisation of a succession of challenges and crises, he personified to his contemporaries the idea of the heroic leader. Isaiah Berlin again testifies to this characterisation of JFK. 'When he talked about foreign policy, my impression was that he thought he was a duelist, with Khrushchev at the other end. There was a tremendous world duel carried on by these two gigantic figures . . . and this is what excited him. And he had a worthy opponent'.[11] Kennedy's assassination embedded such an image of him in the popular mind: an idea of the hero and an ideal of leadership that in its cold war context superseded the memory of FDR and in its turn now became a measure by which his successors might be assessed. But his was also an ambivalent legacy. For amongst the business left unfinished at his death was the issue of growing American involvement in Southeast Asia. America's war in Vietnam was a product of the activist foreign policy which was the defining characteristic of Kennedy's style of presidential leadership. It was also the outcome of a belief in containment: that America should confront communism as part of a comprehensive geopolitical strategy that defined the contemporary international order.

THE RHETORIC OF LEADERSHIP

In articulating the challenges facing the nation during the cold war, America's leaders shaped a persuasive rhetoric that aimed not simply to extol the values of democracy and point out the deficiencies of communism. Whatever their partisan allegiances, presidents – Democrat or Republican – shared a common language of commitment: emphasising the need for America to accept a self-assigned role of international leadership. This, indeed, was the nation's destiny. Compare, for example, the inaugural addresses of Truman in 1949 and Eisenhower in 1953. For these speeches, which gave each president the opportunity to express his political philosophy, vision, and sense of purpose, conjure the sentiment of the times.

Thus for Truman: 'each period of our national history has had its special challenges. Those that confront us now are as momentous as any in the past. Today marks the beginning not only of a new administration, but of a period that will be eventful, perhaps decisive, for us and for the world'. And for Eisenhower: 'the world and we have passed the midway point of a century of continuing challenge. We sense with all our faculties that forces of good and evil are massed and armed and opposed as rarely before in history'. Truman goes on explicitly to contrast the nation's democratic beliefs and 'that false philosophy' of communism. Eisenhower similarly continues by dramatising the nation's struggle in apocalyptic terms.

> Here, then, is joined no argument between slightly differing philosophies. This conflict strikes directly at the faith of our fathers and the lives of our sons. No principle or treasure that we hold, from the spiritual knowledge of our free schools and churches to the creative magic of free labor and capital, nothing lies safely beyond the reach of this struggle. Freedom is pitted against slavery; lightness against the dark.

For Truman, in 'this time of doubt', the rest of the world will 'look to the United States as never before for . . . wise leadership'. America must accept this: as Eisenhower says, 'destiny has laid upon our country the responsibility of the free world's leadership'.[12] Both presidents, therefore, present the struggle against communism as a battle which has to be both joined and won, with the United States leading the charge. But would faith in a providential destiny prove sufficient to the challenge? The language of containment may have been reassuring to those who were confident in the nation's capacity to prevail. From another perspective it begs a question. What if Karl Marx was right?

According to Marx, all societies, America included, were bound by the laws of historical determinism. They would be drawn inexorably towards a socialist future. The predictions – and indeed the predictability – of such an analysis may have offered its adherents a sense of security, bringing an ordered vision to an inchoate world. But this was a future that for Americans emphatically did not work. Faced with that nagging fear that communism was the wave of the future, the United States had to offer to itself and the world a competing historical narrative which could lead the nation towards a different destiny.

The political rhetoric of the 1950s' thus would emphasise American exceptionalism – the idea that the United States was unbound by any laws, sociological, psychological or physical, that might determine the fate of others. Moreover, to confound Marx's interpretation of the dynamics of history, America's own past was studied to endorse the nation's sense of itself as different. The construction of an 'idea of America' in terms of a belief in exceptionalism became the hallmark of the 1950s 'consensus school' of historiography. Such a sense of the unique depended, it was argued, upon the existence of a natural and enduring cultural cohesion which would enable the nation to triumph over the deterministic forces ranged against it, and to keep its historic rendezvous with destiny as the 'last best hope for mankind'. And this mythologised version of the nation's past would be conveniently mined for political rhetoric, not least by John Kennedy, who famously would exploit the seam connecting contemporary America and its historical experience of the frontier.

Americans, however, were not only afraid of communists. They were also scared of the atomic bomb (and naturally enough their fears would be further compounded and intensified when they discovered that there were communists who had the bomb). The anticipation of nuclear conflict as the potential outcome of cold war tensions also framed expectations of national leadership. This fear was compounded by recent memories of other events and their traumatic consequences. So, as William Graebner argues,

> Pearl Harbor, World War II, the Holocaust, the dropping of the atomic bomb, the cold war – produced a culture of profound contingency, in which virtually everything, one's employment, one's values, one's very life, seemed dependent on the vagaries of chance. The sense of contingency that hung over the forties, then, was more than the contingency of capitalism – more, that is, than worries about the state of the economy, inflation, the stability of the banks or the market.[13.]

In this catalogue of shocks, it was the atom bomb that detonated the way to anticipations of a high risk future. As the journalist Edward Murrow put it in 1945, 'seldom, if ever, has a war ended leaving the victors with such a sense of uncertainty and fear, with such a realization that the future is obscure and that survival is not assured'.[14] The cold war dramatised the threat of nuclear apocalypse, and in so doing created a new role for the president as the person who had ultimate control over the nation's fate in the event of such a confrontation.

Fear focused attention on the chief executive's abilities and responsibilities as national leader in a high-risk world. It mattered how successive presidents dealt with the communist threat and the culture of contingency ushered in by the nuclear age. Contemporary political rhetoric in turn emphasised the need for the nation to keep faith with a carefully contrived vision of its past. For if the idea of American exceptionalism affirmed the nation's sense of itself as both different from and superior to others, such a belief would be endorsed in historical accounts of those whose achievements had defined the character of its past.

Yet a history which celebrated America, and which was itself the product of the ideological tensions of the cold war, insofar as it was an artificial construction, and written for a political purpose, was to prove too brittle an artifice to sustain consensus once the war in Vietnam challenged its fundamental assumptions. The potential for its failure was rooted in its origins. Indeed the mood of the 1950s, as Tom Englehardt points out 'was not one of triumph, but of triumphalist despair'.[15] It was a time when, as David Caute observes, 'American liberalism had taken on the coloring of latent hysteria'. In such an atmosphere, the underlying message of consensus history implied two things. First, that anything outside the circumference of agreed ideas, ideals and values was a threat. So dissent would be marginalised, ignored, drowned in a silence of conformist sensibility. And when it did find an issue over which its voice could at last be heard – be that the cause of civil rights or opposition to the Vietnam war – rather than being accepted as legitimate protest within a liberal democracy, it became stereotyped as part of that subversive conspiracy that threatened the ideals of democracy itself. Second, the idea that America's exceptionalist mission was to act as a model and a beacon for the world which was, for Caute, 'particularly rooted in the liberal intelligentsia, . . . was not essentially economic, but rather cultural, idealistic, self righteous, moral'. It would be the liberal supporters of containment – John Kennedy and his advisers among them – moreover, 'who set the United States on the disastrously interventionist and egotistical course that culminated in the horror of the Vietnam war'.[16]

The president stood as the focal point in this 'age of anxiety', of 'hysteria' and 'crisis'. Supplied with the reassuring script of exceptionalist and celebratory history, successive chief executives could deliver panegyrics which emphasised triumphalism rather than despair. But America's war in Vietnam proved a turning point. For Lyndon Johnson and Richard Nixon in particular maintained a political discourse that, step by step, America's failure in Southeast Asia exposed as incredible. Under the pressure of attempting to reconcile the myths of celebratory history with the realities of the Vietnam experience, both presidents faced stresses which not only impacted upon their political abilities but also gave their critics opportunities to characterise them as psychologically damaged if not disturbed. One legacy of Vietnam was thus to expose the limitations of the president's ability to act successfully in the role of heroic leader. Prior to the war in Southeast Asia it had all been different. Then, the story of America's past was a proven quarry for the historians and the speechwriters who crafted the ideas and the rhetoric which sustained and inspired the nation during the cold war. Before, that is, America encountered Vietnam.

CONCLUSION: THE PAST AS PROLOGUE

In October 1952, the United States tested the first hydrogen bomb on the Pacific atoll of Eniwetok. As the author and painter Gilbert Wilson observed: 'only a century after Herman Melville wrote his great book our own American atomic engineers unwittingly selected almost the very spot in the broad Pacific . . . where the fictional *Pequod* was rammed and sunk by the White Whale'.[17] It was Melville, too, who had argued in *White Jacket* (1850) that America was to be 'the ark of the liberties of the world': a nineteenth-century invitation to accept the self-assigned responsibilities of a providential mission. Those consensus historians of the 1950s who endorsed Melville's view constructed – in the descriptive term coined by the French philosopher Jean-François Lyotard – a 'meta-narrative', seeking to explain and endorse America's past and present purpose. This was one strategy that enabled America to confront the contemporary dilemmas of faith and belief engendered by philosophical and scientific relativity: the intellectual basis for the bomb itself.

'Can a people "born equal" ever understand peoples elsewhere that have to become so? Can it ever understand itself?'[18] In 1955, Louis Hartz concluded his influential work of consensus history, *The Liberal Tradition in America*, with two questions that are as relevant to the United States at the end of the cold war as they were at its beginning. For America's conduct during that period of international tension suggests that it has problems not only in appreciating the force of revolutionary change in the world – from China to Cuba, from Vietnam to Iran, – but also in realising that the celebratory historical myths that it has taken to define its contemporary sense of national democratic purpose have distorted its perspective on foreign affairs, and hampered genuine domestic ideological debate.

America's belief in its exceptionalism is confirmed by a distinctive reading of its past. Chapter 2 thus further explores constructions of this 'idea of America' in the writings of the consensus school of American historiography. There were important nuances in the consensus approach to America's history, represented in the work of, among others, Richard Hofstadter, Daniel Boorstin and, notably, Louis Hartz. And yet, such cold war historiography generally was taken to endorse the celebratory version of America's past. The chapter concludes with a consideration of the central metaphor of the frontier as it has characterised America's sense of exceptionalism and mission. The significance of the frontier is linked with concepts of national identity and America's 'manifest destiny' through an interpretation of the changing historical images of the pioneer in the work of Hector St John de Crèvecœur and Frederick Jackson Turner.

This forms the prelude to a discussion of the political implications that lay behind the reworking of the historic myth of the frontier and its heroes in the era of John F. Kennedy's New Frontier: for it was his rhetoric, coupled with his desire to project himself as the nation's heroic leader, which encouraged America's course of international activism on the route towards its eventual denouement in Southeast Asia. Kennedy's approach to the ideological issues raised by the cold war are discussed in Chapter 3 in the context of his contemporary image, with an emphasis on the characterisations of those who, like Norman Mailer, saw him as the embodiment of a Nietzschean existential hero. Kennedy, though, did not define himself unencumbered by his understanding of America's past. And the activism of the New Frontier, his modernisation of the nation's historic sense of mission, led inexorably to active military intervention in Vietnam: the nation's 'mission impossible'.[19]

Lyndon Johnson (LBJ), like John F. Kennedy, believed in the heroic style (Chapter 4). He once argued, 'hero worship is a tremendous force in uplifting and strengthening. Humanity, let us have our heroes. Let us continue to believe that some have been truly great'.[20] Yet he could not project himself in the role of heroic leader while he sought initially to lay claim to the political constituency of his predecessor. For his achievements might be measured only in terms of his capacity to follow a course set by another. As Kennedy's executor, Johnson could not be chief executive in his own right. Only after his election in 1964 could he claim a popular mandate, but as his conduct of the Vietnam war created political divisions within the country and within his own party, he had to contend with those who maintained that the true heir of a Kennedy was one who at least bore the family name. LBJ was a casualty of war: a victim of the myth of JFK, and of the demand for heroic leadership which his predecessor had sought both to articulate and to supply.

Having discussed Johnson's presidency in the context of increasing disillusionment with his prosecution of the war in Vietnam, the book continues (Chapter 5) with a consideration of Richard Nixon, whose presidential career, like that of his immediate predecessor, ended in failure. Nixon, too, believed in the necessity for vigorous presidential leadership. In his memoirs, he recounted his assessment of American political life in 1972.

> I felt that . . . we were at a historical turning point. My reading of history taught me that when all leadership institutions of a nation became paralysed by self-doubt and second thoughts, that nation cannot any longer survive unless those institutions are either reformed, replaced or circumvented. In my second term I was prepared to adopt whichever of these three methods – or whichever combination of them – was necessary.[21]

It is a rare moment of self-revelation. For by opting almost exclusively for the third option – circumvention – Nixon opens the path to an inevitable outcome: Watergate.

Vietnam abroad and the Watergate scandal at home confirmed the collapse of the 'imperial presidency'. The Vietnamese defied and challenged the fundamental myths and beliefs wrapped up in 'the idea of America'. National identity and purpose, re-inforced by an acceptance of ideological unity, rested on the conviction that an exceptional destiny would not admit failure, still less defeat. That experience fractured America's political and cultural consensus, with aftershocks that continue to reverberate through the nation's democratic polity.

Nixon's two immediate successors, Gerald Ford and Jimmy Carter, both adopted different strategies of leadership (Chapter 6.) Gerald Ford, unelected to the office, became in effect the president as national physician: dedicated to restoring health to the body politic after the traumas of Vietnam and Watergate. Using language and metaphors that were reminiscent of Lincoln's rhetoric as he had begun to approach the task of reuniting the nation in the aftermath of the Civil War, Ford nevertheless consciously downplayed the image of the president as a heroic leader. Jimmy Carter too presented himself as an ordinary man who would do his best to deal with the extraordinary legacy he had inherited from his imperial predecessors. And yet ultimately he proved to be an analyst rather than a therapist: a president who articulated problems rather than framing solutions for a nation suffering the post-traumatic stress of its immediate past.

For J. G. A. Pocock,

> when the chosen people failed of their mission, they were by definition apostate, and the jeremiad note so recurrent in American history would be sounded again. It would call for the internal cleansing and regeneration of the 'city on a hill', since the politics of sectarian withdrawal and communal renewal form a standing alternative to those of millennial leadership . . .[22]

The experience of Vietnam quarrelled with America's sense of history and purpose. In the 1980s, however, during the presidency of Ronald Reagan, revisionist historical accounts of America's war in Southeast Asia attempted to overcome the limitations on overseas intervention-ism implied by the self-imposed construction of the 'Vietnam Syn-drome'. Chapter 7 thus continues with an analysis of the way in which Reagan dramatised his presidency as a morality play in which the simple and comforting nostrums of 1950s' consensualism suffused a rhetoric at once optimistic and inspirational. Reagan's approach was to attempt to bury memories of the recent past through repeated exhorta-tions to remember the mythic narratives of America's history that had, until Vietnam, served the nation so well.

If Reagan reinvented the rhetoric of celebratory history, and his presidency was a movie in which he was naturally the star, his successor was unable to emulate such style. In fighting against the 'wimp factor', however, George Bush (Chapter 8) attempted to define his popular image as heroic leader and indeed his presidency through his con-frontation with the Iraqi dictator, Saddam Hussein. The Gulf War in 1991 was also meant to complete Reagan's revisionist project: present-ing America's 'victory' as an atonement for the 'failure' that was Vietnam. And yet, as his re-election campaign faltered, Bush himself resurrected memories of the war in Southeast Asia in suggesting that his opponent's participation in anti-war demonstrations while a student overseas disqualified him from the presidency. Bill Clinton still defeated him. The 1992 campaign thus brought about a generational shift in American politics reminiscent of that which had occurred when Ken-nedy himself was elected in 1960. Chapter 9 evaluates Clinton's achievement and his presidency in terms of the way in which he proved able to confront and overcome a series of personal crises focused upon the issue of 'character', and culminating in the spectacle of the unsuccessful attempt to impeach him. His survival owed much to his ability to reinvent himself in office, to navigate among the shoals and eddies of America's fragmented social consensus in which multi-culturalism on the one hand and fundamentalism on the other had emerged as significant political forces.

In the concluding chapter, then, some connections are made between ideas of heroic leadership, the presidency, the ending of the cold war, and the ways in which interpretations of the past may be used to influence both present and future. Images of the president and the presidency in contemporary Hollywood movies are discussed. The legacy of John F. Kennedy and the continuing impact of Vietnam upon American politics, society and culture are emphasised. The enduring metaphor of the frontier is considered in contextualising American history. And the impact of the idea of heroic leadership on the presidency is explored, tracing its influence from JFK to Bill Clinton.

Throughout this book, the approach taken is based upon interdisciplinary analysis and the discussion is located within a distinctive cultural and historical perspective. In this respect, the work of the novelist Norman Mailer as a cultural commentator is central to the framework of the argument. During the second half of the twentieth century Mailer has placed himself at the heart of contemporary America's intellectual and cultural debates. So, to Robert Solotaroff, for example, 'for all his antics and controversies – perhaps in part because of them – Mailer, as much as any man in the country, occupies the kind of moralist-prophet role that Emerson, Thoreau, and Whitman did'.[23] When he has turned his attention to the presidency, or to such events as Vietnam, through journalism, essays and novels, he has proved himself both a provocative critic and a creative commentator.

Mailer too has had a particular and vicarious fascination for JFK as a character in his fiction. In *An American Dream* (1965), his hero is a contemporary of Kennedy's, first meeting him in November 1946, when they go on a double-date together. In *Harlot's Ghost* (1991), his narrator shares one of President Kennedy's mistresses. And if his identification with Kennedy is imagined in his novels, his connection with another president is reflected in the coincidence that his sixth wife, Barbara, dated Bill Clinton before he was married and became governor of Arkansas.[24]

What, then, did Kennedy say to Clinton, and other members of his group on that July day in 1963? Recalling his recent trip to Europe, the president remarked that he had been

> impressed once again by the strong feeling that most people have . . . that the United States stands for freedom, that the promises in the Constitution and the Declaration of Independence while they may not be fully achieved we are attempting to move to the best of our ability in that direction, that without the United States they would not be free and with the United States they are free, and it is the United States which stands on guard all the way from Berlin to Saigon.

The rhetorical priorities of cold war America are captured in that brief speech, as the president emphasises the nation's global commitment to contain communism, from the divided community of Germany, to the partitioned country of Vietnam. Kennedy also observed: 'we want to welcome you to the White House particularly because this belongs to all of you and because it is so intimately connected with the best in American history . . . all around you is the story of the United States and I think all of us have a pride in our country'.[25]

History as a celebration of America is a prism through which the nation has attempted to understand others even as it has tried to understand itself. The colonial past and the settlement of Puritan New England provided the historical quarry for the construction of the distinctive narrative, defining the American experience, and the nature of the nation's evangelical mission. The dynamic of political and territorial expansion was then dramatised on the changing national frontier. This history was important. JFK's presidential activism was framed in that sense of historical perspective and in response to the demand for heroic leadership during a critical period of the cold war. And so the story that leads to the New Frontier, and beyond to Vietnam, begins with a story about America itself.

NOTES

1. Mailer, 'Superman Comes to the Supermarket', p. 16.
2. Ibid. pp. 18–19.
3. Quoted in Cassirer, *The Myth of the State*, p. 281.
4. Sorensen, *Watchmen in the Night*, p. 142 and preface p. xv.
5. Manchester, *One Brief Shining Moment*, p. 276.
6. Mailer, 'Superman Comes to the Supermarket', p. 19.
7. Schlesinger, 'On JFK', p. 33.
8. De Grazia, 'The Myth of the President', p. 65.

9. Tocqueville, *Democracy in America*, vol. 1, p. 130.
10. Quoted in Combs, *The Reagan Range*, p. 10.
11. Schlesinger, 'On JFK', p. 34.
12. Truman, 'Inaugural Address', Thursday, 20 January 1949; Eisenhower, 'First Inaugural Address', Thursday 20 January 1953 (see Website: Presidential Inaugural Addresses).
13. Graebner, *The Age of Doubt*, p. 19.
14. Quoted in Winkler, *Life under a Cloud*, p. 29.
15. Engelhardt, *The End of Victory Culture*, p. 9.
16. Caute, *The Great Fear*, p. 21.
17. Quoted in Jungk, *Brighter than a Thousand Suns*, pp. 295–6. Wilson also observed that in *Moby Dick* Ahab described the whale in an image reminiscent of the symbol of the atom: 'O trebly hooped and welded hip of power!'.
18. Hartz, *The Liberal Tradition in America*, p. 309.
19. In *Mission Impossible*, first shown on US television in September 1966 when the war in Southeast Asia was at its height, a resourceful team of Americans managed each week to overcome successfully the odds apparently stacked against them. In Vietnam, life would not imitate this art.
20. Quoted in Kearns, *Lyndon Johnson and the American Dream*, p. 64.
21. Nixon, *Memoirs*, p. 763. See also Schlesinger, *The Imperial Presidency*, p. 421.
22. Pocock, *The Machiavellian Moment*, p. 543.
23. Solotaroff, *Down Mailer's Way*, p. viii.
24. See Manso, *Mailer*, p. 566. She remarks (p. 569) that she liked to 'attach myself to people who are on the move – exciting, interesting people like Bill Clinton back in Arkansas, who wasn't yet governor but who had terrific personality, charisma, and possibilities'.
25. *Public Papers of the Presidents: John F. Kennedy (1963)*, pp. 597–8.

CHAPTER TWO

Circling the Wagons:
The Frontier and American History

INTRODUCTION:
CREATING CONSENSUS IN AN 'AGE OF ANXIETY'

In 1948, Richard Hofstadter prefaced his book *The American Political Tradition* with a quotation from the novelist John Dos Passos: 'In times of change and danger when there is a quicksand of fear under men's reasoning, a sense of continuity with generations gone before can stretch like a lifeline across the scary present'.[1] What faced America at the time was not just a 'scary present', but also an uncertain future. As Arthur Schlesinger jr. put it in *The Vital Center* (1949), 'Western man in the middle of the twentieth century is tense, uncertain, adrift. We look upon our epoch as a time of troubles, an age of anxiety'.[2] Faced with the challenge from a totalitarianism of the left – the Soviet Union – and having just fought to help destroy a totalitarianism of the right – Nazi Germany – America's democratic values seemed perpetually under threat.

In this atmosphere, as Peter Novick suggests, ' "consensus" became the key word in postwar attempts to produce a new interpretive framework for American history, focusing attention on what had united Americans rather than what had divided them'.[3] American historical writing thus looked to continuity and consensus as abiding themes in the nation's past, affirming at the same time ideas of both American exceptionalism and American nationalism.

Within consensus historiography, however, there were important nuances of approach which suggest some inherent difficulties in such interpretations of America's past. These can be illustrated through a discussion of works by three of those whom Novick characterises as charter members of this school of American historical writing: Richard Hofstadter, Daniel Boorstin and Louis Hartz. Of the three, it is

Boorstin who provides the most celebratory version of consensus, in his book *The Genius of American Politics* (1953). Louis Hartz, on the other hand, in *The Liberal Tradition in America* (1955), points out some difficulties he sees in a nation where ideological unity precludes sensible political discussion. But it was Richard Hofstadter who in many ways set the tone for those who followed.

RICHARD HOFSTADTER: ESTABLISHING A POLITICAL TRADITION

The following studies in the ideology of American statesmanship have convinced me of the need for a reinterpretation of our political traditions which emphasizes the common climate of American opinion. The existence of such a climate of opinion has been much obscured by the tendency to place political conflict in the foreground of history.

The American Political Tradition signalled a clear departure from the progressive historiography of the early twentieth century. Hofstadter's new thesis implied that any divisions in American society obscure a fundamental political consensus. And in contemporary America, in Schlesinger's time of troubles and anxiety, that fact had to be recognised. The Depression, the New Deal, the Second World War and its aftermath were all historic dislocations that forced a reappraisal of attitudes towards traditional forms of economic organization and the nation's place in world affairs. At the same time, Hofstadter argued, there were still essential continuities that could be teased from the American political tradition.

Above and beyond temporary and local conflicts there has been a common ground, a unity of cultural and political tradition, upon which American civilization has stood. That culture has been intensely nationalistic and for the most part isolationist; it has been fiercely individualistic and capitalistic. In a corporate and consolidated society demanding international responsibility, cohesion, centralization, and planning, the traditional ground is shifting under our feet. It is imperative in a time of cultural crisis to gain fresh perspectives on the past.[4]

The context of consensus history is thus made clear. First there is the perception that America, in the post-war era, is facing new challenges. But more than that, the contemporary atmosphere is one of anxiety or crisis. In response to this, the nation must reflect upon its past: a past where, consensus historians suggested, political and ideological conflicts have been superficial, and where the dominant theme has been one of unity. It is that political tradition which might then be projected from the past to the present and on to the future: wagons should be circled against enemies, both external and internal.

How, then, did Hofstadter reconstruct America's political tradition? The book divides into historical halves, which in essence are almost mirror images of one another. Hofstadter starts with the founding fathers, political pragmatists in an 'age of realism'. In constructing the Constitution and the Bill of Rights, they established the foundations of America's republican polity. America's democratic mould is set then through the formative influences of two presidents, Jefferson and Jackson. Between them they establish the dominant theme in American democratic discussion: the problem of striking a balance between the right of the majority to rule, and the need to preserve the rights of the minority within a republican system of government.

John Calhoun is taken as the foremost critic of the American political tradition as it had emerged by Jackson's time. To Hofstadter he is the 'Marx of the master class', a pointed reference to contemporary times. For Calhoun's challenge to the orthodoxies of American political thought significantly failed. Calhoun, suggests Hofstadter, 'laid down an analysis of American politics and the sectional struggle which foreshadowed some of the seminal ideas of Marx's system'. He foresaw the potential for class conflict and revolution within the American political system, and proposed to forestall it through forging an alliance between the conservative slave-holders of the South and the conservative capitalists of the North. But such common cause was unnecessary. Hofstadter reaches the reassuring conclusion that 'Marx out of optimism and Calhoun out of pessimism both over-estimated the revolutionary capacities of the working class'.[5] The nineteenth-century intellectual challenge to the ideological foundations of the American political tradition fell away.

But there was conflict: Civil War. The first half of Hofstadter's book thus closes with two further biographical sketches: of Abraham Lincoln, the nineteenth-century model of heroic presidential leadership and of a voice of the nation's democratic conscience, the abolitionist Wendell Phillips, the 'patrician as agitator'. The Civil War is thus the watershed in the American political tradition. It is as if the nation pauses, draws breath and starts again. Hofstadter looks at the founding fathers of the new era: 'Spoilsmen in an age of cynicism'. These are the buccaneering capitalists and political manipulators of the 'gilded age' who set the tone of late nineteenth century American economic life.

And yet the essential continuities with the past were preserved. So there was always an echo of traditional democratic idealism. William Jennings Bryan, the standard bearer of the Democrats at the turn of the century, showed in his acceptance speech at the 1896 convention that 'after one hundred years of change in society the Jeffersonian-Jacksonian philosophy was intact'.[6]

In the presidencies of Theodore Roosevelt and Woodrow Wilson, however, Hofstadter sees the formative influences of the modern period. Roosevelt was the nation's lightning conductor.

> His psychological function was to relieve . . . anxieties with a burst of hectic action and to discharge . . . fears by scolding authoritatively the demons that aroused them. Hardened and trained by a long fight with his own insecurity, he was the master therapist of the middle class.[7]

Roosevelt demanded action: the progressive era saw the government beginning to expand both in its domestic and notably in its foreign purposes. Woodrow Wilson then refined both Roosevelt's message and his political approach. He endorsed Roosevelt's support for America's growing international pre-eminence. Whereas Roosevelt had assisted in the quest that had acquired an empire from Spain, however, Wilson's belief was in moral suasion: the imperialism of the 'idea of America' abroad.

After Roosevelt and Wilson, the nation faced its twentieth-century domestic challenge: an economic depression so profound it threatened to shatter the basis of the consensus which had been the hallmark of its political tradition. For Hofstadter, Herbert Hoover, the millionaire businessman-turned-politician, presided over the ending of an old political order: the political baton of the American tradition passed instead to the safe-keeping of his successor, Franklin Roosevelt. FDR, then, was the 'patrician as opportunist'. He capitalised upon crisis. Through his New Deal, and his unique achievement in winning four terms in the White House, he established himself as the major personality of mid-twentieth-century American politics.

Through these successive biographical vignettes, the American political tradition thus emerges largely by default. As Arthur Schlesinger observed in his review of Hofstadter's work, the book is more about the men who made it than the tradition itself.[8] Those who influence America's political tradition do so by redefining it through force of their personalities. It is significant, then, that Hofstadter defines his political tradition with a heavy emphasis on the contribution to it from presidents. From Jefferson onwards, he suggests, it is the chief executive whose leadership and style has affected the character of national politics.

DANIEL BOORSTIN:
CO-OPERATING WITH HISTORY

Consensus history would also help to preserve the reputations of those American historians facing determined anti-communist investigating committees within their own country. Daniel J. Boorstin was to become the distinguished librarian of Congress. In 1953, he appeared before the House Committee on Un-American Activities. According to Peter Novick, 'among historians [Boorstin] was the outstanding example of a co-operative witness'.[9] Boorstin, in addition to 'naming names', explained to the committee that although he had briefly been a member of the communist party, now the expression of his anti-communist feelings took two forms:

> First, the form of an affirmative participation in religious activities, because I think religion is a bulwark against Communism . . . The second form of my opposition has been an attempt to discover and explain to students, in my teaching and in my writing, the unique virtues of American democracy. I have done this partly in my Jefferson book, which, by the way, was bitterly attacked in the *Daily Worker* as something defending the ruling classes in America, and in a forthcoming book called *The Genius of American Politics*.[10]

Boorstin thus used his historiographical approach as an affirmation of his anti-communism.

The Genius of American Politics lies in the way in which it professes not to take an overtly ideological position, and relies instead upon the wisdoms of historical experience. Boorstin uses the nation's past to deny explicitly the contemporary relevance of ideological argument. Nor indeed is there any need to enter into an ideological debate with any proponents of communism, at home or abroad. So 'America's democracy is unique. It possesses a "genius" all its own'. Such 'genius' is 'the tutelary spirit assigned to our nation at birth and presiding over its destiny' or, more simply still, 'a characteristic disposition of our culture'.[11] This view of the nation's past is informed by a profound nostalgia: that Jefferson in 1776 had written America's democratic charter, and the founding fathers in 1787 had arranged things well. The subsequent task for Americans was to attempt to live up to the ideas and ideals bequeathed them by such political forebears.

Boorstin, too, is an advocate of the centrist path between the extremes of right and left. Americans can draw strength from the fact that 'we have become the exemplars of the continuity of history and of the fruits which come from cultivating institutions suited to a time and place, in continuity with the past'.[12] This organic and conservative approach to the development of the nation's political institutions is to be contrasted with the situation elsewhere in the world, and in particular in the old world, Europe. America indeed stands apart from European political traditions, and has avoided the contagions of extremist ideologies – fascism and communism – that see salvation in the centralised and omnipotent state.

Why has America not been drawn to such ideological extremism? For Boorstin it is a result of 'givenness', the 'belief that values in America are in some way or other automatically defined: *given* by certain facts of geography or history peculiar to us'. In effect, the idea of 'givenness', the unique contribution of the American environment in the shaping of the nation's political attitudes and institutions, and indeed the 'national character' itself, is a reworking of a familiar theme. As Boorstin acknowledges, 'it is surely no accident that the most influential, if not the only significant, general interpretation of our history has been that of Frederick Jackson Turner . . . He found the special virtues of our institutions and of our national character in the uniquely recurrent conditions of our frontier'. But the frontier closed at the end of the nineteenth century. Did this mean that 'the historical skill and poetic imagination of Frederick Jackson Turner then produced an interpretation that was more an autopsy than an anatomy of our institutions'? For if this was the case, the argument followed that 'Turner's famous lecture . . . was a declaration of the uniqueness of the American past. It was equally a prophecy of a lack of uniqueness in the American future'.[13] For America to retain its claim that its past had rendered it exceptional among nations, Turner's prophecy had to be proven to be mistaken.

'Even before the first World War, actually as early as the turn of the century, there were attempts to provide a philosophical substitute for the frontier'.[14] Now, after the Second World War, Boorstin advanced his idea of 'givenness' in an attempt to revitalise Turner's argument that environment had a crucial importance in explaining the nature of America's historical development. 'Givenness' had made ideological abstractions and theoretical models of an ideal society superfluous. Look what had happened to the Puritans – the one group of colonists who had come to America with a plan. They had moved from 'providence to pride': their original dogmas had been weakened by their encounter with the opportunities afforded them by the American environment. They had come to take the credit for their achievements, seduced by the generosity of their new-found surroundings in providing them with a lifestyle – spiritual and material – that in Europe they might only have imagined.

Even dislocations in American history had been more apparent than real. The War of Independence had been no revolution: it had been fought to conserve the rights which Americans had thought were their historical due. Similarly the Civil War was the result of different ideas as to the nature of America's constitutional settlement of 1787, rather than a clash of radical and opposed ideological persuasions. The hallmark of American political thought had been the breaking down and consequent rejection of dogmatic systems of belief, reflected in the mingling of the nation's religious and political attitudes. But therein lay a possible danger. Boorstin suggested that America might suffer from a form of 'cultural hypochondria': a suspicion that something was wrong simply because, in comparison with Europe, the nation appeared disinterested in ideological patterns of systematic thinking. Yet, instead, America should revel in its uniqueness, the continuity of its history and the ideological consensus that underpinned it. For that, indeed, was the genius of its politics.

Boorstin's book is celebratory of America's past. The War of Independence and the Civil War, both of which in other times, and indeed in other countries, might be seen as severe historical disruptions here are reworked in such a way as to become part of the seamless, if not the flawless, flow of America's history. And America's task is to go with that flow. In a pointed reference, contrasting the historical approaches of the United States and the Soviet Union, for example, Boorstin argues: 'we have already made a new society without a plan . . . why should *we* make a five-year plan for ourselves when God seems to have had a thousand-year plan ready-made for us?'[15] The echoes of cold war rhetoric reverberate throughout the work: a piece of historical advocacy that Boorstin indeed could draw to the attention of the House Committee on Un-American Activities with confidence that it both proved and improved his anti-communist credentials.

LOUIS HARTZ: QUARRELLING WITH HISTORY

Consensus history provided celebratory and self-satisfying images of the nation's past; and the sub-text of the denial of the significance of ideological argument was that America might thereby escape the threatening fate of a deterministic Marxist history. But did America's sense of its own past equip it to understand the history and the contemporary aspirations of others? In *The Liberal Tradition in America*, Louis Hartz added a powerful voice to the chorus of consensus history. Nevertheless, he pointed too to the problems that could arise from the aggressive maintenance of ideological unity in a world where American exceptionalism might render the nation not only unique but also an isolated actor in world affairs.

Unlike the celebratory images of the American past presented by Hofstadter and Boorstin, the 'idea of America' explored in Hartz's work *The Liberal Tradition in America* is the subject of a subtle critique. And the issue that concerns Hartz is the issue of ideology. Whereas other 'consensus' historians were content to explore those unique and exceptional conditions that might render ideological debate in America irrelevant, Hartz moves the problem of ideology to centre stage within the American political tradition. It is a problem, moreover, since America's unique ideological development has left it incapable of appreciating the force of ideologically inspired revolutionary change elsewhere. So Hartz, too, presents the central dilemma of consensus history: can American exceptionalism, even though it may protect the nation against the contagions of foreign – un-American – ideology – equip the United States for ideological confrontations in the cold war world? Where Boorstin, for example, had taken a neo-isolationist stance, arguing that America's unique democracy could not be replicated abroad, Hartz confronts the dilemma head on. Indeed, he sees internationalism as a force that could potentially break through the national cocoon of ideological security, and force the United States to engage in the political arguments which its liberal tradition had hitherto left untouched.

Hartz's thesis is that the unique circumstances of the founding of American society, and specifically the fact that there was no need to face there the inheritances of a European feudal past, has led to a narrowing of the ideological spectrum. Liberalism in America had been able either to absorb or to ignore challenges from the right (conservatism) or the left (socialism). This closing of the American ideological mind had been accompanied by the flowering of the American version of liberalism. Thus,

> one of the central characteristics of a nonfeudal society is that it lacks a genuine revolutionary tradition . . . And this being the case, it also lacks a

tradition of reaction . . . But the matter is curiously broader than this, for a society which begins with Locke, thus transforms him, stays with Locke, by virtue of an absolute and irrational attachment it develops for him, and becomes as indifferent to the challenge of socialism in the later era as it was unfamiliar with the heritage of feudalism in the earlier one. It has within it, as it were, a kind of self-completing mechanism, which insures the universality of the liberal idea'.[16]

Hartz does not celebrate this triumph of the liberal persuasion in capturing the American political mind. Rather, he sees the dangers that lie in national conformity to a particular and narrow ideological outlook.

Ironically, 'liberalism' is a stranger in the land of its greatest realization and fulfilment. But this is not all. Here is a doctrine which everywhere in the West has been a glorious symbol of individual liberty, yet in America its compulsive power has been so great that it has posed a threat to liberty itself . . . I believe that this is the basic ethical problem of a liberal society: not the danger of the majority which has been its conscious fear, but the danger of unanimity, which has slumbered unconsciously behind it.[17]

It is this inability to appreciate any political argument but that which is presented within the narrowed parameters of American liberal debate which makes the United States impervious to ideological criticisms from the right or the left, but at the same time vulnerable to over-reactions to perceived threats to its liberal way of life: and in particular the so-called 'redscare' of the 1950s.

The Liberal Tradition in America thus traces the political outcomes of the triumph of American liberalism in the absence of American feudalism. The War of Independence and the revolutionary period itself becomes a time of colonial separation rather than social or class upheaval.

Revolution . . . means to murder and create, but the American experience has been projected strangely in the realm of creation alone. The destruction of forests and Indian tribes – heroic, bloody, legendary as it was – cannot be compared with the destruction of a social order to which one belongs oneself.[18]

The founding period was followed, moreover, by the rapid triumph of the political norms of American liberal democracy, built upon the alliance forged between those of a Hamiltonian persuasion, who retained his 'grandiose capitalist dream', and those who believed in the 'Jeffersonian concept of equal opportunity'. 'The result was to electrify the democratic individual with a passion for great achievement and to produce a personality type that was neither Hamiltonian nor Jeffersonian but a strange mixture of them both.'[19] The capitalist American dream combined with the commitment to political equality, given substance in documents such as the Declaration of Independence itself, came to characterise the prevailing ethos of America's liberal community. Notably after the Civil War, when the 'feudal dream' of the South had collapsed under the weight of its internal ideological contradictions, there was no philosophical counterweight in American society to this aggressive combination of liberal democracy and capitalist enterprise.

The American democrat, whom Hartz characterises as a 'petit-bourgeois giant', 'because he had never contrasted his liberal creed with an opposing set of values, had never infected it with the European ethos of class and revolution'. So the American was 'impervious to that ethos when the disciples of Marx advanced it to him'.[20] The United States emerged into the twentieth century confirmed in its ideological commitment to the shared values of its liberal society. Attacks on its political consensus from the right – the Southern reactionary enlightenment – had been comprehensively beaten off through Civil War. Attacks from the socialist left were deemed to be irrelevant. And yet, that could not be the end of the matter. For the cold war was, at core, an ideological struggle. So could this unique liberal society, dominated by its attachment to a single ideological perspective, hope to compete on the world stage with another ideology – communism – which could present itself as more relevant to the aspirations of those nations not so fortunate as to have been 'born equal'?

Hartz argued this point in the context of McCarthyism: the reaction of American society to the perceived threat of communism which was directed at the heart of its liberal community in the 1950s. He wrote:

> the psychic heritage of a nation 'born equal' is, as we have abundantly seen, the death by atrophy of the philosophic impulse. And in a war of ideas this frame of mind has two automatic effects: it hampers creative action abroad by identifying the alien with the unintelligible, and it inspires hysteria at home by generating the anxiety that unintelligible things produce. The redscare, in other words, is not only our domestic problem: it is our international problem as well.

Hartz himself was optimistic. In confronting the challenges of the outside world, he believed that America might face up to the dangers of ideological conformity which afflicted its domestic democratic polity. Indeed, 'America must look to its contact with other nations to provide that spark of philosophy, that grain of relative insight that its own history has denied it'.[21] And yet, whatever the prospects for internationalism as the remedy for the parochialism of America's political ideas, Hartz's insight was to see the limitations of America's ideological approach to the cold war. Consensus, continuity, exceptionalism and the unique patterns of American political thought and development might not be the cause for celebration that others had made them.

In 1968, as the Vietnam war unravelled America's political consensus at home, Hartz testified before the Senate Committee on Foreign Relations, giving evidence on 'The Nature of Revolution'. There he explored in more detail some of the themes he had outlined in *The Liberal Tradition in America*. In particular, he argued that it was the American experience of migration, in effect the escape from feudal Europe, that had led it to avoid a genuine experience of social revolution, with inevitable consequences when it was forced to confront the reality of social change elsewhere. So 'American liberal culture was established by the Puritan migration of the 17th century, rather than by a social revolution, and this fact has made it difficult for us to understand the movement of social revolution abroad'. What migration to America and then across the American continent represents is the 'psychology of escape' which was 'America's substitute for the European psychology of social revolution'. Moreover, that escapist impulse 'not only projected our ancestors out of Europe but across the entire American continent also'.[22]

It was this act of escape that meant that the United States had avoided the ideological fragmentation of post-feudal Europe, and the class-consciousness which had inspired revolutionary movements elsewhere.

> Due to the fact that we established a certain way of life successfully in this country by leaving other ways of life behind in Europe, we have only had familiarity with this one way of life, which I have called liberal, Puritan, Jeffersonian, however you want to use these terms.

America had never had to confront the issues of ideological argument that had inspired modern European political debate. So the question remained: what happened when the United States no longer ran away from European battles, but turned instead to face the world it had left behind? Hartz argued that 'when a country has had experience only with a single way of life . . . and that country is thrown back into the world and has to deal with other people, the inevitable instinct of the country is to spread its way of life to others'. And yet, the fact remained that 'the basic migration, out of which this country arose, narrowed the vision of the country in some fundamental sense'.[23] America's desire to remake the world in its own image, while a natural consequence of the unique circumstances of its historical development, was nevertheless also the result of a profound lack of ideological imagination: an inability to appreciate that others might not share the 'first new nation's' political priorities.

As J. P. Diggins pointed out, Hartz 'remained deeply troubled by the thought that America's uniqueness cut it off from Europe and rendered American political thought all but useless to the Old World'. Moreover, his 'ultimate aim or hope was not to establish the depths of the liberal tradition but somehow to find a way out of it'. In 1955, he saw the prospect of American internationalism as forcing the nation to accept that its love affair with liberalism might have to end on the world stage of ideological confrontation: that the experience of political argument abroad with those of different political persuasions might spark the domestic debate over the meanings of American liberalism that had thus far been avoided. By 1968, testifying to the Senate, it appeared, however, that Hartz was even more convinced that America's historical experience persuaded it to avoid confrontation; seeking instead to convert the alien and the unintelligible rather than to co-exist with it. Thus, too, 'the theme of estrangement is the other and more disturbing side of the theme of exceptionalism. Hartz makes us aware that America's uniqueness is to be lamented and pondered rather than simply celebrated'.[24] By the mid-1950s, therefore, the simple celebratory versions of American history, and the encouragement to be derived in a threatening world from America's continuity and consensus, appeared to raise as many problems as they avoided. Hartz's work should be read more as critique than celebration, and his concern with the problems of ideological uniformity and conformity was shared by others. Indeed, it is a brief journey from Hartz's analysis of the historical impulses which influence the national political mind to the belief that contemporary America was characterised by increasing complacency and self-satisfaction. And the ultimate beneficiary of this increasing disillusionment with the political conformity hitherto celebrated by consensus history was to be the new idol of the intellectuals, JFK. Yet at the same time, Kennedy's rhetoric would derive its appeal from the use it made of an image of

America's past that for many defined the nation's exceptional and separate destiny: the frontier.

CREATING AN AMERICAN ADAM:
REGENERATION AND THE FRONTIER

The celebratory history of America sees the new world as a place of unique opportunity, where European immigrants become a different people: Americans. Moreover, by co-opting the frontier as the place where this transformation takes place, by implication America's nine-teenth-century expansion across the continent under the driving im-pulse of manifest destiny is justified. Frederick Jackson Turner's contribution to this historical account was crucial. It is still a common-place that it was on the frontier that, in the words of Arthur Schlesinger jr., 'the pre-Civil War immigrants steadily turned into Americans'.[25]

Yet consider the myth. For during the nineteenth century, the site of personal transformation – the place where Europeans become Amer-icans – seems to change from the area behind the advancing frontier, civilisation, to the frontier itself. This small, but crucial shift of emphasis is clear if the celebratory version of American history outlined in the colonial period by Hector St John de Crèvecœur, for example, is contrasted with that advanced by Turner in his essay on 'The Sig-nificance of the Frontier in American History' (1893).

'What then is the American, this new man?' Crèvecœur's rhetorical question has been taken widely as the starting point for considerations of America as both the 'first new nation' and the 'last best hope for mankind'. And his response to it, 'here individuals of all nations are melted into a new race of men' is, for Schlesinger among others, 'still a good answer – still the best hope'.[26] But how does Crèvecœur's new man become an American? It is a transformation achieved not simply through the act of emigration. Rather the process of socialisation and acculturation takes place in America, and over a period of time, and is only complete when the European has become Crèvecœur's model citizen: a settler and a farmer. Although the frontier has a role in this, moreover, it is not that which was later to be celebrated in Turner's work.

> Urged by a variety of motives, here they came. Every thing has tended to regenerate them; new laws, a new mode of living, a new social system; here they are become men: in Europe they were so many useless plants, wanting vegetative mould, and refreshing showers; they withered, and were mowed

down by want, hunger, and war; but now by the power of transplantation, like all other plants they have taken root and flourished.

This is Crèvecœur's version of the idea of America as a new Garden of Eden. It is included in the extract from his letter 'What is an American' that is reproduced frequently in relevant readers and anthologies. The extract is ended typically at the point in the correspondence where Crèvecœur concludes: 'This is an American'.[27]

But the letter continues. And in the less often reproduced and read section of it, Crèvecœur explains in more detail the impact of the frontier on individuals, and the entirely more haphazard process by which some are indeed regenerated by the frontier experience, while far more are destroyed by it. The celebratory mood changes. Crèvecœur becomes more candid.

> He who would wish to see America in its proper light, and have a true idea of its feeble beginnings and barbarous rudiments, must visit our extended line of frontiers where the last settlers dwell . . . where men are wholly left dependent on their native tempers, and on the spur of uncertain industry, which often fails when not sanctified by the efficacy of a few moral rules. There, remote from the power of example and check of shame, many families exhibit the most hideous parts of our society. They are a kind of forlorn hope, preceding by ten or twelve years the most respectable army of veterans which come after them.[28]

So those who first encounter the frontier are often overwhelmed by it rather than transformed: they are the vanguard who pave the way for others to come after them; and the pioneers remain often those whom the promise of American life has failed.

The letter recounts a complex process of transformation, in which the original pioneer, far from being Americanised as a result of an encounter with the frontier, is quite likely to become an individual whose life is spent escaping from the advance of civilisation in America. The 'true' American is the settler, who comes after the pioneer and is prepared to build upon the – often rudimentary – start which has been made in tackling the wilderness that lies on the frontier. Crèvecœur's model citizen is a farmer – himself – or the pioneer who survived to become a farmer – his father. Others may perform a useful function in signposting the way for those who follow, but they are unlikely to 'have taken root and flourished' in the American wilderness. As Crèvecœur puts it: 'Thus are our first steps trod, thus are our first trees felled, in general, by the most vicious of our people; and thus the path is opened for the arrival of a second and better class, the true American free-holders; the most respectable set of people in this part of the world'.[29]

It is Crèvecœur's simple celebratory vision of America as the melting-pot which is most often recalled, rather than this account of the impact of the frontier upon those who first confronted it. For contained in his optimistic argument is the assumption that whereas in Europe the population is in the grip of a degenerating society, in America individuals are indeed presented with the opportunity of personal regeneration. The New World thus becomes a place of potential transformation; but this is because of 'new laws, a new mode of living, a new social system' that exist there, rather than because the frontier awaits the civilising hand of the pioneer. Rather, the frontier for Crèvecœur is initially a place that threatens civilisation, morality, religion and the rule of law. 'There men appear to be no better than carnivorous animals of a superior rank, living on the flesh of wild animals when they can catch them, and when they are not able, they subsist on grain'.[30] This is a pioneer American.

Nevertheless, Crèvecœur's letter, and in particular its early part, is an important source for what has become the celebratory version of American history. So too is Frederick Jackson Turner's essay. And in the hundred years that separates the publication of the American edition of the *Letters from an American Farmer*, and Turner's presentation of his thesis, assessments of the significance of the frontier in American life altered. This transition from Crèvecœur's account to Turner's interpretation of the frontier experience marks its evolution as a pivotal metaphor in American historiography. In accounts of the nineteenth century, the frontier was to become a place where, rather than often failing in an attempt to build a new life, pioneers now could seize the great opportunities afforded for personal growth and transformation. By the twentieth century, that change in perspective was complete. Henry Nash Smith, for example, in examining the American West as both symbol and myth in *Virgin Land*, begins his work with Crèvecœur's famous question, 'What is an American?', and then immediately recalls that

> one of the most persistent generalizations concerning American life and character is the notion that our society has been shaped by the pull of a vacant continent drawing population westward through the passes of the Alleghenies, across the Mississippi Valley, over the high plains and mountains of the Far West to the Pacific Coast.

It is, as he admits, the axiomatic view of America's past which 'comes to us bearing the personal imprint of . . . Frederick Jackson Turner'.[31]

THE PIONEER AS HERO:
TRANSFORMATIONS ON TURNER'S FRONTIER

In 1893, Turner used the frontier experience as a metaphor effectively to hijack interpretations of American history. His thesis has subsequently 'functioned as the most influential set of ideas yet presented in American historiography'. Furthermore, 'there is great intuitive appeal in this theory, and few are willing to abandon it entirely'.[32] Why should this be so? In part because it presented Americans with a celebratory version of their past which could also act as an impulse to future action. It also retained a certain attraction for later historiography, in particular in the cold war period, for within it are echoes of ideas of exceptionalism, America's capacity to resist external threats to its security, and indeed the concept of containment itself as a counterpoint to inherent expansionist tendencies.

> The existence of an area of free land, its continuous recession, and the advance of American settlement westward, explain American development . . . The perennial rebirth, this fluidity of American life, this expansion westward with its new opportunities, its continuous touch with the simplicity of primitive society, furnish the forces dominating American character . . . The frontier is the line of most rapid and effective Americanization.[33]

Turner argued that expansionism across the continent not only contributed to the vitality of American society, but also rendered the American historical experience unique in comparative terms.

In Europe, a nation bent on a policy of expansion would immediately confront the territorial claims of neighbouring countries. America, however, was able to expand into 'free land'. Although Turner does acknowledge the presence of an indigenous population, he turns it to the further advantage of his argument. 'The effect of the Indian frontier as a consolidating agent in our history is important . . . The Indian was a common danger, demanding action'. He writes of 'the importance of the frontier . . . as a military training school, keeping alive the power of resistance to aggression'.[34] Here again, the language which turns the pioneering American, intent on pushing back the frontier, into the victim who must resist against Indian 'aggression' is redolent of later cold war rhetoric.

Expansion, the desire for more land, appears as an irresistible impulse. European immigrants became American migrants. Yet any nation which expands must ultimately be constrained. Turner quotes the German historian Grund, writing in 1836:

it appears then that the universal disposition of Americans to emigrate to the western wilderness, in order to enlarge their dominion over inanimate nature, is actually the result of an expansive power which is inherent in them, and which by continually agitating all classes of society is constantly throwing a large portion of the whole population on the extreme confines of the State, in order to gain space for its development. Hardly is a new State or Territory formed before the same principle manifests itself again and gives rise to a further emigration; and so it is destined to go on until a physical barrier must finally obstruct its progress.[35]

It is an analysis reminiscent of George Kennan's assessment of 'the sources of Soviet conduct' in 1947: a nation expands until it meets a finite obstacle or a source of implacable resistance: a continental limit in the American case; a military threat – the doctrine of containment – in the Soviet one.

Indeed, Kennan's Soviets would fulfil much the same role in the twentieth century as had Turner's Indians in the nineteenth. The 'thoughtful observer of Russian American relations', he argued in his famous 'X' article in *Foreign Affairs*,

will rather experience a certain gratitude to Providence which, by providing the American people with this implacable challenge, has made their entire security as a nation dependent on their pulling themselves together and accepting the responsibilities of moral and political leadership that history plainly intended them to bear.[36]

A common enemy would again unify the nation in the pursuit of a manifest destiny.

Turner also provided an account, implicitly of the pioneer's role in the attempt to realise the nation's manifest destiny, and explicitly of the impact of the expanding frontier on the character and nature of American civilisation itself. His essay is thus not only to be identified with the establishment of the frontier as a significant metaphor and influence upon American historiography. It is also about the possibilities for personal transformation that can take place there. And as Turner's American Adam is regenerated continually and successfully on the advancing frontier, the essay could be taken to be a powerful plea for the continuity of America's expansionist mission. For what is important in the nation's historical development is to find and overcome the challenges of new frontiers.

What has providence in store, then, for Turner's pioneer American? It is a tough prospect. 'The wilderness masters the colonist. It finds him a European in dress, industries, tools, modes of travel and thought. It takes him from the railroad car and puts him in the birch canoe. It strips off the garments of civilization and arrays him in the hunting shirt and the moccasin'. Like Crèvecœur's pioneer, Turner's colonist can be overwhelmed by the experience: 'at the frontier the environment is at first too strong for the man'. And yet, 'little by little he transforms the wilderness, but the outcome is not the old Europe . . . here is a new product that is American'.[37] This is a classic statement of frontier regeneration. Crucially, for Turner, it is on the frontier that the European immigrant becomes Crèvecœur's 'new man': an American. The frontier operates as a kind of military boot-camp, a site for basic training. It first strips away the veneer of European civilisation, and as the pioneer 'transforms the wilderness', so the frontier reconstructs the pioneer.

This powerful force of Americanisation becomes stronger as the western expansion of the United States progresses.

> At first, the frontier was the Atlantic coast. It was the frontier of Europe in a very real sense. Moving westwards, the frontier became more and more American . . . Thus the advance of the frontier has meant a steady movement away from the influence of Europe, a steady growth of independence on American lines.[38]

Turner, then, is making the case for American exceptionalism, at a time when, significantly, the impact of the closing of the frontier – the exhausting of the resource of 'free land' – appeared to some to argue that America's fate was to be not too different from Europe's after all. During the 1890s, economic recession, social and political unrest, the Haymarket Riot and demands for an end to the 'plutocracy of wealth' created a situation in which, as Turner's biographer, Ray Billington, notes: 'to many Americans there were disturbing portents of a future in a frontierless land. Class conflict and revolutionary demands threatened to transform the United States into another Europe'.[39] The significance of Turner's essay lies not least in the way he argues that American exceptionalism can be preserved in a frontierless age.

FRONTIER AS METAPHOR

As Tiziano Bonazzi suggests, the meaning of the frontier thesis 'does not simply lie in a new interpretation of the past, but in a new use of the past for the present'.[40] In analysing Turner's essay, Bonazzi points to an inner contradiction, which nevertheless is necessary for the thesis to operate as a gateway to America's future, rather than as a lament for its lost past. On the one hand, the advance of the frontier westwards marks the nation's evolution and progress. On the other, at each stage of the move west, a new frontier offers a fresh opportunity for individual regeneration. But such personal reconstruction also involves that initial deconstruction that strips away inherited 'civilised' values, and moulds them anew in the confrontation with the wilderness. And it is this dynamic process that adapts the American character to new environments, enabling it to overcome fresh challenges. Turner's American does not progress smoothly. Rather, it is necessary constantly to take a step back – to be born again on the frontier – to be able to advance further. America advances confidently across the continent: but Americans make progress in fits and starts. The question remains: how does this contradiction point the way to America's future in the age of the closed frontier?

Influenced by the intellectual currents of the times, Turner's idea of the frontier as the prime force shaping the American character at one level operates as a simple model of historical evolution. Moreover, drawing upon such influences as Walter Bagehot's *Physics and Politics* (1872), Turner argues effectively that the pioneer experience sets the tone for American development: that the qualities seen in the successful pioneer – the fittest survivor in the contest with the frontier – become the formative influences of the national character. In Bagehot's words:

> a sort of type of character arose from the difficulties of struggling with the wilderness; and this type has given its shape to the mass of characters because the mass of characters have unconsciously imitated it. Many of the American characteristics are plainly useful in such a life, and consequent upon such a life. The eager restlessness, the highly-strung nervous organisation are useful in continual struggle, and also are promoted by it.

The pioneer was the American exemplar. Bagehot argues that 'when once the predominant type was determined, the copying propensity of man did the rest'.[41] As Billington suggests, 'Bagehot believed that the American character was shaped by the centuries-long struggle against the wilderness: those who led the assault became the nation's folk heroes, and their traits, acquired in their conquest, became the traits of all'.[42]

Compare Turner.

> From the conditions of frontier life came intellectual traits of profound importance . . . The result is that to the frontier the American intellect owes

its striking characteristics. That coarseness and strength combined with
acuteness and inquisitiveness; that practical, inventive turn of mind, quick
to find expedients; that masterful grasp of material things, lacking in the
artistic but powerful to effect great ends; that restless, nervous energy; that
dominant individualism, working for good and evil, and withal that buoy-
ancy and exuberance which comes with freedom.[43]

For Bonazzi, therefore,

the Frontier Thesis is meant to be a gateway to a consciousness of historical
continuity through change. Turner constructed it in order to show his
countrymen that their basic political ideals, individualism and democracy,
are not secured once and for ever, but exist only as a result of successful
adaptations to ever-changing environments.[44]

The implication of this argument is that in order to maintain such
ideals, the challenges of fresh frontiers constantly must be sought: for it
is in the regenerative opportunity afforded by the frontier experience
that the American character is refreshed and imbued with its dynamic
energy.

CONCLUSION: 'STORYBOOK TRUTHS'

Some two centuries after the settlement of New England, Tocqueville
wrote: 'I think I see the destiny of America embodied in the first Puritan
who landed on those shores, just as the whole human race was
represented by the first man',[45] He was sketching the outline of what
Louis Hartz suggested 'might be called the storybook truth about
American history: that America was settled by men who fled from
the feudal and clerical oppressions of the Old World'. This was an
interpretation of America's past, argued Hartz, that was 'as old as the
national folklore itself'.[46] The Puritan experience in New England came
to exercise, both historically and intellectually, a unique hold over the
American political and cultural imagination. For it was the Puritans'
'idea of America' that came to sustain the idea of the United States
itself. New England's sense of its special destiny, and its mission to fulfil
a providential purpose could be broadened into an interpretation of
American exceptionalism, and could form the basis of a theory of
American nationalism. The legacy of Puritanism would act as a cultural
catalyst, welding disparate American states in common cause.

There is another 'storybook truth' about America's past. Tocqueville, again, outlined it in a couple of familiar vignettes: 'the European

leaves his cottage for the transatlantic shores, and the American, who is born on that very coast, plunges in his turn into the wilds of central America'. The formative experience of American life was seen to be the outcome of such patterns of immigration and migration. So, 'millions of men are marching at once towards the same horizon; their language, their religion, their manners differ; their object is the same. Fortune has been promised to them somewhere in the West, and to the West they go to find it'.[47] As Hartz too observed: 'the legend of the covered wagon supplements, in a secondary way, the legend of the *Mayflower*'.[48]

'Our fate', Richard Hofstadter observed of America, 'is not to have an ideology but to be one'.[49] The 'idea of America' and a belief in exceptionalism is an extrapolation of the experiences of Puritans and pioneers in the New World. John Winthrop's image of the 'City Upon a Hill' still resonates as an American utopian vision. The Puritans' purpose, to redeem the world they had left behind, can be transmuted into America's secular destiny: to re-create that world in the image of its democratic republic. Presented as this 'errand into the wilderness' there is a sense in which American history ends as the first Puritan colonists successfully negotiate their way across the Atlantic. From that point on, historiography – interpreting the nation's past – has more to do with affirming a myth which encourages ideological unity and political consensus than with exploring reality. For the 'idea of America' is at the core of the ideology of American nationalism.

The pioneer carried the 'idea of America' westwards. In recounting that journey, historians could reinforce the analysis of a separate and distinct American identity formed by repeated encounters with the wilderness on the ever-advancing frontier. Frederick Jackson Turner's interpretation of 'The Significance of the Frontier in American History' dominates the nation's historiography. Richard Slotkin has summarised 'the complex of traditional ideas that had accumulated around the idea of the "Frontier" since colonial times'. These included

> the concept of pioneering as a defining national mission, a 'Manifest Destiny', and the vision of the westward settlements as a refuge from tyranny and corruption, a safety valve for metropolitan discontents, a land of golden opportunity for enterprising individualists, and an inexhaustible reservoir of natural wealth on which a future of limitless prosperity could be based.[50]

So the pioneers would be part of that 'great experiment' in democracy and republican government, which would establish Jefferson's 'Empire of Liberty' across the United States. And the idea that the immigrant could be reborn as an American as a result of the pioneering experience would contribute to the belief that thereby the nation was different, exceptional, and unencumbered by the historical and ideological baggage that had been left behind elsewhere.

These 'storybook truths' of American history are powerful myths: they are 'the stories', as John Hellmann puts it, 'containing a people's image of themselves in history'.[51] The 'idea of America' is embedded in the spiritual foundations of a colonial past. It becomes the philosophical inspiration of the United States itself. And it is part of the historical dynamic that dramatises expansionism as the natural fulfilment of a providential design. As Reinhold Niebuhr and Alan Heimert argue,

> our pressure on all previous sovereignties who shared the hemisphere with us, and the tenacity of our land hunger under the moral sanction of what our patriots called 'manifest destiny', may have given the first intimation of the formation of a unique national characteristic or trait of character, namely the expression of a vital impulse in the name of an ideal.[52]

Expansion was an essential part of the process of creating America's sense of national identity, such that even after the territorial integrity of the nation was assured, the dynamism of the principles that energised the republic endured.

Once established, moreover, these mythic 'truths' are substitutes for further ideological debate about the nation's purpose: the 'first new nation' becomes the 'last best hope for mankind'. The myths may contain, for many, indisputable and uncontroversial evidence not only of the promise of American life, but also of the nation's triumphant progress towards its transcontinental and then international pre-eminence. In the words of J. G. A. Pocock,

> 'in the beginning', Locke had written – inadvertently earning his place as a prophet of the new apocalypse – 'all the world was America'; and if in the end all the world should be America again, the mission of a chosen people would have been fulfilled.[53]

The recounting of 'storybook truths' thus forms the basis of much of American political rhetoric and also much of American historiography during the formative years of the cold war. Such myths substituted for ideological debates in the recounting of America's past. And they serve a political purpose.

'Each age', wrote Turner in 1891, 'writes the history of the past anew with reference to the conditions uppermost in its own time'.[54] In this respect, he was intensely suspicious of contemporary 'bolshevism'. In a memorandum written in 1918 about the future prospects for the League of Nations, he hoped to 'keep the Bolshevik's serpent out of the American Eden'.[55] By elevating the frontier to a central explanatory position in his account of America's historical development, he provided Americans not only with an insight into their past, but with an important myth that might justify their future conduct in a country where the movable frontier was becoming at last a fixed border. In that comment he points also the way to the historiographical method of the consensus historians who, sixty years on, were to recast America's past in the light of their contemporary concern: not the closing of the frontier, but the opening of the cold war, and the nation's rise to globalism. And he suggests too the method by which John F. Kennedy would attempt to revitalise America's belief in its providential mission – its manifest destiny – through reworking the historical myth into the dynamic political metaphor of the New Frontier.

NOTES

1. Hofstadter, *The American Political Tradition*, p. v.
2. Schlesinger, *The Vital Center*, p. 1.
3. Novick, *That Noble Dream*, p. 333.
4. Hofstadter, *The American Political Tradition*, pp. vii and x.
5. Ibid. pp. 68 and 87.
6. Ibid. p. 190.
7. Ibid. pp. 227–8.
8. Schlesinger, 'Review of Richard Hofstadter', pp. 612–13.
9. Novick, *That Noble Dream*, p. 327.
10. Quoted ibid. p. 328. *The Genius of American Politics* was the published product of a series of lectures which Boorstin gave at the University of Chicago in 1952 as the result of an invitation from the Walgreen Foundation for the Study of American Institutions, which had been created 'to teach a better appreciation of the American way of life'. Its sponsor, Charles Walgreen, who had made his fortune from drugstores, was 'a keen anticommunist'. See Wilkinson, *American Social Character*, pp. 6–7.
11. Boorstin, *The Genius of American Politics*, p. 1.
12. Ibid. p. 6.
13. Ibid. pp. 9, 25–6 and 163.
14. Ibid. p. 165.

15. Ibid. p. 179.
16. Hartz, *The Liberal Tradition in America*, pp. 5–6.
17. Ibid. p. 11.
18. Ibid. p. 65.
19. Ibid. p. 111.
20. Ibid. pp. 204–5.
21. Ibid. pp. 285 and 287.
22. Hartz, 'The Nature of Revolution', pp. 110 and 112.
23. Ibid. pp. 129–30 and 147.
24. Diggins, 'Knowledge and Sorrow', pp. 363 and 372.
25. Schlesinger, *The Disuniting of America*, p. 30.
26. Ibid. pp. 12 and 138.
27. Crèvecœur, *Letters from an American Farmer*, Letter III, pp. 42 and 44. The shortened version of the letter is reproduced in, for example, Commager, *Living Ideas in America*; Levy, *Political Thought in America*; Bailey and Kennedy, *The American Spirit*, vol. 1; and Stourzh and Lerner, *Readings in American Democracy*.
28. Crèvecœur, 'What is an American', in his *Letters from an American Farmer*, pp. 46–7.
29. Ibid. p. 55.
30. Ibid. p. 46.
31. Smith, *Virgin Land*, p. 3.
32. Benson, 'The Historian as Mythmaker', pp. 18–19 and Lee, 'The Turner Thesis Re-examined', p. 66.
33. Turner, *The Frontier in American History*, pp. 1–4.
34. Ibid. p. 15.
35. Ibid. p. 7.
36. Kennan, 'The Sources of Soviet Conduct', p. 868.
37. Turner, *The Frontier in American History*, p. 4.
38. Ibid. p. 4.
39. Billington, *Frederick Jackson Turner*, p. 109.
40. Bonazzi, 'Frederick Jackson Turner's Frontier Thesis', p. 151.
41. Bagehot, *Physics and Politics*, pp. 36 and 38.
42. Billington, *Frederick Jackson Turner*, p. 120.
43. Turner, *The Frontier in American History*, p. 37.
44. Bonazzi, 'Frederick Jackson Turner's Frontier Thesis', p. 163.
45. Tocqueville, *Democracy in America*, vol. 1, p. 301.
46. Hartz, *The Liberal Tradition in America*, p. 3.
47. Tocqueville, *Democracy in America*, vol. 1, p. 303.
48. Hartz, 'The Nature of Revolution', p. 112.
49. Quoted in Cunliffe, 'New World, Old World' p. 19.
50. Slotkin, *Gunfighter Nation*, p. 30.
51. Hellmann, *American Myth and the Legacy of Vietnam*, p. ix.
52. Neibuhr and Heimert, *A Nation So Conceived*, p. 9.

53. Pocock, *The Machiavellian Moment*, p. 542.
54. Quoted in Novick, *That Noble Dream*, p. 103.
55. Turner, 'International Political Parties in a Durable League of Nations', p. 550.

CHAPTER THREE

John F. Kennedy: Hero

INTRODUCTION: AMERICAN SUPERMAN

Norman Mailer's first novel, *The Naked and the Dead* (1948), was published in the same year as Richard Hofstadter's *The American Political Tradition*. In it, Mailer has his character Major General Cummings observe that 'there's a popular misconception of man as something between a brute and an angel. Actually man is in transit between brute and God'.[1] It is a reference to the work of the German philosopher Friedrich Nietzsche. The General's remark, as Robert Solotaroff argues, 'clearly derives from Zarathustra's "man is a rope stretched between the animal and the Superman"'.[2] The connection is made more obvious in the subsequent discussion with Lieutenant Hearn, who asks the rhetorical question: 'Man's deepest urge is omnipotence?' As Cummings makes that case, he concludes that 'the only morality of the future is a power morality, and a man who cannot find his adjustment to it is doomed'.[3] This, in effect, is a version of Nietzsche's idea of the 'will to power', the basic impulse of humanity that transcends all moral codes and becomes 'the chant of a reborn man, and it is all about rebirth – the rebirth of the individual, the rebirth of humanity at large'.[4] Is it, as Cummings claims and Mailer hints, the time for the American Adam to recognise and co-operate with that impulse in the impending era of ideological confrontation and cold war?

For Mailer, Nietzsche was the philosopher for the nuclear age: a time when the world was on the verge of apocalyptic confrontation, and contemporary ideologies had to do battle in the shadow of the atomic bomb. By the end of the 1950s, moreover, in common with other American intellectuals, he would see the United States as suffering from a failure of both nerve and leadership in its opposition to Soviet communism. Enter Nietzsche again. Those individuals who can muster sufficient 'will to power' were, he had argued, exceptional in an age of democratic egalitarianism. But they are to be 'encountered in the most widely different places and cultures: here we really do find a *higher type*, which is, in relation to mankind as a whole, a kind of *Übermensch*':[5] the 'overman' or 'superman'.

Such ideas moulded Mailer's initial reaction to John F. Kennedy's campaign for the presidency. His view mirrored that of his contemporaries – notably among the 'best and the brightest' who became the candidate's most ardent fans. JFK became a Nietzschean *Übermensch*: the 'superman' who would be able to redefine America's sense of national purpose, reasserting mastery after the drift of the Eisenhower years. Yet in attempting such a redefinition, Kennedy himself merely co-opted an American historical myth. Moreover, it was the promise of the New Frontier, which, coupled with the new president's desire for international activism, set the nation on course for its rendezvous in Vietnam.

Walt Whitman, Nietzsche's nineteenth-century contemporary, assessed the political challenges facing America in 1856 in language that might not have seemed misplaced a century later.

> The times are full of great portents in these States and in the whole world. Freedom against slavery is not issuing here alone, but is issuing everywhere. The horizon rises, it divides I perceive, for a more august drama than any of the past. Old men have played their parts, the act suitable to them is closed, and if they will not withdraw voluntarily, must be bid to do so with unmistakeable voice.

In 1957, with Eisenhower's concluding term in the White House drawing to its inexorable close, the Soviet Union's launch of Sputnik immediately raised the technological stakes of the cold war. Could the United States cover this new bet? As Whitman had asked, 'who shall play the hand for America in these tremendous games?'.[6]

The poet had looked forward to a 'Redeemer President', 'some heroic, shrewd, fully informed, healthy bodied, middle-aged, beard-faced American blacksmith or boatman come down from the West across the Alleghenies, and walk into the Presidency'.[7] But Kennedy was no Lincoln, in background, style nor partisan allegiance. Whitman's redeemer hero came from the ordinary people, the democratic mass in whom the poet invested his faith. Kennedy was cast in a different mould.

Nietzsche's 'overman' 'is the person who not only chooses between good and evil, but who himself *establishes new values and affirms the significance of life in so doing*:'[8] in Mailer's terms, the 'hipster', an existential hero. This, then, was Kennedy. In 'Superman Comes to the Supermarket', he is described thus: 'Kennedy's most characteristic quality is the remote and private air of a man who has traversed some lonely terrain of experience, of loss and gain, of nearness to death, which leaves him isolated from the mass of others'. Already JFK appeared different: a difference confirmed in Mailer's interview with the candidate. There, Kennedy had shown his knowledge of Mailer's work. ' "I've read *The Deer Park* and . . . the others" ', which, the novelist confesses, 'startled me for it was the first time in a hundred similar situations, talking to someone whose knowledge of my work was casual, that the sentence did not come out, "I've read *The Naked and the Dead* . . . and the others" '.[9]

For Arthur Schlesinger jr., this was merely Kennedy's 'faithful expression of an idiosyncratic taste'.[10] But in terms of Mailer's discussion, the conversation is significant. By recording it, he appears to be identifying JFK with the existential philosophy that he had more fully developed in his third novel than in his first: an existentialism that he later defined as having 'no precedents, no traditions, no disciplines, no books, no guides sufficiently familiar with the situation to take you through'.[11] Moreover, as Norman Podhoretz argued, it was with *The Deer Park* that 'for the first time in Mailer, . . . victory over the system has become possible to those who can see through it and who are sufficiently brave to act on what they see'.[12] In 1960, Kennedy represented himself as a political 'outsider', a challenger to the Democrats' establishment and the traditional 'smoke-filled rooms' of the political power-brokers at the Convention. And yet, he did not pursue the politics of existentialism to the extent of rejecting political precedents, traditions and disciplines wholly in favour of intuitive actions. Rather he defined himself, and could be defined, within the parameters of established American historical myth.

It is here, though, that Mailer's interpretation of twentieth-century American history also has some relevance. Since the First World War, he argued, the nation's past had 'moved on two rivers, one visible, one underground'. The surface history of politics had been 'concrete, factual, practical and unbelievably dull', but there was also 'a subterranean river of untapped, ferocious, lonely and romantic desires, that concentration of ecstasy and violence which is the dream life of the nation'. By the 1950s, the political and the mythic life of the nation had diverged too far, for 'there was nothing to return them to one another, no common danger, no cause, no desire, and most essentially, no hero'.[13] This, then, is what Kennedy promised: the reconciliation of politics and myth.

Mailer thus offers the leitmotiv for Kennedy's campaign in 1960 in writing the epitaph for the previous decade.

> America's need in those years was to take an existential turn, to walk into the nightmare, to face into that terrible logic of history which demanded that the country and its people must become more extraordinary and more adventurous, or else perish, since the only alternative was to offer a false security in the power and the panacea of organized religion, family, and the FBI, a totalitarianization of the psyche by the stultifying techniques of the mass media which would seep into everyone's most powerful associations and so leave the country powerless against the Russians even if the denouement were to take fifty years, for in a competition between totalitarianisms the first maxim of the prizefight manager would doubtless apply: 'Hungry fighters win fights'.[14]

As Solotaroff observes, the suggestion was 'that a truly heroic president could turn the stagnating population back toward its historic quest for growth and adventure'.[15] Kennedy might be that hero. Mailer's essay was the overture for the New Frontier.

PROFILES IN COURAGE

Some of Kennedy's own ideas about the challenges of contemporary American politics can be gathered from his Pulitzer prizewinning history *Profiles in Courage*, first published in 1955. It was written at a time when JFK was intent on rehabilitating his political career in the aftermath of serious illness and his coincident – and to some fortuitous – absence from the Senate when it voted to censure Joe McCarthy. Courage, then, is 'that most admirable of human virtues . . . "Grace under pressure", Ernest Hemingway defined it'.[16] Moreover, such a quality is the essential requirement for a cold war leader. So,

> in the days ahead, only the very courageous will be able to take the hard and unpopular decisions necessary for our survival in the struggle with a powerful enemy – an enemy with leaders who need give little thought to the popularity of their course, who need pay little tribute to the public opinion they themselves manipulate, and who may force, without fear of retaliation at the polls, their citizens to sacrifice present laughter for future glory.[17]

Kennedy then gives the examples of those Senators whose acts of political courage he admires, and thus by implication would emulate.

He begins with John Quincy Adams, from his home state of Massachusetts, and a man whose strong Puritan convictions made him an outsider in terms of the temper of his times. In addition to a religious belief which distinguished him from his contemporaries, Adams appears in other ways to be much like JFK himself. 'The son of an unpopular father, a renegade in his party and rather brash for a freshman senator . . .'.[18] Adams, facing a choice between supporting President Jefferson or maintaining his party allegiance, put what he saw as the national interest above partisan popularity. He retained the support of his father – the former president. Kennedy emphasises the importance of Adams' family values. Significantly, too, Adams went on from the Senate to the White House itself. JFK, by analogy, appears to project himself vicariously into the presidency through choosing to profile his eminent predecessor.

Daniel Webster, another native of Massachusetts, and Kennedy's second biographical vignette, sought to articulate and define a national consensus in the face of sectional rivalries. JFK's admiration is reserved for a political maverick, and for politicians who reject partisan considerations for a greater good. The same criteria governs his choice of courageous Senators from the South: Thomas Hart Benton and Sam Houston. Like Webster, their fascination appears to lie as much in the quality of their rhetoric as in the courage of their actions. In the political crisis that defined American politics in the nineteenth century, they sacrificed popularity for what they identified as the greater cause of maintaining the Union.

After the Civil War, Edmund Ross of Kansas, in supplying the crucial vote in the Senate to prevent the successful impeachment of President Andrew Johnson, like Adams sided with the executive in a struggle with the legislature. Once more the national interest overcomes partisan persuasion. Finally from the nineteenth century, Kennedy resurrects the career of Lucius Lamar, 'the most gifted statesman given by the South to the nation from the close of the Civil War to the turn of the century',[19] and who like Webster, Benton and Houston had tried to reconcile the sectional divisions within the country. It is as if, in these examples, he is hinting at a historical parallel, warning of the political courage that both legislature and executive would need to confront the contemporary issue of civil rights. The Supreme Court had handed down the Brown versus Board of Education decision ending segregation in 1954, the year before JFK's book was published. Like these nineteenth-century leaders, contemporary politicians would have to seek and be able to articulate the need for a fresh consensus. Kennedy's call to Martin Luther King's wife while the civil rights leader was imprisoned – a gesture that helped him win the presidency – was to be an act of political courage reminiscent of those he explored in his book.

Two twentieth-century senators also have a courageous profile. George Norris, suggested as an example by Theodore Sorensen, who was also from Nebraska, is again a significant choice in terms of Kennedy's presidential aspirations. One of his principled actions was to support Al Smith for president in 1928, despite the fact that Norris was a Republican and Smith a Democrat. And Norris was a Protestant, Smith a Catholic. Kennedy quotes Norris: 'it is our duty as patriots to cast out this Un-American doctrine and rebuke those who have raised the torch of intolerance. All believers of any faith can unite and go forward in our political work to bring about the maximum amount of happiness for our people'.[20] It is an early attempt to confront the religious issue that threatened to dominate his campaign in 1960.

Robert Taft, another Republican, is, at first sight, a curious inclusion. His act of political courage did not even involve confrontation within the Senate. Rather, Kennedy recalls Taft's speech on the constitutionality of the Nuremberg trials in 1946, as 'a bold plea for justice in a time of intolerance and hostility'. It effectively ended his presidential ambitions for the sake of political principle. Yet JFK suggests that Taft had been right to argue that the death sentences passed on Nazi war criminals were unconstitutional because they ran counter to 'the fundamental principle of American law that a man cannot be tried under an *ex post facto* statute'. This, then, may be the closest that Kennedy comes to comment by analogy on McCarthyism. The contrast between McCarthy and his fellow Republican Taft, 'an apostle of strict constitutionalism', is clear.[21] McCarthy's methods, assuming guilt by innuendo, and using the right of silence guaranteed by the fifth amendment as evidence of public confession, demonstrated how he was prepared to destroy the principles of American democracy in order, ostensibly, to save it. He would not, then, find inclusion in Kennedy's pantheon.

An integrated portrait drawn from the material of his book provides a glimpse of Kennedy's idealised politician. The potentially heroic leader is one who puts service to the nation above support of a party or section of the country; one who respects executive power rather than seeking legislative influence; one who is tolerant of racial and religious differences; and one who maintains the rule of law in times of political intolerance. Among his admirers, Kennedy himself would demonstrate such multifaceted political courage: his book could be read as both history and personal manifesto.

RHETORIC AND THE NEW FRONTIER

First Kennedy had to win. According to Richard Foster, Mailer believed that his 'Superman' essay 'was the generative cause for Kennedy's small plurality over Nixon in the election'.[22] The question facing America in 1960 was whether it would be 'brave enough to enlist the romantic dream of itself, would it vote for the image in the mirror of its unconsciousness'?[23] Mailer may have thought that his contribution tipped the balance. Arthur Schlesinger, on the other hand, believed that, when presented in such fashion, this was also the question 'which frightened the nation when it began to fall away from Kennedy in the last days before the election'.[24] In the event, America's Nietzschean 'superman' captured the White House by the narrowest of margins.

Mailer misread Kennedy, as he later admitted. According to Schlesinger, what the novelist had omitted from his assessment of the candidate and the presidency 'was the paradox of power – that the exercise of power is necessary to fulfil purpose, yet the world of power dooms many purposes to frustration'.[25] Yet Schlesinger himself also was attracted still by Mailer's idea of Kennedy's potential as an existential *Übermensch*. So the candidate may have tried to act in the presidency according to 'his own determination, as Norman Mailer said in a flash of insight, to define 'the nature of our reality for us by his actions'' '. And in this sense, the president was 'the existential hero, though the term would have amused or depressed him'. On the other hand, Schlesinger, like Mailer, can only pursue the analogy so far. For his 'superman' did not exercise his 'will to power' free from the encumbrances of his interpretation of the prevailing orthodoxies of cold war American historiography.

The problem thus lies in the New Frontier. In his acceptance speech at the Los Angeles Convention, Kennedy proclaimed:

> We stand today on the edge of a New Frontier, the frontier of the 1960s, a frontier of unknown opportunities and perils, a frontier of unfulfilled hopes and threats. But the New Frontier of which I speak is not a set of promises, it is a set of challenges. It sums up not what I intend to offer the American people, but what I intend to ask of them. It appeals to their pride, not their pocketbook – it holds out the promise of more sacrifice instead of more security.[26]

Theodore Sorensen claims that 'the basic concept of the New Frontier – and the term itself – were new to this speech. I know of no outsider who suggested that expression, although the theme of the Frontier was contained in more than one draft'.[27] Kennedy, in articulating this slogan, which became the popular catchphrase of his administration, was not seeking, however, fundamentally to redefine the nature of American politics. Interpretations of the significance of the frontier were and had remained a cornerstone of the nation's historiography.

Kennedy undoubtedly had a sense of this history. Allan Nevins, writing the introduction to the edition of *Profiles in Courage* that was published to coincide with its author's inauguration as president, suggested that 'as we confront the murky future, it should reassure Americans to know that their president understands so well the utility of the lamp of the Past in guiding our feet'.[28] And yet, that understanding had profound political consequences. Ernst Cassirer, summarising the nature of modern political myths, argued that they 'do not grow up freely; they are not wild fruits of an exuberant imagination. They are things fabricated by very skilful and cunning artisans'.[29] As William Appleman Williams observed, 'Kennedy and his advisers had the brilliant perception to talk about empire in the classic idiom of the frontier. That propaganda gem is of itself almost enough to justify honouring them as the cleverest imperial leaders of their generation'.[30] In co-opting America's frontier myth, therefore, Kennedy was able to package his political agenda of renewed cold war activism as a fresh phase in the nation's historic mission. As John Hellmann puts it: 'the New Frontier proclaimed that the western frontier . . . could remain in its metaphorical dimensions an open landscape of challenge and opportunity. In this symbolic frontier America could regenerate its traditional virtues while serving future progress'.[31]

In these terms, major initiatives of the New Frontier reflected Kennedy's desire to confront what were perceived in cold war America as the immediate threats and challenges posed by international communism. The Alliance for Progress was to forestall the spread of the ideology in Latin America. The Peace Corps was 'born out of America's historic sense of mission to protect liberty at home and spread it abroad'.[32] And the space race – the most visible indication of exploring fresh frontiers – was the product of the fear that the Russians might compound the success of Sputnik and the first manned orbital flight, made on 12 April 1961, soon after Kennedy had become President. As Lyndon Johnson said in a speech to Congress two years later, to raise funds for the proposed American lunar landing: 'I, for one, don't want to go to bed by the light of a Communist moon'.[33]

The ethos of the administration promoted the idea that extraordinary individuals could confront and overcome these challenges set for the nation by its president. After the debacle of the Bay of Pigs, for example, Kennedy had committed America to the goal of a moon landing. The first group of American astronauts, according to Tom Wolfe, 'had now become the personal symbols not only of America's Cold War struggle with the Soviets but also of Kennedy's own political comeback. They had become *the* pioneers of the New Frontier, recycled version'.[34] And it was the 'best and the brightest', the president's immediate entourage, who were responsible for formulating the administration's policies, not least towards Vietnam. The Peace Corps were missionaries for American democratic ideas and technological prowess. Furthermore, it was Kennedy himself who now took an interest in the establishment of an elite military force that would be responsible for counter-insurgency in Southeast Asia.

Hellmann suggests that 'as a single hero representing the ideal answer of the New Frontier to the calls for renewal, the Green Beret of the periodical press occupied in a single timeless moment the whole of American myth'.[35] And it is this identification of the pioneer as hero – whether as an astronaut or a Green Beret; or more prosaically as one of a new breed of political pragmatists directing the nation's affairs, or as a volunteer with the Peace Corps, which is the hallmark of the Kennedy administration. The president, reworking American historical myth in such a way as to elevate the expectations of his contemporaries – that America had both the capacity and ability successfully to prosecute its cold war mission – was the example: Mailer's superman was the first among equals in this nation of potential heroes. Such was the prevailing political mood. Kennedy exhorted his fellow Americans, in the most famous lines of his inaugural address, to 'ask not what your country can do for you, but what you can do for your country'.[36] The words are reminiscent of

> the Nietzschean conclusion that 'the decisive issue is surely always one's readiness to sacrifice and not the object of sacrifice' . . . duty, was not understood as a matter of enlightened self-interest or contractual obligation; it was an absolute moral value that demonstrated one's inner strength and superiority to materialism and natural determination. It was the beginning of freedom and creativity.[37]

The truly democratic individual might embrace the ideas of duty and service to the nation: James Madison's 'republican virtue' was once more in vogue.

This, then, was what Kennedy and his New Frontier represented. As Schlesinger put it:

> his 'coolness' was itself a new frontier. It meant freedom from the stereo-typed responses of the past. It promised the deliverance of American idealism, buried deep in the national character but imprisoned by the knowingness and calculations of American society in the 'fifties. It held out to the young the possibility that they could become more than stock-holders in a satisfied nation. It offered hope for spontaneity in a country drowning in its own passivity – passive because it had come to accept the theory of its own impotence. This was what Norman Mailer caught at Los Angeles in 1960 – Kennedy's existential quality, the sense that he was in some way beyond conventional politics, that he could touch emotions and hopes thwarted by the bland and mechanized society.[38]

But the New Frontier disintegrated, not simply in an instant in Dallas in November 1963, but at greater length, and with ultimately more far-reaching results, in Vietnam.

KENNEDY AND VIETNAM

In May 1961, after his summit meeting with Khrushchev, and on his way back from Vienna, Kennedy went to Paris, where he met with President de Gaulle. In the course of their conversation, de Gaulle warned: 'the ideology that you invoke will not change anything . . . You Americans wanted, yesterday, to take our place in Indo-China, you want to assume a succession to rekindle a war that we ended. I predict to you that you will, step by step, be sucked into a bottomless military and political quagmire'.[39]

Nevertheless, Kennedy's administration, motivated by the pragmatic activist mood of the New Frontier, effectively closed off the avenues whereby America might escape from an undertaking to pursue its self-assigned mission to its inexorable conclusion. De Gaulle's prediction was the outcome of France's own defeat, and the loss of its empire in Indo-China. But Kennedy ignored it. And in looking at the 'lessons' apparently learnt from Vietnam, in a later era of revisionism, it might appear that some American presidents in office in the post-Vietnam war period continued to lean towards Kennedy's persuasion rather than de Gaulle's. As the anti-war critic George Ball suggested, for some Americans after Vietnam, in T. S. Eliot's words, 'we had the experience but missed the meaning'.[40]

Kennedy's role in the making of America's war in Vietnam is

sometimes presented as peripheral. Frances FitzGerald, for example, in her dispassionate account of the folly of the American mission, *Fire in the Lake* (1972), entitled one chapter 'The United States Enters the War'. And it starts with the account of Lyndon Johnson's commitment of ground troops to Southeast Asia. Nevertheless, as FitzGerald had made abundantly clear in the earlier part of her book, American involvement in Vietnam pre-dated the Johnson administration. Stanley Karnow, in *Vietnam: A History* (1983), has chapters entitled 'LBJ Goes to War' and 'Nixon's War', while Kennedy's role in the unfolding drama of American involvement is subsumed within the narrative.

Similarly, Michael Maclear in *Vietnam: The 10,000 Day War* (1981), a book which by its title suggests accurately that the conflict began just after the hostilities of the Second World War ended, nevertheless portrays the Johnson administration as facing the 'Days of Decision'. If the defeat of the French at Dien Bien Phu in 1954 marked the end of their war in Vietnam, it still leaves years to account for before LBJ would face Maclear's time to decide upon the nature of America's involvement in Vietnam. During that time, first the Eisenhower administration, and then, in particular, the Kennedy administration had not left Vietnam to its own devices.

By the time Johnson took office the principled commitment to contain communism in South Vietnam had been made and made again. And Kennedy's part in the process by which the United States was sucked inexorably into de Gaulle's 'quagmire' was thus pivotal. Nevertheless, JFK is more often exonerated rather than blamed for setting a trap into which LBJ then walked. Kennedy's was, after all, a short administration and the military escalation of the war did not come until later. Furthermore, by marginalising his involvement in the decisions which led to America's war, it is possible to avoid tainting the Kennedy myth with failure. This can lead to the revisionist sentiment that if he had survived, things would have been different. They may have been: but America would have still been twisting in the winds of the dilemmas of a commitment to South Vietnam that Kennedy's policies had done nothing to resolve. But following from the 'leader lost' idea is the fact that it suits a number of members of the New Frontier – Schlesinger and Sorensen are key witnesses in this respect – to blame two of their traditional political opponents, Johnson and Nixon, as responsible for the war, particularly in the light of their support for Robert Kennedy's election campaign of 1968, fought in part on an anti-war platform.

So, as Thomas Brown observes,

Kennedy's role in the Vietnam War is unsurprisingly the most controversial aspect of his public image and record. Equally unsurprisingly, it is the aspect that has been subjected to the greatest number of revisions by Kennedy's admirers. Such reinterpretations were of course due to the felt need to insulate JFK from the disastrous consequences of the American venture in Southeast Asia.[41]

Had America's mission in Vietnam been a success, then undoubtedly Kennedy would share the credit for his resolute support of cold war containment, and his active part in fighting communist inspired 'wars of national liberation'. As it was, by November 1963, in Neil Sheehan's words,

> John Kennedy had raised the Stars and Stripes and shed blood and enveloped in the protection and self-esteem of the United States that half of Vietnam below the 17th Parallel which the 1954 Geneva Agreements had said was just a truce zone but which American statesmen had pronounced a sovereign state and called South Vietnam.[42]

As president, he had made the commitment to 'bear any burden' to 'assure the survival and the success of liberty'. Sheehan again points out that 'liberty as defined by John Kennedy and the statesmen of his Presidency had meant an American-imposed order in Kennedy's "New Frontier" beyond America's shores'.[43]

As a senator, in the 1950s, his tone had been at first less strident. In 1954, at the time of Dien Bien Phu, American foreign policymakers had contemplated intervention in Indo-China. Kennedy, in a speech in the Senate, had argued for united rather than unilateral action. After France had been forced to acknowledge the independence of Indochina, and to end its colonial influence there, JFK looked to the indigenous peoples to join in the battle against communism. In that crusade, they could rely on American support. But, Kennedy suggested,

> to pour money, materiel, and men into the jungles of Indochina without at least a remote prospect of victory would be dangerously futile and self destructive . . . I am frankly of the belief that no amount of American military assistance in Indochina can conquer an enemy which is everywhere and at the same time nowhere, 'an enemy of the people' which has the sympathy and covert support of the people.[44]

Despite the somewhat dubious image of an 'enemy of the people' which could nevertheless rely on their 'covert support', Kennedy's argument seemed sound. Yet it ignored the fact that, if not with materiel and men, the United States had certainly supported the French colonial war with money. And now it would continue to attempt to buy time with further injections of aid to build a nation where none had existed before. South Vietnam was invented, and so, in many ways, was the career of its leader, Ngo Dinh Diem.

By 1956, Kennedy, as keynote speaker at a symposium organised by the American Friends of Vietnam, of which he was a member, was changing the emphasis he placed on America's self-assigned role in Southeast Asia. No longer was he seeking 'united action' against communism. Now he saw South Vietnam as representing 'the cornerstone of the Free World in Southeast Asia, the keystone to the arch, the finger in the dike'. In this way, and not differentiating even between the North and South, Kennedy asserted that 'Vietnam represents a proving ground of democracy in Asia'. Furthermore, 'the United States is directly responsible for this experiment – it is playing an important role in the laboratory where it is being conducted. We cannot permit that experiment to fail'. He argued now that 'Vietnam represents a test of American responsibility and determination in Asia, . . . This is our offspring – we cannot abandon it, we cannot ignore its needs'. This was because 'the key position of Vietnam in Southeast Asia, . . . makes inevitable the involvement of this nation's security in any new outbreak of trouble'.[45]

The metaphors Kennedy used are revealing. Vietnam becomes an American child: to be nurtured, and given help as it grows into a healthy democracy. America would help to build 'democratic character' into its offspring. It would teach values, influence attitudes, impart ideas. The hidden trap in 'nation-building' is revealed. For if the child-nation does not respond in the anticipated fashion, and proves incapable in its task of defending itself against communist incursions, then its parent-mentor, both wiser and more capable, must do the job itself. Trapped in its diminutive status, Vietnam was always likely not to live up to America's expectations. By the time Kennedy had taken office, this view of South Vietnam as America's adopted Asian child had hardened to the extent that the country was seen, according to David Halberstam, 'through the prism of American experience, American needs and American capacities. American purpose with *Americans* doing the right things could affect the destinies of these people. The Vietnamese were secondary, a small and unimportant people waiting to be told what to do by wiser, more subtle foreigners'.[46] Halberstam, indeed, refers to South Vietnam on more than one occasion as America's 'tar-baby'. 'Nation-building' would carry within it the seeds of an escalating effort to try repeatedly to invent South Vietnam as a democratic country in the face of manifest failure to do so.

Moreover, Kennedy's Vietnam is also an experiment, in the same way that America itself had been the 'great experiment' in republican government in the nineteenth century. That had been experiment as risk: the survival of which hung in the balance at least until the outcome of the Civil War had decided the fundamental shape of modern America's democratic polity. But in a scientific and technocratic age, Vietnam has become a laboratory experiment – something that is planned, controlled and in which outcomes should be predictable. As George Ball observed, by the time Kennedy took office as president, 'the prospect of leading the Third World into the twentieth century offered almost unlimited scope for experimentation not only to economists but also to sociologists, psychologists, city planners, agronomists, political scientists, and experts in chicken diseases'. The last reference may be a sly reminder of Tom Knox, a character in William Lederer and Eugene Burdick's book, *The Ugly American* (1958), whose improvements in third world poultry breeding techniques are ultimately sabotaged by American officialdom. That book had impressed Senator Kennedy sufficiently for him to send a copy to every member of the Senate. Still, as Ball suggests, the Kennedy years became 'the golden age for development theorists'. And 'the most presumptuous undertaking of all was "nation-building", which suggested that American professors could make bricks without the straw of experience and with indifferent and infinitely various kinds of clay. *Hubris* was endemic in Washington'.[47]

In similar vein, William Gibson points out:

> Vietnam as the laboratory for weapons development and military science, Vietnam as the laboratory for 'social systems engineering', Vietnam as the laboratory for economic modernization: the country had become completely abstracted into the universal space of positive science. It was *the* 'test-case', and that scientific status subsequently became mapped onto the political world.[48]

Again, in *The Backroom Boys* (1973), Noam Chomsky uses the familiar metaphor:

> Vietnam was seen as a great experiment, challenging and almost exhilarating, a laboratory of counter-insurgency and a test of the feasibility of 'wars of national liberation' – by definition, inspired by 'international communism' when they take place within the 'free world'.[49]

'Nation-building' involved its practitioners in an artificial use of language, and the aims they sought to achieve bore little relation to the reality which emerged from their efforts.

So America invented a client state in South Vietnam. Halberstam contrasts the situation north and south of the 17th parallel dividing the country.

> Ho did not need foreign aid to hold power, his base had deep roots in the peasant society which had driven out foreigners. Diem could not have survived for a week without foreign aid; he was an American creation which fit American political needs and desires, not Vietnamese ones.[50]

But as Denis Warner recounts, America's approach to 'nation-building' in South Vietnam did bring with it short-term gains.

> No analysis of the early years of the Diem regime can ignore the major role of the United States. United States aid kept Diem in power and manned the barricades against his adversaries. It reconstructed roads and railways, put goods in shop windows, caused modest improvements in agriculture, and some even more modest industrial development.[51]

It also gave cold war America something to boast about.

> By the summer of 1959, official American optimism about the situation had become unlimited and unrestrained. Experts wrote books and magazine articles which referred to the 'miracle' of South Vietnam. American military advisers and diplomats threw caution out of the window. The Communist threat had been reduced to the past tense, something that could be looked back on, a nightmare now only half remembered.[52]

An example of George Ball's hubris was undoubtedly present in the pages of one of America's most prestigious foreign policy journals, *Foreign Affairs*. In the only article published specifically on South Vietnam between 1954 and 1961, the establishment of the American-backed regime of Ngo Dinh Diem is presented as a success story that has happened against all odds. However, the author, William Henderson, has at times to put a public relations spin on the unsavoury aspects of South Vietnamese government. The article, 'South Viet Nam Finds Itself' (1957), is a revealing insight into contemporary American thinking about Southeast Asia. So after the Geneva Accords, 'the general expectation was that South Viet Nam would quickly succumb to Communist pressures'. But far from collapsing, the government of Ngo Dinh Diem . . . has made remarkable progress in putting its house in order and establishing the bases of stability and future progress. Today South Viet Nam is very much in business, and barring the catastrophe of a third world war in the foreseeable future, is likely to remain in business.

The credit for this 'wholly unexpected political miracle' should go to Diem: 'history may yet adjudge Diem as one of the great figures of twentieth century Asia'. What sort of regime had been constructed? The image of an orderly and peaceful nation is somewhat undermined as Henderson, without trace of irony, admits that 'from the beginning Diem has ruled virtually as a dictator. South Viet Nam is today a quasi-police state characterized by arbitrary arrests and imprisonment, strict censorship of the press and the absence of an effective political opposition'. Moreover, there is another candid insight that 'Diem could never have survived without American support'.

But at least this is not a communist regime. That fact allows a comforting prediction to be made.

Today the Communists could still cause a lot of trouble in South Viet Nam. They could isolate extensive if fairly remote areas in the event of a renewed outbreak of civil war. But barring outside aid in the form of an invasion from the North, it is doubtful if they could any longer seriously challenge the authority of the Diem regime over most of its territory.[53]

The Eisenhower years were punctuated by such laudatory references to Diem's supposed achievement. In 1955, the Democrat senator Mike Mansfield argued that South Vietnam's situation had improved 'largely through the dedication and the courage of Ngo Dinh Diem'.[54] And in November 1960, Professor Rupert Emerson of Howard University, in an article which dealt with 'The Erosion of Democracy' in parts of Asia, nevertheless suggested that

in South Vietnam, Ngo Dinh Diem, far exceeding the expectations of most observers, made excellent use of the opportunities which peace and independence offered him for a non-Communist reconstruction of his country. Power has, however, been gathered tightly into his own hands and the democratic trimmings of his regime represent rather a hope for the future than a present working reality.[55]

If Diem had really done so much, and the prospect for a developing democracy existed in South Vietnam by the end of Eisenhower's administration, as such expert comment would imply, the question is begged: why did things collapse so quickly just after Kennedy entered the White House?

The view of Diem that developed in the 1950s was built on self-delusion and wish-fulfilment. As Frances FitzGerald points out, by 1956 'U.S. officials were lyrical in their reports to the press and to Congress, asserting that the Diem regime was on the way to rebuilding the economy and solving the social problems caused by a decade of war'.[56] 'Like water turning to ice', for Halberstam, 'the illusion crystallized and became a reality, not because that which existed in South Vietnam was real, but because it became real in powerful men's minds'.[57] The acceptance of the myth that Diem's regime represented a powerful bulwark against the spread of communism in Southeast Asia allowed Americans to believe that their policy of containment was working.

Schlesinger in his account of Kennedy's administration, *A Thousand Days* (1965), admits that Vietnam was the most intractable problem which American policymakers were to face in the post-Eisenhower period. Yet 'the commitment to South Vietnam . . . followed directly from the Dulles conception of the world as irrevocably split into two unified and hostile blocs. In such a world, the threat of communism was indivisible and the obligation to oppose that threat unlimited'.[58] And it is in that failure to recognise that the perspectives of the Eisenhower era might not be appropriate to the world inherited by a new Democrat administration that the limited vision of the 'best and the brightest' is revealed. For if, as Halberstam suggests, 'the essence of good foreign policy is constant re-examination', then it is also revealing that

the Kennedy Administration did not re-evaluate any of the Eisenhower conceptions in Asia (conceptions which Dulles had tailored carefully to the disposition of the McCarthy group in the Senate); if anything, the Kennedy people would set out to upgrade and modernize the means of carrying out those policies.[59]

As Diem's regime floundered and foundered, the Kennedy team emerged as, on the whole, unreconstructed cold warriors, intent on galvanising America's self-assigned mission to oppose communism. Their achievement would be to transform the war in Vietnam into an American enterprise.

At first, Kennedy himself seemed prepared to accept the official view that America's protégé in Vietnam was firmly in control of events there. In the aftermath of the French withdrawal, he claimed, 'a determined band of patriotic Vietnamese around one man of faith, President Diem' had tapped into and directed 'the latent power of nationalism to create an independent, anti-Communist Vietnam'.[60] Despite this, and a litany of other similar endorsements from other political leaders in the United States, however, it was evident that 'in spite of considerable American economic and military aid, Diem was in trouble by 1959'.[61] So, as president, Kennedy was confronted immediately with a steadily worsening situation in South Vietnam. But what had gone wrong with Diem?

The answer was that little had been right with Diem from the start. But it suited American officials and political leaders – and Kennedy was an accomplice to this conceit – to present South Vietnam as a cold war success story. Their version of Diem's achievement was unquestioned, because, as Frances FitzGerald observed, until 1961 at least, few American journalists went to Vietnam to report at first hand the nature of the regime in the South. In this way, 'for the first six years information about the Diem regime came largely from U.S. government sources'. Furthermore, 'by far the most prolific of these government sources was the team from Michigan State University led by Diem's earliest supporter, Dr. Wesley Fishel'. And 'as Dr. Fishel himself explained, one had to know the whole history and culture of a country in order to understand its process of political and economic development. As the head of the team, Dr. Fishel himself took over the task of explaining how and in what manner the Diem regime was a democracy'.[62]

It was an early example of 'explaining' Vietnam through an appeal to the special knowledge that might be gained only by visiting the country: the idea that a privatised truth was apparent to those who witnessed it at first hand. Others might defer to such experience and expertise. But the implications of relying upon such an official source are apparent in Halberstam's assessment of the deteriorating situation in South Vietnam. 'The American policy was to trust Diem and not to cross him; thus the American military mission saw its job as getting along with Diem, so his reporting became our reporting, his statistics our statistics, finally his lies our lies'.[63]

As the political situation in South Vietnam, viewed from an American perspective, deteriorated in 1960 and 1961, the Kennedy administration, already beset by foreign policy confrontations – the Vienna summit, the Bay of Pigs invasion, tension in Berlin – was forced to turn its attention to the problems engendered by its policy there. The principal goal had been established. Given the underlying force of

Kennedy's imperialist persuasion, and the prevailing assumptions of cold war ideology, the purpose of American involvement was simple. It was to prevent communist control of South Vietnam. Debates centred around the mechanisms whereby South Vietnam could be 'saved'; not indeed around the question of whether America should 'save' it. South Vietnam was an example of traditional containment policy: the linear descendant of Greece in 1947 and Korea in 1950, with the 'loss' of China in 1949 forever lurking in the background.

Diem is the pivotal figure in any assessments of the Kennedy administration's pursuit of its mission in South Vietnam. And the ambiguities of the relationship between America's nominated leader and his sponsors in the United States are well illustrated when one of Kennedy's closest aides comes to write about this period. Theodore Sorensen in *Kennedy* (1965) claims that Diem saved the South from political disintegration after partition. 'American aid, Vietnamese energy and the vigorous administrative talents of South Vietnam's President Ngo Dinh Diem prevented that collapse and in fact produced more economic and educational gains than the North.' But a page later, in an effort to absolve JFK from expanding America's involvement in the war he continues:

> the principal responsibility for that expansion lies not with Kennedy but with the Communists, who, beginning in the late 1950s, vastly expanded their efforts to take over the country. The dimensions of our efforts also had to be increased, unfortunately, to compensate for the political weaknesses of the Diem regime.[64]

So the energetic and vigorous administrator of the mid-1950s, within a couple of years and a page of memoirs has become politically emasculated. The United States was thus forced to react to increased communist activity in Vietnam. The disingenuous use of the word 'unfortunately' to describe America's escalating military commitment to South Vietnam is a revealing insight into Sorensen's political persuasion.

Kennedy, then, was not to be blamed. If the communists were one scapegoat, testing what Sorensen claims was Kennedy's principal objective, to make South Vietnam 'neither a Cold War pawn nor a hot war battleground', then Lyndon Johnson might be another. Kennedy sent his vice-president on a tour to Vietnam in 1961, where, with classic Texan hyperbole, he was moved to describe Diem as the 'Winston Churchill of South-East Asia'. But this allows Sorensen to suggest that it was Johnson's report which helped to persuade Kennedy to support the fight against communism. 'The key to what is done by Asians, he said, is confidence in the United States, in our power, our will and our understanding.' But Kennedy was 'unwilling to commit American troops to fighting Asians on the Asian mainland for speculative psychological reasons'.[65] For Sorensen, then, Kennedy was being forced reluctantly into war: an interpretation that can be sustained only through suspending belief in the administration's rhetoric in an effort to provide political absolution for its president's actions. For, as Halberstam observes, 'the problems were political, but the response was military'.[66] Kennedy's choice to oversee the administration's policy on Vietnam was Robert McNamara, secretary of defence, rather than Dean Rusk, his secretary of state. The idea that this was not yet, in any sense, an American war is belied by McNamara's confident statement on a visit to Vietnam in 1962: 'every quantitative measure . . . shows that we are winning the war'. It is 'our war'. As the *New York Times* argued in a contemporary editorial, the war in Vietnam 'is a struggle this country cannot shirk'.[67]

In 1963, in his State of the Union address, Kennedy argued that 'the spearpoint of aggression has been blunted in South Vietnam'.[68] In the run-up to the 1964 election, it was important to appear in control. Halberstam, again, sums up the approach:

> if the reporters would not write up-beat stories, the Kennedy Administration, facile, particularly good at public relations, would generate its own positive accounts. Thus optimism amd optimistic statements became a major and deliberate part of the policy; warfare by public relations, one more reflection of the Kennedy era.[69]

It was an era that was about to end.

The *coup* and the assassination of Diem early in November 1963 are taken to have concentrated Kennedy's mind on his administration's record in South Vietnam. Schlesinger argues that this made Kennedy realise 'that Vietnam was his great failure in foreign policy, and that he had never given it his full attention'. The implication is that had Kennedy made the containment of communism in South Vietnam his highest priority, that failure might have been avoided. But his strategy of expanding the American military role in South Vietnam, while attempting to keep the commitment of American personnel limited encouraged Diem to continue on an ultimately self-destructive path, while leading the nation to believe that here was a burden that might be easily borne. Kennedy's rhetoric, combined with his policies, narrowed the options for his successor: he established the mission that would prove impossible. And yet as Lyndon Johnson inherited the presidency, he did so with an avowed intention. 'I am not going to lose Vietnam . . . I am not going to be the President who saw South-East Asia go the way China went'.[70] Along with his immediate successors in the White House, he did.

CONCLUSION: SUPERMAN AS HEROIC LEADER

The Will to Power is by nature aggressive; it goes forth in search of obstacles, it seeks to compare, master, conquer, and destroy.[71]

For Charles Morris, 'there is no doubt that Kennedy's militarism helped him gain his razor thin election victory'.[72] His 'thousand days' in office were marked by the abortive attempt to invade Cuba in the Bay of Pigs, the brinkmanship of the missile crisis, and the inexorable commitment of military force to the political problem of Vietnam. It was in this sphere of military involvement overseas, then, that the two parts of Kennedy's political identity – the Nietzschean existentialist, defining himself through action, and the New Frontier rhetoritician, seeking fresh challenges abroad – were most thoroughly integrated. The adventure of the Bay of Pigs ended in early defeat. The Cuban Missile crisis, following soon afterwards, demonstrated to both the Soviet Union and the United States the potential risks of such confrontations. But there remained alternative strategies. As Kennedy put it on his return from his disastrous summit meeting with Khrushchev in Vienna in 1961, 'now we have the problem of making our power credible, and Vietnam looks like the place'.[73] Southeast Asia was where the existential hero as president was prepared to assert his 'will to power' in the cause of containing communism.

As Richard Slotkin observes, Kennedy's 'inaugural address, and the policy formulations that followed it, framed the New Frontier's project as one of personal moral regeneration achieved through action in a particular heroic style'.[74] So it was not just leadership which the United States required, it was heroic leadership. And in this context, Arthur Schlesinger also provided a philosophical justification for Kennedy's style in an argument reminiscent of Mailer's Nietzschean analysis, in an article published in *Encounter* a month after Kennedy had won the presidential election. Schlesinger's investigation was ostensibly concerned with the problem of political leadership in the developing world, but an image of JFK appears to underlie much of what he has to say. So classical democratic theory has a problem with the concept of leadership: Lockean ideas of majority rule, and the egalitarian ethic that underpins the ideal of democracy tend to denigrate the role of the leader. But, as Schlesinger observes, whatever the theory, in practice the United States has recognised 'democracy's functional need for leadership' from the founding period onwards.[75]

It is when his discussion moves to a moral justification for strong leadership, however, that Schlesinger conflates the idea of the hero with the idea of the leader, and a vignette of Kennedy can be teased from his argument. Writing in a cold war idiom which saw a fundamental dichotomy between democratic concepts of free will, and Marxist beliefs in historical determinism, Schlesinger proposes that

> the heroic leader has the Promethean responsibility to affirm human freedom against the supposed inevitabilities of history. As he does this, he combats the infection of fatalism which might otherwise paralyse mass democracy. Without heroic leaders, a society would tend to acquiesce in the drift of history. Such acquiescence is easy enough; the great appeal of fatalism, indeed, is as a refuge from the terrors of responsibility.

The heroic leader can operate, in certain circumstances, even beyond the pale of constitutional government. Faced with crises of 'war, revolution, or economic chaos', the heroic leader should take command, for 'what makes short-run authoritarianism possible in . . . the United States is precisely the strength of the antecedent tradition of liberty' which will reassert itself after the crisis has passed.[76] The nation might need Nietzsche's superman rather than Whitman's democratic hero. Schlesinger's conception of the heroic leader – Kennedy – suggests what Slotkin calls 'the paradox of the New Frontier . . . it aimed at achieving democratic goals through structures and methods that were elite-dominated and command-oriented'.[77] The desire not simply for a leader, but one cast in such a heroic mould was due to the enormity of the cold war challenges that in 1960 many Americans believed their country faced.

As Ralph Waldo Emerson had observed, 'whoso is heroic will always find crises to try his edge'.[78] In *Profiles in Courage*, JFK had written that 'great crises produce great men, and great deeds of courage'.[79] He presented himself to his contemporaries as president at a time of acute – almost apocalyptic – challenge. In his inaugural address, he referred to his generation's almost unique historical role 'of defending freedom in its hour of maximum danger'. Similar imagery suffused his first State of the Union address, made shortly afterwards. 'I speak today in an hour of national peril and national opportunity. Before my term has ended, we shall have to test anew whether a nation organized and governed such as ours can endure.' The echoes of Lincoln's Gettysburg address nevertheless preceded a note of caution: 'the outcome is by no means certain. The answers are by no means clear'. Later, Kennedy appears even more pessimistic.

> No man entering upon this office, regardless of his party, regardless of his previous service in Washington, could fail to be staggered upon learning – even in this brief ten day period – the harsh enormity of the trials through which we must pass in the next four years. Each day the crises multiply. Each day their solution grows more difficult. Each day we draw nearer the hour of maximum danger, as weapons spread and hostile forces grow stronger.[80]

Even allowing for rhetorical exaggeration, the imagery is that of an Emersonian hero deliberately creating the atmosphere of crisis in which his leadership will be tested, repeatedly, during the pilgrimage of his presidency. It was this challenge that Kennedy appeared to relish. As Slotkin suggests, 'his heroic style was that of the warrior'.[81] Both New England transcendentalist and German philosopher would have approved. 'Sensitive, intelligent, scholarly, poetic and solitary, Emerson admires, as Nietzsche with a similar temperament would after him, men of action'.[82] JFK seemed to his contemporaries to be such a man.

In assessments of the new president, then, a recurrent theme is of Kennedy as a potentially heroic leader. Nietzschean images in such a portrayal seem to be never far away. As the historian James McGregor Burns put it: 'He is omniscient . . . He is omnipresent . . . He is omnipotent . . . He's Superman!'[83] But for the image to retain its political resonance, Kennedy had to maintain the atmosphere of challenge and confrontation that characterised his administration. Henry Fairlie captured this mood when he suggested that throughout Kennedy's time in the White House America 'lived in an atmosphere of perpetual crisis and recurring crises . . . policy was subjected to crisis, and crisis was used in turn to stimulate the response of the people . . . So they lived for a thousand days in expectation of danger, and of rescue from it'.[84] Kennedy's supporters would thus follow him as he tiptoed into Vietnam, only to exonerate him later from his error, clinging to the belief that had he survived, things would have been both different and better.

The Nietzschean superman as president had re-emphasised the role of the pioneer as the democratic hero of American history: the self-reliant individual who could survive in the hostile environment of the New Frontier. Kennedy had the ability to catch and thus define within his own political persona the transient spirit of his age. Yet the Vietnam war fractured the political consensus of the United States in the 1960s, and after Kennedy's assassination that conflict now led a generation of Americans to challenge the worship of such traditional icons, and in turn all but destroyed the nation's belief in its established historical myths. As Hellmann writes:

> Kennedy had energized Americans with his vision of their heroic possibilities on a New Frontier. He had celebrated the American mythic landscape in a poetic image that called for imaginatively transforming the idea bound up in America's past geographical drive West into a many-leveled pursuit of national adventure and mission . . . but a decade after his death Vietnam seemed to have cut Americans off from both their past and future frontiers.[85]

Such was the legacy of the 'hipster' as president.

NOTES

1. Mailer, *The Naked and the Dead*, p. 282.
2. Solotaroff, *Down Mailer's Way*, p. 16.
3. Mailer, *The Naked and the Dead*, p. 282.
4. Lea, *The Tragic Philosopher*, p. 185.
5. Quoted in Richard Schacht, *Nietzsche*, pp. 329–30.
6. Whitman, 'The Eighteenth Presidency', pp. 112 and 113.
7. Ibid. p. 93.
8. Molina, *Existentialism as Philosophy*, p. 24.
9. Mailer, 'Superman Comes to the Supermarket', p. 24.
10. Schlesinger, *A Thousand Days,* p. 57.
11. Mailer, '*Playboy* Interview', p. 272.
12. Podhoretz, 'Norman Mailer', p. 79.
13. Mailer, 'Superman Comes to the Supermarket', pp. 15–18.
14. Ibid. p. 20.
15. Solotaroff, *Down Mailer's Way*, p. 125.
16. Kennedy, *Profiles in Courage*, p. 1.
17. Ibid. p. 19.
18. Ibid. p. 42.
19. Ibid. p. 177.
20. Ibid. p. 208.
21. Ibid. pp. 215, 218, 223.

22. Foster, 'Norman Mailer', p. 44.
23. Mailer, 'Superman Comes to the Supermarket', p. 36.
24. Schlesinger, *A Thousand Days*, p. 105.
25. Ibid. pp. 105 and 649.
26. Quoted in O'Donnell and Power, *Johnny We Hardly Knew Ye*, p. 199.
27. Sorensen, *Kennedy*, p. 167. Compare, however, Pilger, 'Bobby', pp. 121–2: 'It was [Richard] Goodwin who was said to have coined "the New Frontier" for John Kennedy's campaign . . .'.
28. Nevins, introduction to J. F. Kennedy, *Profiles in Courage*, pp. xix–xx.
29. Cassirer, *The Myth of the State*, p. 282.
30. Williams, *Empire as a Way of Life*, p. 198.
31. Hellmann, *American Myth and the Legacy of Vietnam*, p. 36.
32. Fuchs, *Those Peculiar Americans*, p. 11.
33. Quoted in Wolfe, *The Right Stuff*, pp. 400–1.
34. Ibid. p. 275.
35. Hellmann, *American Myth and the Legacy of Vietnam*, p. 47.
36. Kennedy, 'Inaugural Address', Friday, 20 January 1961' (see Website: Presidential Inaugural Addresses).
37. Fukuyama, *The End of History and the Last Man*, p. 333.
38. Schlesinger, *A Thousand Days*, pp. 104–5.
39. Quoted in Michael Maclear, *Vietnam*, p. 59.
40. Ball, *The Past Has Another Pattern*, p. 422.
41. Brown, *JFK*, pp. 34–5.
42. Sheehan, *A Bright Shining Lie*, p. 375.
43. Ibid. p. 12.
44. Gibbons, *The US Government and the Vietnam War*, pt 1, p. 204.
45. Ibid. pp. 303–4.
46. Halberstam, *The Best and the Brightest*, p. 168.
47. Ball, *The Past Has Another Pattern*, p. 183.
48. Gibson, *The Perfect War*, pp. 80–1.
49. Chomsky, *The Backroom Boys*, p. 28.
50. Halberstam, *The Best and the Brightest*, p. 182.
51. Warner, *The Last Confucian*, p. 125.
52. Ibid. p. 125.
53. Henderson, 'South Viet Nam Finds Itself', pp. 283–94, *passim*.
54. Gibbons, *The US Government and the Vietnam War*, pt. 1, p. 300.
55. Emerson, 'The Erosion of Democracy', p. 2.
56. FitzGerald, *Fire in the Lake*, p. 85.
57. Halberstam, *The Best and the Brightest*, p. 184.
58. Schlesinger, *A Thousand Days*, p. 467.
59. Halberstam, *The Best and the Brightest*, p. 151.
60. Quoted in Bassett and Petz, 'The Failed Search for Victory', p. 226.
61. Ibid. p. 226.
62. FitzGerald, *Fire in the Lake*, p. 86.

63. Halberstam, *The Best and the Brightest*, p. 226.
64. Sorensen, *Kennedy*, pp. 650 and 651.
65. Ibid. p. 653.
66. Halberstam, *The Best and the Brightest*, p. 225.
67. Quoted in Karnow, *Vietnam*, pp. 271 and 272.
68. *Public Papers of the Presidents: John F. Kennedy (1963)*, 'Annual Message to Congress on the State of the Union', p. 11.
69. Halberstam, *The Best and the Brightest*, p. 255.
70. Quoted in VanDeMark, *Into the Quagmire*, p. 25.
71. Lea, *The Tragic Philosopher*, p. 198.
72. Morris, *A Time of Passion*, p. 21.
73. Kennedy to James Reston, quoted in Halberstam, *The Best and the Brightest*, p. 97.
74. Slotkin, *Gunfighter Nation*, p. 499.
75. Schlesinger, 'On Heroic Leadership' p. 4.
76. Ibid. pp. 5 and 9–10.
77. Slotkin, *Gunfighter Nation*, p. 500.
78. Emerson, 'Heroism', p. 110.
79. Kennedy, *Profiles in Courage*, p. 55.
80. Kennedy, 'Inaugural Address' and *Public Papers of the Presidents of the United States: John F. Kennedy (1961)*, 'Annual Message to Congress on the State of the Union', pp. 19–28.
81. Slotkin, *Gunfighter Nation*, p. 497.
82. Stack, *Nietzsche and Emerson*, p. 129.
83. Quoted in Halberstam, *The Best and the Brightest*, p. 52.
84. Quoted in Price, *With Nixon*, p. 80. Price observes (ibid.) that 'Nixon sought . . . on taking office: to move, as he put it, from crisis management to crisis prevention'.
85. Hellmann, *American Myth and the Legacy of Vietnam*, p. 95.

CHAPTER FOUR

Lyndon Johnson: Casualty of War

INTRODUCTION: PARANOIA AND THE PRESIDENCY

Robert Dallek, in his biography of Lyndon Johnson, *Lone Star Rising* (1991), recounts President de Gaulle's remark at John Kennedy's funeral in 1963: 'This man Kennedy, de Gaulle said, was the country's mask. But this man Johnson is the country's real face'.[1] Kennedy had supplied American politics with a fleeting existential veneer, and had re-packaged the mythology of the frontier to galvanise the nation's sense of mission in the midst of its cold war confrontation with the Soviet Union. In Robert McNamara's estimation, his successor was 'a towering, powerful, paradoxical figure, reminding me of a verse from Walt Whitman's "Song of Myself": *Do I contradict myself?/Very well then I contradict myself;/I am large, I contain multitudes*'.[2] With Lyndon Johnson (LBJ) in the White House, the restless energy, pragmatism, self-confidence and sense of purpose of Frederick Jackson Turner's typical pioneer found its outlets in the hubris of the Great Society, and ultimately in the wreckage of Vietnam.

LBJ, a 'child of the passing frontier',[3] continued the pursuit of an overseas adventure that would undermine traditional beliefs in the mythic landscape of American history, and would fracture too the nation's political consensus. And he suffered as a result. As Stephen Oates suggested in 1985,

> maybe Johnson has become so hated in our time that Americans want him reduced to caricature, want him presented as . . . [someone] who took away *our* idealism and *our* humanity in the flames of Vietnam. Maybe Johnson has become a scapegoat for our collective guilt over the war, and all our woes and shattered dreams that followed.[4]

Johnson's perceived failure as chief executive, moreover, represented a defeat for the idea of the heroic president. And yet, for his critics, it was not the institution that was at fault. Rather Johnson's conduct as president, like Nixon's after him, would be measured and assessed in terms of his personality and indeed his mental health. Both LBJ and his immediate successor, as Vietnam unravelled the cultural consensus of cold war America, would be regarded by some of their political opponents as significantly and psychologically flawed.

The image of a paranoid president is part of a discernible political demonology, rooted not simply in the broader concerns of the 'paranoid style' that Richard Hofstadter, for example, had used as a historical characterisation of American political culture. Fear of nuclear war, in which survival techniques were based upon comforting nostrums such as 'duck and cover', underpinned American cold war culture as an ever-present, tangible concern. In this atmosphere, any war – Vietnam included – would become a drama played out against the background of a heightened expectation of the possibility that the denouement of the cold war would be nuclear conflict. Who would decide that fate? America needed calm, rational, emotionally stable leaders: those who – in the analogy of the hero as astronaut – were celebrated by Tom Wolfe as having 'the right stuff'. But what would happen if a madman gained power? Portraying presidential aspirants as psychologically unstable extremists became part of the contemporary currency of political campaigns.

If the launch of Sputnik in 1957 had demonstrated the potential of Soviet rocket technology, five years later the Cuban missile crisis, as well as being a showpiece of nuclear brinkmanship, compounded popular fears of atomic war. This was reflected in contemporary popular culture. In 1962, the same year that Kennedy confronted Khrushchev over Cuba, Eugene Burdick and Harvey Wheeler published *Fail Safe*, a novel in which the American president, modelled evidently on JFK (and played in the movie by the calm and trustworthy Henry Fonda), makes a wholly rational decision to use nuclear bombs to destroy New York, after a technological malfunction has sent bombers on a mission to Moscow. The novel aimed to undermine misplaced and complacent faith in the mystique that nuclear systems were infallible. Chance accidents could occur. If they do, as the plot unfolds, it becomes chillingly clear that the rational responses of game theory as applied to nuclear strategy will lead to the apocalyptic moment. The president has to sacrifice an American city to forestall a wider conflict. A year later, Stanley Kubrick's film *Dr Strangelove* (1963) was another cultural response to this pervading sense of anxiety. For David Halberstam, indeed, it represented 'an important bench mark; it attacked not so much the other side as the total mindlessness of nuclear war, portraying how the irrational had become the rational'.[5] Cold war critics of the film failed to appreciate its satirical message: *Dr Strangelove* dared to make fun of what Burdick and Wheeler had shown was the potentially devastating outcome of a situation where the smallest error could result in a chain reaction that might lead to war.

This heightened fear of nuclear confrontation was compounded when, in October 1964, China exploded an atomic device. In a public address on 18 October, Johnson, in the last stages of campaigning against Barry Goldwater for the presidency, interpreted the event.

> No American should treat this matter lightly. Until this week, only four powers had entered the dangerous world of nuclear explosions. Whatever their differences, all four are sober and serious states, with long experience as major powers in the modern world. Communist China has no such experience.[6]

So China's communists were naive and fanatical; fanatics were irrational; now reckless and unpredictable gamblers could play nuclear poker.

Johnson subtly played upon the pervasive popular anxiety over nuclear warfare, effectively challenging Americans to confront the perennial question of cold war presidential politics: who would be responsible for controlling the nation's atomic arsenal? In private, he was convinced that Goldwater was psychologically unfit to be president: in *Taking Charge* (1997), Michael Beschloss transcribes tapes of LBJ's White House conversations in which he routinely refers to his Republican opponent as a madman. At one point, Johnson says, 'I just shudder to think what would happen if Goldwater won it. He's a man that's had two nervous breakdowns. He's not a stable fellow at all . . .'.[7] In public, he was more restrained, but lost no opportunity to question the Republican candidate's ability to lead cold war America. So, in Ohio, on 16 October 1964, before China's nuclear test, for LBJ,

> one important question, and there has been a good deal of attention to this one, is whose hand and whose thumb is going to be trusted by the American people with control of the most awesome power, the mightiest power, the world has ever known? When you get ready to push that button, whose thumb do you want on that button?

Again, at Los Angeles City Hall on 28 October, he was even more dramatic:

the only real issue in this campaign, the only thing you ought to be concerned about at all, is who can best keep the peace? In the nuclear age the president doesn't get a second chance to make a second guess. If he mashes that button – that is it.[8]

LBJ, who had seen at first hand how Kennedy had responded to the missiles in Cuba, portrayed himself as experienced in handling potential nuclear crises.

In contrast, right-wing belligerence would lead to nuclear catastrophe. Goldwater was dangerously unpredictable. The Republican slogan 'in your heart you know he's right' was transformed tellingly into the Democrat retort, 'in your guts you know he's nuts'. Theodore White recalls one of the 'masterpieces of political television' devised by Johnson's campaign team.

The famous Daisy girl spot . . . which began with a close-up of a tow-haired muppet plucking petals from a daisy, babbling her count as she went, until the film faded through her eyes to a countdown of an atomic testing site and the entire scene dissolved in a mushroom cloud. The film mentioned neither Goldwater nor the Republicans specifically – but the shriek of Republican indignation fastened the bomb message on them more tightly than any calculation could have expected.[9]

Johnson recalls in his memoirs that Goldwater in 1964 made

a series of statements implying that he would more than willingly threaten to use, or even use, nuclear weapons to gain American ends. Statements such as 'I want to lob one into the men's room of the Kremlin and make sure I hit it' created the image of an impulsive man who shoots from the hip, who talks and acts first and thinks afterwards.[10]

Goldwater's sentiment may have been designed as an appeal to those frustrated by their fears of living constantly in the shadow of nuclear confrontation: those to whom resolution of an ever present threat was better than the constant uncertainty of contemporary life. But such a constituency was small. The threat to use nuclear force was easily presented as more dangerous when power was in the hands of a Republican extremist than when it was given to a trustworthy Democrat committed to maintain the integrity and the security of the 'vital center'.

Electoral considerations aside, as Brian VanDeMark observes, China's new-found nuclear capability did have important strategic dimensions for US policymakers. 'Pentagon officials, who vividly recalled

China's punishing intervention in the Korean War, now faced an army of two and a half million, equipped with nuclear weapons. The combination appeared a potent threat, no longer checked by an American nuclear advantage'. The psychological impact of China's technological achievement was no less significant. 'By becoming the first Asian nation to master the atom, U.S. officials believed China had dramatically strengthened its influence in a region – Southeast Asia – which many considered a crucial ideological battleground between Peking and Washington'.[11] In terms of America's growing involvement in the Vietnam war, China's emergence as a nuclear power was critical not only in its timing, but also in terms of defining the parameters of the conflict.

Decisions to escalate America's military presence in Vietnam would thus be made in the context of the recurrent concern that China, too, might be drawn into the conflict. If Johnson's assessment of China's leadership was correct – that it lacked the international maturity to behave responsibly in the nuclear age – in turn that would open the possibility of a war of containment spiralling out of control. And yet, if China's nuclear capacity focused American's attention on the responsibilities of their own leaders in deciding whether or when to use the nation's nuclear weapons, and made the 1964 election campaign in part a referendum on the psychological health of the candidates, it would be Vietnam that in turn would turn the spotlight during the subsequent four years on the state of mind of the president – LBJ.

THE WAR AND JOHNSON'S MIND

With America's sons in the fields far away, with America's future under challenge right here at home, with our hopes and the world's hopes for peace in the balance every day, I do not believe that I should devote an hour or a day of my time to any personal partisan causes or to any duties other than the awesome duties of this office – the Presidency of your country. Accordingly, I shall not seek, and I will not accept, the nomination of my party for another term as your President.[12]

On 31 March 1968, in announcing that he would not be a candidate for re-election, Lyndon Johnson resigned from the American presidency in just as an effective manner, if not as spectacularly, as did his successor, Richard Nixon, some six years later. He left the White House with his fellow Americans rioting in the streets: his ambition to be regarded as the greatest president since Franklin Roosevelt crushed by war in Southeast Asia. He became, indeed, a casualty of war.

Two years earlier, Arthur Schlesinger jr. had published *The Bitter Heritage* as part of an attempt, co-ordinated with two other Kennedy stalwarts, Richard Goodwin and John Kenneth Galbraith, to stir American public opinion against Johnson's prosecution of the war. Despite his opposition to LBJ's policy in Southeast Asia, at that time Schlesinger wrote that 'the Vietnam story is a tragedy without villains'.[13] In his biography of *Robert Kennedy and His Times* (1978), however, he found a scapegoat. There he characterised – even pilloried – Johnson in the language of psychological disturbance. Schlesinger quotes Henry Kissinger leaving Washington in 1967 'with a conviction that LBJ's resistance to negotiation verges on a sort of madness'. Similarly Robert McNamara had 'concluded that Johnson was no longer capable of objective judgment'. For Bill Moyers 'Johnson . . . was by now well sealed off from reality; the White House atmosphere was "impenetrable" . . . Moyers used the word "paranoid" '.[14]

Such a portrayal of LBJ has to do with a concern to avoid Vietnam contaminating the Kennedy mystique. But it is not simply that. It enables Schlesinger, for example, to reconcile his earlier support for an aggressive cold war resistance to threatened communist expansionism, and his desire for a heroic leader in that struggle, with his later opposition to the war in Southeast Asia.[15] Whatever the provenance of this characterisation of presidential neurosis, its attraction for those who wish to preserve the myth of Kennedy's Camelot, and for those who are impressed by counter-factual interpretations of the history of the 1960s, is self-evident. The argument is straightforward. Vietnam becomes an egregious error: the president who countenanced such events must thus have had significant flaws in his character. A retrospective diagnosis of executive neurosis – with a hint, indeed of insanity – is thus useful in helping to explain the apparent absence of rational judgements and the suspension of moral sensibilities during a critical period in American history. There is also the implied speculation that if John F. Kennedy had lived, events would have been handled not simply in a different way, but with significantly better outcomes.

Bernard Brodie in *War and Politics* (1973) offers one such perspective on the role of chance in shaping history. For 'when a man like Lyndon B. Johnson can become President of the United States by virtue of the fact that an otherwise insignificant person full of rage happened to be able to fire a rifle bullet accurately . . . then surely we are dealing with a large measure of caprice'. It may be, of course, as capricious to assume that Jack Kennedy might have dodged the bullet in Dallas, but Brodie is concerned to make the case that Vietnam would not have been such an intractable problem had Kennedy survived. Thus, it is 'next to impossible to imagine . . . President Kennedy stubbornly escalating the commitment (to Vietnam) . . . and persisting in a course that over time abundantly exposed its own bankruptcy'. JFK had 'a far more subtle intelligence' than LBJ.[16] The argument relies more upon faith than logic. Yet for obvious reasons it appeals to those who also have contributed to the creation of the myth that Kennedy could and would have rescued the country from the debacle of Vietnam. Arthur Schlesinger jr. described Brodie's book as 'brilliant'.[17]

In picturing Johnson as paranoid, Schlesinger took Brodie's analysis a stage further. In so doing, he effectively reinforced the idea that Kennedy's assassination in some way warped the course of American politics. JFK did not show signs of the mental instability that he suggested affected the judgement of his successor, who became president only by default. If he had survived, therefore, it is only natural to assume that the politics of sanity would have kept America from sinking further and further into the quagmire of Vietnam.

Consider, then, Schlesinger writing about Lyndon Johnson in the latter stages of his presidency.

> In private, as the Vietnam debate grew more bitter, the President became driven, irascible, inflamed by wild suspicions . . . White House aides, Doris Kearns wrote, 'were frightened by what seemed to them signs of paranoia.' The president would enter into a compulsive monologue, punctuated by irrelevant laughs: . . . It was hard to make out. Was this merely an eccentric mode of relaxation? Or did he really believe what he was saying? If the latter, Goodwin and Moyers wondered what could be done. They thought of asking for psychiatric investigation. But, as Goodwin said, he would just talk calmly and rationally to a panel of psychiatrists, 'and everyone would think we were the ones who were crazy'.[18]

Schlesinger's portrait of Johnson is of a beleaguered president, besieged in the White House, and maddened by the war.

Richard Goodwin is a principal witness to Johnson's apparent neurosis. In a previous work Schlesinger described him as 'the archetypal New Frontiersman' who, apart from Theodore Sorensen, 'was Kennedy's best writer'.[19] Uneasy in his dealings with JFK's successor, Goodwin worked formally in the Johnson White House for only nine months, leaving in September 1965. Three years later he would help Eugene McCarthy in the New Hampshire primary election before joining Robert Kennedy's presidential campaign team. An ardent Kennedy supporter, then, he broke with Johnson early over the issue of Vietnam. His reminiscences on the state of LBJ's mind were given to Schlesinger in an interview some twelve years after the event.

Goodwin's discussion with Bill Moyers was a conversation with another disillusioned Johnson aide. Moyers had been an assistant to LBJ during his time in the Senate, but he was, according to David Halberstam, 'a Kennedy-style Texan', who during JFK's administration became deputy director of the Peace Corps. As a presidential aide to Lyndon Johnson, Moyers 'showed his own doubts on Vietnam largely by encouraging other doubters to speak and by trying to put doubters in touch with one another'. Having replaced George Reedy as Johnson's press secretary in 1965, he became 'a casualty of the war, . . . wounded at Credibility Gap' and left the White House during the following year.[20]

So in recounting this assessment of Johnson's paranoia, which appeared sufficiently worrying to have his aides wondering whether to seek psychiatric help, Schlesinger is relying upon the testimony of two committed anti-war Kennedy supporters, whose views are coloured not simply by their experience of working for Johnson, but also because of their fundamental disagreements with him about his policy on Vietnam. Yet equally supporting – and damaging – evidence of the way in which the Vietnam war and the pressures of the presidency worked upon Johnson's psyche is given by his other source, Doris Kearns. The account of the president's rambling monologue is taken from Schlesinger's reading of the manuscript copy of Kearn's psychobiography of Johnson. That work, then, appears to add further weight to Kennedy's friends' speculation as to LBJ's mental health.

FREUD AND LYNDON JOHNSON

Doris Kearns's relationship with Lyndon Johnson was complex. A doctoral student at Harvard and an anti-war activist, she joined the White House staff on a fellowship programme in 1967. She remained as a member of the president's personal entourage when he left the White House, helping him work on his book of memoirs. She married Richard Goodwin. By the standards of presidential biographies, her work *Lyndon Johnson and the American Dream* is possibly unique. The president, in his retirement, talked to his biographer because 'I reminded him of his dead mother. In talking with me, he had come to imagine he was also talking with her, unraveling the story of his life'.[21] In places, the book suggests that Johnson was using a form of psychotherapy in recounting some of his recurrent dreams: such material allows Kearns to use 'psychiatric knowledge . . . as a means of understanding the formation of Johnson's behavior'.[22] In so doing, however, Kearns is imitating to some extent the techniques employed in an earlier attempt at a 'psychological study' of another president, the controversial and speculative collaboration between Sigmund Freud and William Bullitt, *Thomas Woodrow Wilson*, published finally in 1967.

There are parallels between the two works. Whereas the greatest formative influence in Woodrow Wilson's life was his father, the Reverend Joseph Ruggles Wilson, for Lyndon Johnson it was his mother. Thus, 'from his position of primacy in his mother's home, Johnson seemed to develop what Freud has called "the feeling of a conqueror, that confidence of success that often induces real success"'.[23] Both Wilson and Johnson, however, had to grapple with what Freud considered to be the common challenge to the individual's psyche. 'Every human newcomer has been set the task of mastering the Oedipus complex . . . Whoever cannot manage it falls prey to neurosis'.[24] Freud and Bullitt's Wilson and Kearns's Johnson, in their separate ways, become presidents traumatised by self-induced neuroses emanating from their upbringing.

Freud and Bullitt's work, understandably, is couched in terms of Wilson's confrontation with the Oedipus complex, 'the most difficult problem that faces a child of man in his psychic development'. They suggest further that it was as a result of the drive of his super-ego that Wilson 'slipped many times towards neurosis, [and] . . . finally toward the end of his career he nearly plunged into psychosis'.[25] Kearns similarly infers from a childhood dream of Johnson's, in which he found himself paralysed in the face of stampeding cattle, that 'the boy's paralysis presents one solution, albeit powerful, to the fear of acting out the forbidden Oedipal wish to eliminate the father and take the mother'.[26] Wilson overachieved in his effort to live up to his childhood image of his father; Johnson sought preferment in deference to the future imagined for him by his mother. Both men reached the White House with the neuroses that stemmed from their early psychological developments intact. Moreover, their presidential careers appear to converge in failure, as Woodrow Wilson was unable to convince the nation of the benefits of the new world order negotiated at Versailles, and as Lyndon Johnson succumbed to the stresses of fighting an unpopular war in Vietnam.

The connection between the two presidents is made explicit by Kearns. In recurrent dreams which followed his heart attack in

1955, and again after the Tet offensive in 1968, Johnson 'became' Woodrow Wilson.

> In the dream, he [LBJ] was lying in a bed in the Red Room. His head was still his, but from the neck down his body was dead, victim of that paralysis which had held both Wilson and his grandmother in their final years. In the next room, he could hear all his assistants squabbling over who would get what parts of his power. He could neither talk nor walk and not a single aide tried to protect him.

As president, and terrified by this dream, Johnson developed a ritual.

> Lying in the dark, he could find no peace until he got out of bed, and, by the light of a small flashlight, walked the halls of the White House to the place where Woodrow Wilson's portrait hung. He found something soothing in the act of touching Wilson's picture; he could sleep again. He was still Lyndon Johnson, and he was still alive and moving; it was Woodrow Wilson who was dead.[27]

According to Kearns, therefore, Johnson's decision 'to go into Vietnam covertly, with force and with overtures of benevolent intentions, was an act of will that almost seems to sum up the character of the man'. But the psychological pressures induced by the domestic turmoil that came in the wake of direct American intervention in Southeast Asia impacted directly upon Johnson's already disintegrated personality. As that decision proves wrong, moreover, the embattled president becomes besieged within the White House, and his psychological problems are both magnified and manifest. Thus,

> it is characteristic of obsessional, delusional thinking to piece together bits of fact . . . in the past Johnson had displayed a fine sense of discrimination about his political opponents, recognizing that his enemies today might be his allies tomorrow. Now he became unrestrained and reckless, creating a fantasy world of heroes and villains. Members of the White House staff who had listened to the President's violent name-calling were frightened by what seemed to them signs of paranoia. Suddenly in the middle of a conversation, the President's voice would become intense and low-keyed. He would laugh inappropriately and his thoughts would assume a random, almost incoherent quality, as he began to spin a vast web of accusations.[28]

The implication is that Vietnam had unbuttoned the president's mind.

After recounting this monologue (which was the source Schlesinger quoted in his portrait of LBJ), Kearns comments that 'sometimes it seemed as if Johnson himself did not believe what he was saying, as if all the surmises were a bizarre recreation, a way to relax. But at other times Johnson's voice carried so much conviction that his words produced an almost hypnotic effect'. This obsession with the conspiracy he thought surrounded him came to dominate LBJ's life, and all but destroyed his grasp upon reality. Moreover, the institutional framework of his presidency contributed to his paranoid style.

> In typical circumstances, of course, people who slip into fantasy are quickly set straight by the adverse criticism of those around them, which forces them to face the truth. In Johnson's White House there were no such correctives. To the contrary, his every self-deception was repeatedly confirmed in the men around him.[29]

Kearns documents LBJ's fear of paralysis, fear of rejection, fear of being alone; his craving for affection, his competitiveness, both political and sexual; his deceit, conceit, energy and ambition. These traits contributed to Johnson's personal and political style and were brought to bear in his decision to commit more and more resources to the Vietnam war and in his method of prosecuting it. Her Freudian reading of Johnson as president illuminates the creative and also the destructive impulses of his compulsive personality. And it allows Schlesinger, for example, also to question the president's sanity as the Vietnam war impacted upon him.

THE INSTITUTIONALISATION OF NEUROSIS

Kearns's argument that there was no countervailing force within the White House that could jerk a delusioned president back to reality owes much to George Reedy, who resigned as Johnson's press secretary during the escalation of the Vietnam war. In *The Twilight of the Presidency* (1970), he suggested that the institution itself was a magnifying glass which would reveal any latent neuroses affecting its incumbent. And although he does not explicitly describe Johnson as mad, the thought of LBJ is never far from mind. Thus 'in the Senate . . . even the most neurotic of personalities must make some obeisance to reality' because political accommodations have to be reached among and between the hundred members.[30] This, then, was an arena in which Johnson had been held in check: indeed one in which he had been able to excel. The executive branch is different, its incumbent isolated, remote, but preternaturally able to dominate the political process.

In such a situation, Reedy argues, 'a highly irrational personality, who under other circumstances might be medically certifiable for treatment, could take over the White House and this event never be known with any degree of assurance'.[31] Moreover, this is not a remote possibility.

> Politics and neurosis are inextricably mingled because the neurotic personality is usually more articulate and more logical in expressing stands on the great issues of the day . . . What keeps most political leaders from rushing headlong into catastrophe is the fact that their own neurotic drives must clash with the neurotic drives of others and in the conflict certain forms of social sanity are bound to emerge. The presidential office, however, exists in an environment which is free of many of the restraints with which all other political leaders must contend . . . It is certain that whatever neurotic drives a president takes with him into the White House will be fostered and enhanced during his tenancy.[32]

So all politicians are potentially neurotic, and indeed the more successful the politician the deeper the neurosis may be. In an institution like the Senate, the American system of checks and balances works to the extent that politicians have to interact with each other, for out of collective neurosis, 'social sanity' – whatever that may be – can emerge. But the president, free from the need to sublimate psychological affliction to achieve political objectives, can give full reign to whatever fantasy life he takes with him to the White House. The structure of the institution encourages the indulgence of neurosis. Reedy's argument provides an institutional context for Kearns' psychological investigation and for Schlesinger's portrayal of a paranoid president.

LBJ AND THE AMERICAN PSYCHE

Michael Maclear considers that 'Johnson's revelations to Doris Kearns about his Vietnam motivations are essential to any understanding of America's sudden plunge into war'.[33] If LBJ bears responsibility for America's 'sudden' immersion in the Vietnam conflict, it was still the case that under Kennedy the nation had stood poised with its toe in the water. Johnson's first line of defence when faced with criticism of his actions in Southeast Asia always was to establish the continuity of an approach endorsed by his predecessor.[34] Nevertheless, Maclear correctly highlights the centrality of Kearns's work to any assessment of Johnson's character, and his approach to the presidency and decision-making.

Yet LBJ, as de Gaulle suggested, was also an American everyman.

He was a product of the society which, in the traumatic aftermath of Kennedy's assassination, looked to him to provide political leadership. As Hugh Sidey observes, LBJ would 'hold the country together. He pursued that goal with a singlemindedness and skill that no other man in high office could have mustered . . . Lyndon Johnson worked methodically and knowingly and – in the short term at least – produced a near-miracle in a storm center of anguish' .[35] In the same way that he had stamped his initials on his wife, his daughters, his pet dog and his ranch, however, so too did he conceive of himself now as the figurative father of the national tribe, whose assets were his to use as he wished.

So his style of leadership was personal – for Hugh Sidey, indeed, 'very personal'. 'His' boys would bomb Vietnam as their president selected the targets for them. He even had a proprietary interest in some of the technology they used. In 1948, Johnson had campaigned for the Senate using a helicopter built by the Bell Aerospace corporation. As Ronnie Dugger recounts,

> Bell aircraft . . . moved its entire helicopter operation to north Texas during the Korean war and became established as the world's largest builder of helicopters. By 1967 the Texas plant had eleven thousand employees producing two hundred helicopters a month, four fifths of them military.[36]

Johnson had looked after some of his home-state family. And as he said to an officer who was about to redirect him from one machine to another, following a review of marines *en route* for Vietnam, 'Son, they are all my helicopters'.[37] The comment condenses some of Johnson's assumptions about his position, his power and his responsibility.

He was, as Hugh Sidey notes, 'the great consumer, . . . an inveterate gadget man, reveling in all the labor-saving devices produced by United States technology'.[38] But Lyndon Johnson's fascination with machines had a psychological dimension as well. They allowed him, in the isolation of the presidency, to rediscover some of the former political benefits of life in the Senate: the club where he had become the ultimate 'insider' as majority leader in the 1950s. So 'one can imagine that in surrounding himself with ticker tape machines and triple-set television arrays and by reaching every spare moment for the phone Johnson was trying to recreate the flow, immediacy, and intimacy of his former political arena'.[39] Technology kept Johnson in communication with his American Empire – in touch and in charge. It is significant that when the technology of communication failed in the aftermath of the Tet offensive in 1968, Johnson was left politically floundering: his Vietnam policy exposed as veering out of control.

Barbara Tuchman argues that

> in the nervous tension of his sudden accession, Johnson felt he had to be 'strong', to show himself in command, especially to overshadow the aura of the Kennedys, both the dead and the living. He did not feel a comparable impulse to be wise; to examine options before he spoke.[40]

Yet as Hugh Sidey points out, in terms of the commitment to Southeast Asia,

> there were two basic options open to the President. He could get out of Vietnam or he could send a major force of combat troops to take the offensive – to fight toward some kind of victory, even though not clearly defined. Actually, there was only one option, given the state of Lyndon Johnson's mind and, indeed, of the national mentality. The United States did not quit and run.[41]

Here again the psychological make-up, of Johnson, and by extension of the country as a whole, points in the direction of the inevitability of a decision to continue to intervene overseas.

In Billy Lee Brammer's novel *The Gay Place*, published in 1961, Roy Sherwood stands outside Governor Arthur Fenstemaker's office. Sherwood is one of Fenstemaker's acolytes: the Governor is a thinly veiled caricature of Lyndon Johnson. In asking himself what he is doing there, Sherwood recalls that the same question 'had come to him once in Alaska, as he stalked a bear, cold and blinded with tears, on a hunting trip with his father . . .'.[42] Coincidentally Norman Mailer explores a similar metaphorical terrain in his 1967 work *Why Are We in Vietnam?*, a 'case study', as John Aldridge observed, 'of the individual and national pyschosis which, in its most virulent pathological extension, seems to him to have created the Vietnam war'.[43]

From this perspective, an appreciation of Johnson's psychology – his presidential 'character'- might thus become a way of interpreting too the collective psyche of the nation which, between 1961 and 1967, pursued its providential mission overseas and thereby destroyed its cultural consensus at home. Saul Frielander in *History and Psychoanalysis* (1978) poses a speculative question.

> Could we not say that major political decisions . . . result from the convergence of a social structure, the evolution of a personality, the profound beliefs of a collective identity and perhaps, in the case of choices with

universal implications, a set of archetypal configurations buried deep in the deepest regions of human experience?[44]

If so, LBJ as leader was in a sense merely following the collective cultural consensus of the time; a consensus of which he was both a product and a representative. America did not want to fail a cold war test any more than did Lyndon Johnson.

In his address to a joint session of Congress shortly after his predecessor's assassination, Johnson freely borrowed from Lincoln's Gettysburg address: 'so let us here highly resolve that John Fitzgerald Kennedy did not live – or die – in vain'.[45] Lincoln had rededicated the republic to its democratic purpose. But the impact of Kennedy's death was different to that of even Civil War. A national sense of purpose – 'ask not what your country can do for you . . .' – seemed temporarily shattered. Or as John Aldridge put it, in the wake of the events in Dallas, 'in our frustration and rage we have quite simply gone berserk'.[46] In such a situation, it may be that, as Richard Godden observes, 'war or its promise tightens the consensual accords'.[47] Vietnam becomes not so much the legacy of John F. Kennedy, as of his assassination. Many initially supported America's intensified military commitment to Southeast Asia. Only when the mission proved impossible did that consensus fracture.

> I have heard it said about the difference between results and consequences that results are what we expect, consequences are what we get. This certainly applies to our assumptions about Vietnam in the summer and fall of 1965. Reality collided with expectations. We had no sooner begun to carry out the plan to increase dramatically U.S. forces in Vietnam than it became clear there was reason to question the strategy on which the plan was based. Slowly, the sobering, frustrating, tormenting limitations of military operations in Vietnam became painfully apparent.[48]

Robert McNamara's realisation that the Johnson administration's policy in Southeast Asia was flawed did not prevent him trying to retrieve the mistake until, disillusioned, he left the Pentagon on 29 February 1968, a month before the president himself announced he would not seek another term in office. During that time the number of American troops in Vietnam had steadily increased, anti-war opposition within the United States had become more and more vociferous, and finally, the Tet offensive in 1968 had marked a psychological turning point: dramatically illustrating the tenacity with which the North Vietnamese continued to fight the war.

Freud, in *Totem and Taboo*, quotes J. G. Frazer's observation that a ruler 'must not only be guarded, he must also be guarded against'.[49] Johnson's tenure as president, to his critics, would bear out the wisdom of that remark. Yet whatever LBJ's personal commitment to the war in Vietnam, the domestic fracturing of political, social and cultural consensus caused by American involvement there eventually overwhelmed him. By 1968, as Doris Kearns put it, 'abdication was thus the last remaining way to restore control, to turn rout into dignity, collapse into order . . . He [LBJ] decided to retreat with honor'.[50] Johnson left the White House with his 'Great Society' disintegrating, under siege in the streets of America's major cities: his tenure as president punctuated by the assassinations of the nation's political leaders – literally in the cases of the Kennedy brothers, and Martin Luther King, metaphorically in terms of LBJ's own political career.

As Johnson committed America to fight a land war in Southeast Asia, Michael Maclear observes that 'circumstances forced his [LBJ's] decisions – *or was it the reverse?*'.[51] America's cold war mentality, nurtured in the conformist and consensus-dominated 1950s and coupled with Aldridge's 'frustration and rage' contributed thus to a national mood in which large scale intervention in Vietnam did not at first appear to be the act of folly it later seemed to be. Indeed, the repression of domestic political divisions in the consensus-minded years following the Second World War – the 'end of ideology' – might have played a part too in the build-up to Lyndon Johnson's adventure in Vietnam. As Carl-Gustav Jung put it in his essay 'The Fight with the Shadow' (1946):

> anything that disappears from your psychological inventory is apt to turn up in the guise of a hostile neighbour, who will inevitably arouse your anger and make you aggressive. It is surely better to know that your worst enemy is right there in your heart. Man's war-like instincts are ineradicable – therefore a state of perfect peace is unthinkable. Moreover peace is uncanny because it breeds war. True democracy is a highly psychological institution which takes account of human nature as it is and makes allowances for the necessity of conflict within its own national boundaries.[52]

The suppression of political conflict at home, most visible in the development of a bi-partisan approach to foreign policy – which Johnson as majority leader in the Senate supported during the Eisenhower years – endorsed confidence in the projection of America's military power abroad, even after the experience of Korea had hinted at the possibility of failure.

In his study of Freud's political and social thought, Paul Roazen explores the idea that

> war caused a malignant regression, both within the contending countries and within each individual. It lifted restraints all across the board. Aggression was sanctioned now, murder was legitimized, and those impulses within men which had been held under control were reactivated. . . . Outside events can always reawaken those most elemental drives of men.[53]

If the war in Vietnam would allow the release of such energies, however, it would also confirm the tendency of many in modern society towards alienation from the political and social system which appeared to condone such conduct. Zbigniew Brzezinski, writing in 1966, argued indeed that the cultural and political fragmentation of American society was a product of the times, and that sentiment opposed to the American involvement in the Vietnam war was a symptom rather than a cause of alienation.

> In some respects the alienated anti-Viet Nam war demonstrators are a portent of things to come. Their attitude as well as their personal behavior are a manifestation of a psychological crisis inherent in modern society. Viet Nam provides an outlet for basic cravings and fears, and if that issue did not exist, some other one would provide an excuse for the expression of personal and political abdication.[54]

It was as if some of the generation to whom Kennedy had pitched his appeal, after his death, were taking another existential step along the path of Nietzschean nihilism and alienation. Why, then, was America in Vietnam?

WHY ARE WE IN VIETNAM?

In Joseph Campbell's words there is an 'irresistible compulsion to make war: the impulse to destroy the father is continually transforming itself into public violence'.[55] And it was Norman Mailer once more who explored this Freudian predilection to engage in combat. For John Aldridge, Norman Mailer's novel, *Why Are We in Vietnam?* (1967) is 'an outlandish comic parable of our national tragedy, a grotesque anatomy of our psychic melancholy, a nightmare map of LBJ's certain route to disaster'.[56] The narrator D.J., 'broadcasting from Texas, from Dallas, Big D in Tex', [57] is located in Johnson's home state, where LBJ had made his wealth from owning broadcasting franchises; in the city where Kennedy had been assassinated. Mailer's novel explores the psychological pressures that are helping to drive the president and the nation towards war in Vietnam. D.J. becomes metaphorically one of LBJ's 'sons', who will fight 'Mr. Johnson's war' in Southeast Asia. In 1960, Mailer had described the Lyndon Johnson

> who has compromised too many contradictions and now the contradictions were in his face: when he smiled the corners of his mouth squeezed gloom; when he was pious, his eyes twinkled irony; when he spoke in a righteous tone, he looked corrupt; when he jested, the ham in his jowls looked to quiver. He was not convincing.[58]

In *Why Are We in Vietnam?* he presents another caricature of an LBJ-like personality in describing the narrator D.J.'s father, Rutherford 'Rusty' Jethroe. Rusty appears as 'a heroic-looking figure of a Texan, 6½, 194, red-brown lean keen of color, eyes gray-green-yellow-brown . . . he look like a high-breed crossing between Dwight D. Eisenhower and Henry Cabot Lodge'.[59] Eisenhower and Lodge in themselves symbolised the bi-partisan approach to the wider world. The president, a Republican, but one who projected himself as 'above' partisan politics – leaving such battles to his lieutenant, Richard Nixon – and Lodge, again Republican, but one who would serve the Kennedy administration as ambassador to South Vietnam.

But Rusty is also a representative of a corrupt corporate America, and 'the most competitive prick there is'[60], whose battles with his son underscore the Freudian relationship which is central to the novel. On the hunting trip to Alaska, once home to the Russian bear, but now American-owned and a playground in which the nation's corporate rich can relax, Rusty and D.J. act out the Oedipal complex. As they pursue a bear together, D.J. recalls Rusty beating him as a child, seeing the boy as a rival. During the hunt,

> death is on him, memory of father near to murdering the son, . . . and then on the trail came a presence, no longer the fear of death but concentration, murder between the two men came to rest, for murder was outside them now, same murder which had been beaming in to D.J. while he thinking of murdering his father, the two men turned to contemplate the beast.[61]

Yet the rite of passage of the hunting trip does not resolve the Oedipal tensions between father and son: Rusty's American competitiveness prevents such a psychological catharsis. Their hunt is successful. But back at camp, they asked at last who had got the bear, and D.J., in the silence which followed, said, 'Well, we both sent shots home, but I reckon Rusty got it', and Rusty didn't contradict him – one more long silence – and Rusty said, 'Yeah, I guess it's mine, but one of its sweet legs belongs to D.J.'. Whew. Final end of love of one son for one father.

Later, the desire for patricide re-emerges. 'D.J. was in such a murder ball of sick disgusted piss-on-dad after Rusty took claim of the bear that he couldn't sleep for fear he'd somnambulate long enough to beat in Rusty's head'.[62] Hunting together does not defuse the familial conflicts nor deflect them towards an external source. But war, as the ultimate rite of passage, and one in which such psychic dilemmas may be worked out, offers a final solution to the rivalries between the father and son, corporate America and its progeny, authority and alienation. For 'God was a beast, not a man, and God said, "Go out and kill – fulfill my will, go and kill" . . . Vietnam, hot damn'.[63]

CONCLUSION: THE SHADOW OF THE KENNEDYS

On 1 April, the day after he had announced his decision not to run for re-election, Lyndon Johnson went to Chicago to address the National Association of Broadcasters. His remarks, which were broadcast nationally, reveal his sense of betrayal: that he had suffered from misrepresentation in the media. The broadcast industry thus had 'the power to clarify and . . . the power to confuse' in a world where accuracy might be sacrificed to immediacy. For 'unlike the printed media, television writes on the wind'. Vietnam was a case in point. What impact did images of war have upon the American people? 'No one can say exactly what effect those vivid scenes have on American opinion.' Johnson implied that the broadcast media preferred the drama of war to the search for peace. 'Peace, in the news sense, is a "condition." War is an "event" '. But more than that, in helping mould public opinion against the war, television news had compromised its objectivity. Instead, Johnson warned,

> you must defend your media against the spirit of faction, against the works of divisiveness and bigotry, against the evils of partisanship in any guise. For America's press, as for the American Presidency, the integrity and the responsibility and the freedom – the freedom to know the truth and let the truth make us free – must never be compromised or diluted or destroyed.[64]

The game was over. Johnson's 'credibility gap' – the distance that had to be travelled from his rhetoric to the reality of what was happening in Southeast Asia – had been exposed and exploited by the media, for whom the war now appeared to be an exercise in futility. In his remarks to the broadcasters, the president tried to argue for consensus where it no longer existed and objectivity where it was no longer possible. The president had lost control of his message, and that had effectively ended his political career. If he could not have predicted the circumstances in which he would inherit the presidency, Johnson might not have imagined the manner in which he would be forced to leave it.

Kennedy's election had thus represented a generational shift in American political leadership. The energy associated with his administration was a function of the age of those who joined him on the New Frontier. Lyndon Johnson was the antithesis of the telegenic ironic existentialist who captivated the imagination of American liberals and who then, in the tragedy of his early death, left them with the powerful myth of a promise unfulfilled. Yet if the institution of the presidency was the fulcrum on which the cold war consensus and the rhetoric of the New Frontier had turned, then the assassination of President Kennedy symbolised a direct attack upon the 'vital center' of the American political system itself. Johnson, however, immediately and self-consciously projected a style of leadership that reiterated the need for both cultural consensus and political unity as the basis of the 'idea of America' both at home and abroad. As he wrote in his memoirs: 'any hesitation or wavering, any false step, any sign of self-doubt, could have been disastrous. The nation was in a state of shock and grief. The times cried out for leadership'.[65] Such leadership was to be inclusive rather than exclusive: in time it would involve a heroic attempt to extend the values of American democracy to a far greater cross-section of the community than had hitherto enjoyed its benefits: Johnson's idealism was to find practical expression in the programmes of his Great Society.

Nevertheless, for all his efforts to foster a radical and liberal consensus in terms of his domestic policy, Johnson would ultimately be judged in the light of his decisions on Vietnam. Here he was the one person who was not allowed the luxury of a change of mind. Instead he was forced through political exigency to persist in a course of action in which the rhetoric of American exceptionalism eventually no longer could be sustained. At this point, the liberal consensus collapsed into the vacuum of the 'credibility gap', and Kennedy's former supporters felt free to question not simply Johnson's actions, but also his mental health.

Yet, at another point, this besieged and psychologically disturbed president re-emerges as a western hero who realises that the time has come to face his nemesis. According to Arthur Schlesinger jr., therefore, Johnson had 'always known that, as in the classic Hollywood western, there would be the inevitable walkdown through the long silent street at high noon, and Robert Kennedy would be waiting for him'.[66] This putative showdown would presumably have taken place somewhere on the New Frontier.

The battle between Johnson and Kennedy for the mantle of heroic leader was one which would never take place. Johnson had lost stomach for the fight. But while it was a possibility, in the two weeks that elapsed between Kennedy's announcement that he would run for office, and Johnson's decision that he would vacate it, the contest could be dramatised as one that pitted the new existentialist hero, Bobby, against the self-proclaimed representative of consensus, LBJ. And it would have been about interpretations of leadership; for what was at stake, as Kennedy put it in the statement of his intention to challenge Johnson, was 'not simply the leadership of our party or even our country – it is our right to moral leadership on this planet'.[67]

It was Robert Kennedy, then, who was politically the most significant among those who constructed the myth that would seek to define the memory of the assassinated president in popular thought. Through the experience of his brother's assassination, he reinvented himself in the image of JFK. His first major public speech after the trauma of Dallas was in March 1964, where he evoked his brother's legacy in the words of the poem celebrating the Irish patriot Owen Roe O'Neill. The final verse was at once a eulogy and a personal statement of grief.

> We're sheep without a shepherd,
> When the snow shuts out the sky –
> Oh! why did you leave us, Owen?
> Why did you die?

Thereafter, in the nine speeches collected, for example, in the book *Rights for Americans*, and made between March and June 1964, Bobby either mentioned or quoted from his brother, to whom he always referred as 'President Kennedy', in all but one. More often he evoked the memory of JFK in terms of his commitment to civil rights, to the poor, and to the young.[68]

In his book *Heroes*, the journalist John Pilger recalls a conversation with Bobby Kennedy on a flight to Los Angeles during what would be his final presidential primary campaign in California in 1968.

> Maybe I can never suffer like the blacks, the Indians and the chicanos do. But Jesus Christ, I'm the one to stand up for them'.
> 'Why?'
> 'I can be President of the United States'.
> 'So can Hubert Humphrey or Richard Nixon'.
> 'They can't be President Kennedy . . .'[69]

It was this intuitive appreciation of the symbolism of his name that encouraged Robert Kennedy to project himself as a potentially heroic leader in the image of his brother, the existential superman, rather than in the mould of Lyndon Johnson, America's everyman. By contrast, for Kennedy's supporters Johnson's supposed psychological disintegration in the face of political pressures confirmed his inability to assume the role of heroic leader. In the construction of the Great Society he had sought to outstrip the achievements of Franklin Roosevelt. Instead LBJ quit with the sense that he had been the victim of a raw deal. As he left Washington, now it was Richard Nixon who would play the hand for America in a political game, the rules of which had been changed utterly by the seemingly intractable war in Vietnam.

NOTES

1. Dallek, *Lone Star Rising*, p. 7.
2. McNamara, *In Retrospect*, p. 98.
3. Kearns, *Lyndon Johnson and the American Dream*, p. 64.
4. Quoted in Dallek, *Lone Star Rising*, p. 4.
5. Halberstam, *The Best and the Brightest*, p. 519.
6. *Public Papers of the Presidents: Lyndon B. Johnson, (1963–64)*, p. 1378.
7. Beschloss, *Taking Charge*, p. 470.
8. *Public Papers of the Presidents: Lyndon B. Johnson (1963–64)*, pp. 1370 and 1498. The quotation from the Los Angeles speech is taken from White, *The Making of the President, 1964*, p. 374.
9. White, *The Making of the President, 1964*, p. 322.
10. Johnson, *The Vantage Point*, p. 102.
11. VanDeMark, *Into the Quagmire*, p. 25.
12. *Public Papers of the Presidents: Lyndon B. Johnson(1968–69)*, p. 476.
13. Schlesinger, *The Bitter Heritage*, pp. 58–9.
14. Schlesinger, *Robert Kennedy and His Times*, pp. 823–4, 845 and 848.
15. See, for example, Schlesinger, *The Vital Center*. Novick, *That Noble Dream*, p. 341, describes this as Schlesinger's 'anti-Communist Manifesto'.

16. Brodie, *War and Politics*, pp. 187–8.
17. Schlesinger, *Robert Kennedy and His Times*, p. 968.
18. Ibid. p. 741.
19. Schlesinger, *A Thousand Days*, pp. 192 and 598.
20. Halberstam, *The Best and the Brightest*, pp. 53, 603 and 777.
21. Kearns, *Lyndon Johnson and the American Dream*, p. 18.
22. Ibid. p. 22.
23. Ibid. p. 25.
24. Quoted in Gay, *Freud: A Life for Our Times*, p. 332.
25. Freud and Bullitt, *Thomas Woodrow Wilson*, pp. 35 and 55.
26. Kearns, *Lyndon Johnson and the American Dream*, p. 32.
27. Ibid. pp. 23 and 342.
28. Ibid. pp. 284 and 315–16.
29. Ibid. p. 317.
30. Reedy, *The Twilight of the Presidency*, p. xi.
31. Ibid. p. 160.
32. Ibid. pp. 165–6.
33. Maclear, *Vietnam*, p. 85.
34. See, for example, Johnson, *The Vantage Point*, p. 116: 'My first decision on Vietnam . . . [was] to reaffirm President Kennedy's policies'.
35. Sidey, *A Very Personal Presidency*, p. 34.
36. Dugger, *The Politician*, p. 318.
37. Recounted ibid. and Sidey, *A Very Personal Presidency*, p. 98.
38. Sidey, *A Very Personal Presidency*, p. 97.
39. Heinrichs, 'Lyndon Johnson', p. 20.
40. Tuchman, *The March of Folly*, p. 388.
41. Sidey, *A Very Personal Presidency*, p. 220.
42. Brammer, *The Gay Place*, pp. 111–12.
43. Aldridge, 'From Vietnam to Obscenity', p. 185. Mailer says there is 'no connection' between Brammer's work and his novel (personal communication).
44. Frielander, *History and Psychoanalysis*, p. 69.
45. *Public Papers of the Presidents: Lyndon B. Johnson (1963–64)*, p. 10.
46. Aldridge, 'From Vietnam to Obscenity', p. 188.
47. Godden, *Fictions of Capital*, p. 177.
48. McNamara, *In Retrospect*, p. 207.
49. Quoted in Freud, 'Totem and Taboo', p. 41.
50. Kearns, *Lyndon Johnson and the American Dream*, pp. 347–8.
51. Maclear, *Vietnam,* p. 85.
52. Jung, 'The Fight with the Shadow', p. 225.
53. Roazen, *Freud*, p. 196.
54. Brzezinski, 'Tomorrow's Agenda', p. 666.
55. Campbell, *The Hero with a Thousand Faces*, p. 155.
56. Aldridge, 'From Vietnam to Obscenity', p. 182.

57. Mailer, *Why Are We in Vietnam?*, p. 9.
58. Mailer, 'Superman Comes to the Supermarket', p. 12.
59. Mailer, *Why Are We in Vietnam?*, p. 31.
60. Ibid. p. 38.
61. Ibid. pp. 137–8.
62. Ibid. pp. 147 and 157.
63. Ibid. pp. 203 and 208.
64. *Public Papers of the Presidents: Lyndon B. Johnson (1968–69)*, pp. 482–6.
65. Johnson, *The Vantage Point*, p. 18.
66. Schlesinger, *Robert Kennedy and His Times*, p. 865.
67. Quoted ibid. p. 855.
68. Hopkins, *Rights for Americans*, p. 198. The remaining speeches are collected in the concluding section of the book, 'Opening to the Future'.
69. Pilger, 'Bobby', p. 126.

CHAPTER FIVE

Richard Nixon: Heroic Failure

INTRODUCTION: THE HEROISM OF RICHARD NIXON

In his closing remarks in the fourth debate between the candidates for the 1960 presidential election, Richard Nixon said: 'in the years to come it will be written that one or the other of us was elected and that he was or was not a great president. What will determine whether Senator Kennedy or I, if I am elected, was a great president? . . . It will be determined to the extent that we represent the deepest ideals, the highest feelings and the faith of the American people'.[1] The new president would be judged by his capacity to articulate a vision and to confront gathering threats, symbolised by the contemporary fears and anxieties engendered by the nuclear age and the cold war. Nixon thus endorsed the idea which would characterise John F. Kennedy's administration: heroic leadership would be defined as a constant battle against crisis: indeed the symbolic significance of crisis was a way of seizing and holding the nation's attention.

Following his defeat in 1960, Nixon was faced with the problem of maintaining public interest in his political career at a time when the spotlight of attention was fixed on Kennedy's White House. His response was to write a book. This work, which came to have a talismanic importance for Nixon, and was recommended reading to his aides, was significant not least in its title. So *Six Crises* is not simply an attempt to join the ranks of politician-intellectual. It is Nixon's howl from the political wilderness. And it shows that he too understood clearly the demand and the need for heroic political leadership during the cold war.

In the introduction to his book, Nixon recalls visiting President

Kennedy after he had taken office, and, incidentally, after the Bay of Pigs crisis.

> When I told him I was considering the possibility of joining the 'literary' ranks, of which he himself is so distinguished a member, he expressed the thought that every public man should write a book at some time in his life, both for the mental discipline and because it tends to elevate him in popular esteem to the respected status of an 'intellectual'.[2]

This observation is used by Arthur Schlesinger jr. in his biography of Kennedy as an example of the president's ironic wit at the expense of a political rival for whom Schlesinger himself had no respect: 'only the solemnity with which Kennedy's remark was received could possibly have exceeded the ambiguity with which it was uttered'.[3] The circumstances of the meeting might explain both Nixon and Kennedy's use of the ironic form: during the election campaign Kennedy had been able to appear more hawkish than Nixon on America's response to the Cuban Revolution. Nixon was unable to reveal that plans for an invasion, which he supported, were already underway. Now one reason why they were together was to discuss its failure.

Six Crises, then, was Nixon's attempt to emulate Kennedy's *Profiles in Courage*, but with no sense of the existential detachment which had characterised JFK's biographical vignettes of a number of distinguished senators. Whereas for JFK, writing a book could be presented as a genuine attempt at historical scholarship, even if that was combined with a calculated act of political self-promotion, Nixon's work was in many ways an emotional catharsis. His book was intensely personal. Garry Wills indeed suggests that 'the whole of *Six Crises* is a saga of moral education'.[4] In it, Nixon attempts to extrapolate from his own experience some more generalised ideas about crisis and its management. But in so doing, he dramatises his political life and experiences in a way which sometimes strains to its very limits the conception of what constitutes a crisis. As Stephen Ambrose puts it, '*Six Crises* was a book written by a great man about small events'.[5] Yet Nixon's attempt at explaining the way in which crisis may be confronted is revealing in its self-analysis. For him, 'crisis can indeed be agony. But it is the exquisite agony which a man might not want to experience again – yet would not for the world have missed'.[6] It is his conduct in these self-defined crises which in turn defines Nixon both to himself and to others.

Nixon's crises are built around confrontations: with individuals

(Alger Hiss, Khrushchev, Kennedy) with groups (the Caracas mob, the press who revealed his 'secret fund' in the 1952 campaign) and with an unexpected event (Eisenhower's heart attack). He divides each crisis into three phases: the period of indecision, when a course of action is debated and decided, the 'easiest period . . . the battle itself', and the aftermath in which, having been exposed to the extreme tensions of the crisis, the individual relaxes in what is, for Nixon, the most dangerous time, when it is necessary to be aware of 'dulled reactions and faulty judgment'.[7] The lessons from early crises are applied to later political dramas. So, as Wills notes,

> The problems that plagued him at the outset of the book are all overcome by the end. In the first four crises, for instance, he suffers from emotional collapse when the crisis has passed. In the last two, he has learnt how to prepare for this danger, and obviate it.[8]

The book, however, fails as a self-help manual for would-be crisis managers. There is little evidence, for example, that JFK reacted to the trauma of crisis and its aftermath in similar fashion. Nixon's lessons reveal more about himself than they provide a guide to crisis conduct.

In dramatising such personal challenges as crises Nixon is able to inflate not only their own importance, but also his political skills in dealing with them. Thus 'one factor common to all six of these crises is that while each was an acute personal problem, each also involved far broader consequences which completely over-shadowed my personal fortunes'.[9] The sentiment is disingenuous. Each of the events Nixon describes is intimately associated with his political career. What the book reveals is an obsession with crises as a way of testing his ability to conduct himself according to the standards which he has set for himself in public life: as a political, and ultimately heroic, leader in cold war America's confrontation with communism.

Three of the crises thus involve and revolve around Nixon's battles with communists. In a process of learning about the communist threat, he confronts his enemy first within the United States, before being ambushed by communists abroad, and finally taking the fight to the citadel of communism itself: Moscow. The Hiss case, the attack by the Caracas mob, and his conversations with Khrushchev thus combine to show Nixon as the most effective – and heroic – leader that America might have in its cold war confrontation with the Soviet Union.

In exposing the Hiss case, moreover, Nixon took on the American liberal establishment and won, catapulting himself into national mythology and to the vice-presidency itself. Without Hiss, Nixon would have been, like Kennedy at the time, another young, ambitious representative in Congress. The Hiss case promoted him temporarily above his political contemporaries. It also defined for him the communist threat and the communist enemy. It was 'a vivid case study of the continuing crisis of our times, a crisis with which we shall be confronted as long as aggressive international Communism is on the loose in the world'. Moreover,

> the Hiss case, for the first time, forcibly demonstrated to the American people that domestic Communism was a real and present danger to the security of the nation . . . The nation finally saw that the magnitude of the threat of Communism in the United States is multiplied a thousandfold because of its direct connection with and support by the massive power of the world Communist conspiracy centered in Moscow.[10]

So Hiss is not history. *Six Crises* makes clear that while Nixon won a battle against communism in 1948, the war continues. But at least one aspiring American political leader had established his heroic credentials in the fight.

In confronting Alger Hiss, Nixon appeared to be playing a high-stakes game with his own political future. When Hiss made his initial appearance before the House Committee on Un-American Activities, to refute the allegations made against him by Whittaker Chambers, Nixon concedes it was 'a virtuoso performance . . . He so dominated the proceedings that by the end of his testimony he had several members of the Committee trying to defend the right of a congressional committee to look into charges of Communism in government'.[11] Furthermore, 'when the Committee reconvened in executive session later that afternoon, it was in a state of virtual shock' and was tempted to end its investigation. Nixon, though, wanted to persevere even though he was in a minority of one. He did, however, have the support of Robert Stripling, the Committee's chief investigator, and an eventual compromise was reached whereby Nixon was appointed as head of a sub-committee to continue the questioning of Chambers.[12] The stage was set:

> when I arrived back in my office that afternoon, I had a natural sense of achievement over my success in preventing the Committee from dropping the case prematurely. But as I thought of the problems ahead of me I realized for the first time that I was up against a crisis which transcended any I had been through before.[13]

As Garry Wills points out, however, the confrontation with Alger Hiss was not quite the dramatic confrontation that *Six Crises* describes. Prior to his public investigation of Hiss, Nixon had already discovered 'information that made the encounter of Whittier College with Harvard Law a kind of rigged bout between David and Goliath'. Nixon's mentor while he investigated the issue of domestic communism was Father John Cronin, who, eighteen months before Whittaker Chambers made his accusations, had told his congressional protégé of Alger Hiss's communist connections. Nixon had prepared his case well before the matter became public. This interpretation explains Nixon's persistence when the House Committee on Un-American Activities almost halted its investigation following Hiss's initial testimony. So 'when Nixon – a first-term congressman, as lowly a creature as exists in Washington – pushed the Hiss case, he seemed to be taking a great risk. It was less than it looked. He had cards all up and down his sleeves and inside his vest'.[14] It was to Hiss's public embarrassment that he encountered in Nixon not a Mississippi riverboat gambler of the McCarthyite variety, but a confident poker player who knew when to bet the limit.

The problem with domestic communists like Hiss was that in appearance they looked like any other American. That was what made them most threatening. They could be identified only through their mistakes or their actions. Otherwise they were anonymous, unseen faces in the lonely crowd. The heroic leader, like Nixon, had the talent to uncover the communist conspirators at home, but he also needed the qualities to win confrontations with communists abroad. The second encounter with communism in *Six Crises* is an account of what was perhaps the most genuine of the challenges Nixon faced. As vice-president, on a 'goodwill tour' of Latin America, and having faced down what was, in his estimation, a communist mob in Peru, his car was attacked by another mob in Caracas, and during a twelve-minute siege in which his motorcade was trapped, his physical security, and that of his entourage, was threatened.

Nixon was face to face with the enemy. In Peru, the leaders of the mob were 'the usual case-hardened, cold-eyed Communist operatives'. When he confronts 'one of the most notorious Communist agitators in Lima', Nixon sees 'a weird-looking character whose bulging eyes seemed to merge with his mouth and nose in one distorted blob'.[15] This, then, is literally the ugly face of communism, where Hiss had been its disguised countenance. Once more, though, Nixon, the consummate poker player, has the measure of his opponents. Americans would 'not put our tails between our legs and run every time some Communist bully tries to bluff us'.[16] This, then, was the philosophy he took to Venezuela, and to his confrontation in Caracas.

> They had used the same slogans, the same words, the same tactics that 'student' demonstrators had used in every country in South America I had visited, which was absolute proof that they were directed and controlled by a central Communist conspiracy.

Nixon's encounter with communism abroad confirms his belief that the fight against the international enemy is a constant battle against a co-ordinated campaign directed from Moscow. Like the Hiss case, therefore, 'Caracas was a much-needed shock treatment which jolted us out of dangerous complacency'.[17] Once again, Nixon's personal crisis focuses the nation's attention upon its cold war enemy and upon his abilities as a political leader in confronting and facing down the communist threat.

Nixon's final confrontation with communism in *Six Crises* comes in Moscow, a direct encounter with the leaders of the international conspiracy itself. He meets Khrushchev, 'Communist man at his most dangerous best', at a time when 'at stake was world peace and the survival of freedom'.[18] In their 'kitchen debate', Nixon stands up to his adversary, refuses to be brow-beaten and gains an unrivalled insight into the character of the communist leader. So Khrushchev 'never plays by the rules. He delights in doing the unexpected'. For all his efforts to entertain his American guest, in negotiations he reveals himself as just another communist operative of the kind Nixon had encountered elsewhere. It is in his eyes. 'His expression never changed. His eyes were as cold as they had been all afternoon'. This, then, is Khrushchev.

> Intelligence, a quick-hitting sense of humor, always on the offensive, colorful in action and words, a tendency to be a show-off, particularly where he has any kind of gallery to play to, a steel-like determination coupled with an almost compulsive tendency to press an advantage . . . to run over anyone who shows any sign of timidity or weakness.[19]

The enemy is finally unmasked.

Nixon, though, has his measure. For in Khrushchev he recognises an aspect of himself: the calculating card player. So

> there is no doubt that Khrushchev would have been a superb poker player. First, he is out to win. Second, like any good poker player, he plans ahead so that he can win the big pots. He likes to bluff, but he knows that if you bluff

on small pots and fail consistently to produce the cards, you must expect your opponent to call your bluff on the big pots.[20]

Through his experience in Moscow, Nixon can project himself as the American leader capable of sitting down at a poker table with the communists in a game played with the prospect of nuclear confrontation should things go awry.

But Americans had rejected him. His last and biggest crisis, as he writes the book, is the election of 1960. It was the first defeat of his political career, throwing into relief his earlier experiences where at times of personal crisis he had managed to emerge successful, with his political reputation enhanced. Now Kennedy had assumed the public role of heroic leader, despite the fact that, as Nixon's book makes clear, his own profile was at least as courageous as that of JFK. He projects himself as the president's equal. As JFK encounters the Bay of Pigs crisis, it is up to Nixon's daughter to speak his mind. The president asks him to the White House. Tricia Nixon relays the message: 'JFK called. I knew it! It wouldn't be long before he would get into trouble and have to call on you for help'.[21] Kennedy's first confrontation with communism had ended in the kind of defeat that Nixon had never encountered in his battles with the conspiracy both at home and abroad. Who then was the more capable heroic leader? For Nixon, finally elected to the White House in 1968, as for others who seek to disentangle the political achievement of JFK from the myth surrounding him, always it would be a question of character.

The 'Plebiscitary Presidency'

For Barbara Tuchman, 'character again was fate. When worked on by the passions of Vietnam, Nixon's character, and that of the associates he recruited, plunged his Administration into the stew that further soured respect for government'.[22] The war in Southeast Asia became the pivot on which the Nixon presidency turns, just as it had been for his predecessor. Indeed Richard Nixon's 'peace with honor' was bought for the price of his political career. For in the five years it took to achieve, his administration was driven underground: covertly pursuing both foreign and domestic policies the results of which would be revealed, finally, in such diverse places as Cambodia and the Watergate offices of the Democrats' national committee. Once his burglars had been caught, moreover, the president predicted the outcome. In his memoirs, Nixon reflects how 'I began to realise the dimensions of the problem we were facing with the media and with Congress regarding Watergate. *Vietnam had found its successor*'.[23] Yet for his liberal critics, and in particular for Arthur Schlesinger jr., Nixon's conduct was a reflection too of his conception of the presidency: an idea that the chief executive embodied – in Weberian terms – a plebiscitary power that should allow for uncontested freedom of political action.

Nixon believed that, as president, he should use Theodore Roosevelt's 'bully pulpit' to fashion, rather than to reflect, political opinion, particularly in the area of foreign policy. As Stephen Ambrose puts it, 'rather than wait for a constituency to develop behind such [foreign] policies, Nixon acted, and by acting, created a constituency for them'.[24] There is nothing new in this. The same aspiration might be ascribed to both Kennedy and Johnson. But Nixon's use of presidential power could be seen by his political opponents as evidence that, in seeking to manipulate consent, he was defining a political persona aloof from a liberal consensus. After his election in 1968, however, the president had to finesse a fundamental dilemma of democratic leadership: to define the course of public policy, while at the same time retaining support among the electorate. Or, more simply, simultaneously telling and giving a divided public what it wanted. For in terms of Vietnam, Americans wanted both success and disengagement.

In the decay of political consensus that marked the transitions from JFK, through LBJ and to Nixon, liberal commentators turned from supporting the president as heroic cold war leader (Kennedy) to suspicion of the chief executive's accumulation of power (Johnson) and finally to the conviction that the presidency itself was at the mercy of corrupt politicians (Nixon). The cold war imperial republic had created the imperial presidency. It is a thesis that neatly traps Nixon in an institutional accident that, according to Schlesinger, was waiting to happen. In this way, '. . . a plebiscitary presidency could be seen as the fulfillment of constitutional democracy'. So,

> Nixon was carrying the imperial presidency toward its ultimate form in the plebiscitary Presidency with the President accountable only once every four years, shielded in the years between elections from congressional and public harassment, empowered by his mandate to make war or to make peace, to spend or to impound, to give out information or to hold it back, superseding congressional legislation by executive order, all in the name of a majority whose choice must prevail till it made another choice four years later – unless it wished to embark on the drastic and improbable course of impeachment.[25]

By this line of argument, Nixon's presidency represented the culmination of historic trends that transcended the era of cold war America.

Thus, 'personalization, the plebiscitary stance, and presidentially induced mass expectations, we are told, began with John Kennedy or, at the earliest, with Franklin Roosevelt'. But Schlesinger immediately absolves two recent Democrat heroes from such responsibility. For

> this notion springs from a curiously foreshortened view of American history. In fact, the Presidency has been a personalized office from the start, both for political reasons – the interests of the President – and for psychological reasons – the emotional needs of the people.[26]

In other words, the office of chief executive has been moulded by both historical circumstance and personality – presidential character. In the cold war, the imperial president defined the institution in a manner which threatened the political integrity of the constitutional system and its animating theory of checks and balances. Nixon's becomes the cathartic administration. It lays bare the realities of the imperial presidency and at the same time, through the president's resignation, preserves the integrity of the Constitution. With Nixon, the imperial presidency disintegrates. But the dilemmas of presidential leadership remain.

Schlesinger's conception of the plebiscitary presidency is reminiscent of Max Weber's analysis of the nature of the democratic process. Thus, 'for Weber, plebiscitary democracy functioned to provide a reliable and efficient selection of rulers, not (to) legitimate political power'. In this way, he defined such a democracy

> as a form of *Führer-Demokratie* (leader-democracy) as 'a variant of charismatic authority, which hides behind a legitimacy that is *formally* derived from the will of the governed' . . . but the real authority of the ruler depends on the trust and commitment of his . . . political followers.[27]

Such a democracy works well, then, when the charismatic appeal of the leader creates a genuine political constituency among the populace. Yet Schlesinger's model of a plebiscitary democracy cannot operate when led by someone who, in his view, fails to command charismatic authority. In this sense, the imperial presidency fails because of Nixon's character: the thesis becomes almost a lament for the loss of charismatic leadership in America – a loss that resulted from the untimely deaths of both John and Robert Kennedy. Indeed, had Bobby survived in 1968 to beat Nixon at the polls and reinherit the political legacy that Johnson had usurped, *The Imperial Presidency* might have remained one of the great unwritten books of American constitutional analysis.

Such a model of presidential power exposes Nixon's shortcomings as a leader in the view of one of his political opponents. Yet underlying the scandal that forced his resignation was not only his personality but also the force of circumstance: the continuing American involvement in Southeast Asia. Indeed, it is easy to find references to Watergate which connect it in some way with Vietnam; as Nixon himself does in his memoirs. So for Kim McQuaid, 'Watergate had flowed from Vietnam and from the polarized domestic politics the failed American war in Indochina had induced'. In Bob Haldeman's view, 'without the Vietnam war there would have been no Watergate'. And in a contemporary account of the Watergate hearings in Congress, Mary McCarthy provided a reason for the link:

> a French friend . . . says he thinks that the Americans are using Watergate to cleanse themselves of guilt for Vietnam. As he says this a light goes on in my mind. Yes, he is right; if it had not been for Vietnam, the scandal of the break-in might have soon dropped from notice like previous scandals – a tempest in a teapot.[28]

Instead Watergate became a shorthand expression for presidential corruption that, for many, stemmed from the flawed morality that successive administrations had used to underscore America's 'mission impossible' in Southeast Asia.

Watergate encapsulated the problems of presidential leadership in a country where ideological consensus is the glue necessary to hold the body politic together. Nixon was aware of the difficulties he faced. In his memoirs, he expresses his 'fears about the American leadership classes' which 'had been confirmed and deepened' during his first term in office. 'In politics, academics, and the arts, and even in the business community and the churches, there was a successful and fashionable negativism . . . The Vietnam war had completed the alienation for this group by undermining the traditional concept of patriotism.' The president also felt he was capable of rebuilding national morale.

> It may seem ironic in view of the scandal that was about to overtake me . . . but in the first few weeks and months of 1973 I was planning to provide America with a positive and, I hoped, inspirational example of leadership that would be both a background and an impetus for a new rebirth of optimism and decisiveness and national pride.[29]

So Nixon saw the need for presidential leadership to redefine a sense of America's mission in the aftermath of the national failure in Vietnam. Yet, like Johnson before him, the political and cultural tensions that cold war adventurism had engendered, when the fight against communism was taken to Vietnam, overwhelmed the aspirations of his administration. At core, neither Johnson nor Nixon could overcome the erosion of presidential credibility, the gap between their rhetoric and their actions by which they were ultimately to be judged.

THE PROBLEM OF CREDIBILITY

On 11 November 1968, Nixon, as president-elect, visited Lyndon Johnson at the White House. In his memoirs, Nixon recounts his conversation with LBJ in the Oval Office: 'he talked with a sense of urgency . . . "you can be sure that I won't criticize you publicly. Eisenhower did the same for me. I know what an enormous burden you will be carrying" '. Nixon continues:

> Johnson and I had been adversaries for many years, but on that day our political and personal differences melted away. As we stood together in the Oval Office, he welcomed me into a club of very exclusive membership, and he made a promise to adhere to a cardinal rule of that membership: stand behind those that succeed you.[30]

The chief executive's club thus was dedicated to a particular code of public conduct. It would maintain a show of political solidarity, given substance by the shared knowledge of the initiated. Only one who had been president could understand the problems of others who achieved the office.

In 1991, reflecting on America's involvement in Southeast Asia, Nixon observed that 'the pressure of waging the war in Vietnam broke Johnson, but I was damned if it were going to break me'.[31] One of his options when he became president might have been to emulate Eisenhower in ending the Korean war. He could have simply withdrawn American forces from Vietnam. It would have been a grand political gesture similar to his decision to open diplomatic links with China. Within a year of his election, with the war continuing, he faced strident opposition not simply within America but also overseas. On 15 October 1969, a quarter of a million people converged on Washington for Vietnam Moratorium Day. Similar demonstrations occurred elsewhere. In London, Bill Clinton 'led a teach-in and served as a marshal' during a protest outside the American embassy.[32]

In his memoirs, Nixon claims that the Moratorium was the catalyst that convinced him to maintain the nation's commitment to Vietnam.

> If a President – any President – allowed his course to be set by those who demonstrate, he would betray the trust of all the rest . . . It would give the decision, not to the majority, and not to those with the strongest arguments, but to those with the loudest voices . . . It would allow every group to test its strength not at the ballot box but through confrontation in the streets.

Despite a memorandum from Mike Mansfield, the Senate majority leader which offered him the political opportunity 'to end "Johnson and Kennedy's war" ' on 3 November 1969, Nixon's reaction instead was to make his 'Silent Majority' speech.[33] He would describe this as 'probably my greatest speaking triumph, apart from the Fund speech, which saved my political career'.[34]

In the speech, Nixon appealed for support from 'the great silent majority of my fellow Americans'. The collapse of consensus undermined American objectives, 'for the more divided we are at home, the less likely the enemy is to negotiate at Paris'. Instead, 'let us be united for peace. Let us also be united against defeat. Because let us understand: North Vietnam cannot defeat or humiliate the United States. Only Americans can do that'.[35] It was Nixon's attempt to re-establish the rhetoric of cold war mission, and in his memoirs he claimed it as a major victory. The silent majority expressed its view with

> the biggest response ever to any presidential speech . . . A Gallup poll taken immediately after the speech showed 77 percent approval . . . I had the public support I needed to continue a policy of waging war in Vietnam and negotiating for peace in Paris until we could bring the war to an honorable and successful conclusion.[36]

Here is Nixon's claim for the mandate to pursue 'peace with honor'. It would take him over three more years to negotiate. On 27 January 1973, a cease-fire effectively ended America's military involvement in Vietnam. Five days earlier, Lyndon Johnson had died.

For Nixon, then,

> the test of great leadership is to lead public opinion, not be led by it. In the case of Vietnam, that loud group of protestors was mistaken for public opinion. If they really were public opinion, I would never have been reelected in 1972 by such a large margin – if at all.

Framing his policy of continuing America's involvement in Southeast Asia in terms of a determination not to be swayed by those who vociferously opposed the war proved to be a high-risk strategy, in keeping with his view that 'greatness comes through the tough decisions with a risk involved, the risk to lose it all . . .'.[37] Nixon's self-conscious image of himself as heroic leader in the Kennedy mould implied that he should take such risks. But to his critics, his intransigence was evidence that, like Johnson, he was psychologically unfit for office.

THE 'MADNESS' OF RICHARD NIXON

Soon after he had inherited the presidency, Johnson had privately expressed his determination not to 'lose' Southeast Asia as China had been 'lost'. 'Mr. Johnson's war' followed. Far from drawing a line under his predecessor's military adventurism, Nixon had defined his political purpose publicly in a hauntingly familiar fashion. In September 1969, even before the Vietnam Moratorium, he told Republican congressional leaders that 'I will not be the first President of the United States to lose a war'.[38] Tom Engelhardt argues, therefore, that,

> nothing drove America's Vietnam presidents, Johnson and Nixon, more ruthlessly than the desire to avoid that most infamous of humiliations. For both, it was an inconceivable fate and yet, to the point of obsession, impossible to stop thinking about. Both, facing the spectre of defeat, embraced a very unpresidential madness.[39]

Whereas, for his critics, Johnson's neuroses were exposed by the war in Vietnam, however, Nixon's 'madness' was more cerebral than elemental. For he deliberately embraced the popular perception of his psychopathological hatred of communism in order to use that image as an instrument of foreign policy.

As Johnson's caricature of Goldwater in 1964 – a 'madman' whose 'finger is on the button' – implied, it was part of the accepted liberal demonology of cold war politics that Republican anti-communist zealots were more likely to use nuclear force than were liberal – rational – Democrats. Nixon turned this mythology to his advantage. Engelhardt suggests that his 'madman theory' may have come from Henry Kissinger, who heard it expounded at a Harvard seminar by Daniel Ellsberg.

> Ellsberg called the theory 'The Political Uses of Madness'. In essence, he described a problem in bargaining theory: what to do when the available

threat is so extreme or costly as to make it seem unlikely that a sane and reasonable person would carry it out . . . Ellsberg postulated that one way of making the threat somewhat credible . . . would be for the person making the threat to appear not to be fully rational.[40]

As Bob Haldeman put it:

the threat was the key, and Nixon coined a phrase for his theory which I'm sure will bring smiles of delight to Nixon-haters everywhere . . . He said, 'I call it the Madman theory, Bob. I want the North Vietnamese to believe I've reached the point where I might do *anything* to stop the war. We'll just slip the word to them that, "for God's sake, you know Nixon is obsessed about Communism. We can't restrain him when he's angry – and he has his hand on the nuclear button" – and Ho Chi Minh himself will be in Paris in two days begging for peace'.[41]

For Engelhardt, this shows that 'the United States, then, was prepared to confront its enemies with a carefully crafted vision of a mad president'.[42]

There is little evidence to support this view. True, when in April 1969, North Korean jets shot down a US Navy reconnaissance plane, Nixon claims that Kissinger's advice was to retaliate by adopting a version of the 'madman' strategy.

'If we strike back, even though it's risky', he said, 'they will say, "This guy is becoming irrational – we'd better settle with him"'. But if we back down, they'll say, "This guy is the same as his predecessor, and if we wait he'll come to the same end"'.[43]

In the event, Nixon rejected the advice. Similarly, Kissinger relates an incident later that year when Nixon 'told me that I should convey to Dobrynin [the Soviet ambassador to the USA] that the President was "out of control" on Vietnam'. Again, it seems possible that Nixon was seeking to implement his 'madman theory'. But as Kissinger goes on to observe, 'in serving Nixon one owed it to him to discriminate among the orders he issued and to give him another chance at those that were unfulfillable or dangerous. This one was in the latter category'.[44]

Nevertheless, it was Nixon's own readiness to question the psychological health of his political opponents that contributed to the disintegration of his administration in the quagmire of Watergate. Again, Daniel Ellsberg played a pivotal role. After he had leaked the Pentagon Papers to the *New York Times*, documenting the history of America's involvement in the Vietnam war, Ellsberg became a political target. In the pursuit of material which would discredit him, the White House authorised a break-in at the offices of Ellsberg's psychiatrist. It was an early indication of the tactics to be employed in the campaign to re-elect the president.

For Bernard Brodie, 'the personality and character of some of the greatest figures of our national history have until now persistently eluded their biographers'. This is because most biographers 'live in a world unsullied by any of the psychological notions developed by Freud and others'.[45] As the Watergate scandal unravelled his presidency, however, Nixon became, and has remained, an interesting case for psychoanalysis. Again, if the constitutional crisis was a question of individual character, it implies that any sense of collective responsibility for the creation of a political culture in which morality was routinely sacrificed to expediency is expunged. Once more, then, Freudian analysis apparently reveals the fatal flaws in Richard Nixon's personality. Whereas there is a sense in which Johnson, by relating his dreams to Doris Kearns, co-operated in the psychoanalytic portrait which she was able subsequently to draw of him, assessments of Richard Nixon's psyche have remained a matter for conjecture. Yet this did not prevent a number of them being made. Of these, one of the most complete was Fawn Brodie's book, *Richard Nixon: The Shaping of His Character* (1981), a work which resonates with Freudian language and imagery.

'The warping in his capacity for love, and the influence of death in his life, are examined in this volume in detail, as is the evolution of Nixon's lying. All three themes are interwoven with his identity failure and with the grandiose fantasy life'. Thus Brodie traces Nixon's problems directly to his childhood, with chapters entitled 'The Punishing Father', 'The Saintly Mother' and 'The Unsmiling Child'. The traumatic death of two brothers – both more loved and loveable than he – is a formative experience in Nixon's early life, and one which curiously foreshadowed his own political ascent to the presidency, which was in part a consequence of the assassinations of John and Robert Kennedy. 'What one does not know', observed Brodie, 'is whether or not Nixon suffered from an anxiety that the fate helping him was demonic and not divine'.[46] Elsewhere in the book, however, she offers anecdotal evidence that 'a personal feeling of guilt for the death of an assassinated leader can haunt even the innocent'. The basis for this assertion is a footnoted reminiscence:

one of my students confessed that he was consumed with remorse because by accident he had accompanied a friend who took his gun to the home of Siran

[sic] Sirhan and sold it to him. The gun was shortly used to assassinate Robert Kennedy. Had the student somehow blocked the sale, he thought, he would have had a decisive impact for good on history. By not blocking it, he had inadvertently had an evil impact.[47]

Whether that evil impact was simply the assassination, or the subsequent election of Nixon to the presidency is left unsaid. But this story is the foundation for the inference that Nixon, too, was consumed with guilt as a result of the death of the Kennedys.

Nixon also had 'a problem with touching'. His lack of a display of public affection for his wife is taken as a sign of his incapacity for giving or accepting love. This appears as a character defect. Brodie observes that 'Quakers are known for kissing each other freely in public, especially on the cheek', citing in support a book written by one of Nixon's grade school teachers. She goes on to document the occasions in Nixon's memoirs when he is at pains to record his physical affection for his wife as evidence that he realised this criticism and wanted to correct a mistaken and damaging impression.[48] In so doing, she misses Nixon's observation, recording his homecoming as a child after a six-month absence.

> As soon as he saw me alone, my youngest brother, Arthur, greeted me with a solemn kiss on the cheek. I later learned that he had asked my mother if it would be proper for him to kiss me since I had been away. Even at that early age he had acquired our family's reticence about open displays of affection.[49]

In this respect, perhaps the Nixons were not typical Quakers.

Brodie's speculations about Nixon's mental health include the suggestion that, while vice-president, he sought psychiatric help from a physician in New York.

> Dr. Arnold A. Hutschnecker, later called – not altogether incorrectly – 'the President's shrink', was not a psychiatrist but an internist specializing in psychosomatic problems, in what he called 'the emotional conditions – the mystery, tension, the unhappiness', of his patients. Later he called himself 'a psychoanalytically oriented psychotherapist'.

Made aware of the political implications of his actions, Nixon abandoned his visits to Hutschnecker, who subsequently wrote in a book entitled *The Drive for Power* (1974):

> how strange . . . that a man in public life would be allowed, even encouraged, to visit a heart specialist, say, but would be criticized for trying to understand

the emotional undercurrent of his unconscious drives, fears, and conflicts, or possible neurotic hangups.[50]

It is a naive view. Any suspicion of mental health problems would have been politically disastrous – in 1972, George McGovern's challenge to Nixon's second term was destroyed by the revelation that his vice-presidential choice, Thomas Eagleton, had been treated for nervous exhaustion and depression with electric shock therapy. The implication of Brodie's account is clear: even in the 1950s, Nixon's mental health was suspect. Guilt is established by innuendo. Speculation masquerades as analysis from a biographer whom Tom Wicker describes fairly as 'one of Nixon's severest critics'.[51]

For Bruce Mazlish, 'the effort to cast doubt on Richard Nixon's mental stability by vague accusations that he visited a psychotherapist in the late 1950s itself indirectly cast doubt on psychological history'.[52] Nevertheless, the president remained an easy target for psychoanalysts. Ray Price, Nixon's speechwriter, in his book *With Nixon* (1977) describes, for example, meeting a prominent New York psychiatrist, David Abrahamson, who was researching a work on the former president. 'As we talked, it became apparent that he was planning to follow the currently fashionable trend of psychohistory, interpreting a public official's public acts by means of a sort of remote-control Freudian psychoanalysis'. The danger in this, for Price, is that – as in Brodie's case – political prejudice suggests that anything the subject does which is offensive to the psychobiographer becomes 'irrational', and is explicable only in the language of psychological disturbance. Indeed, 'so much for the sanity of politics and the politics of sanity'.[53] And yet, Price misses a point. For the language of Freud is a way of attempting to understand not simply character but also motivation. As such, it is a good vernacular for the dramatisation of biography. Enter Oliver Stone.

THE CELLULOID NIXON

Fawn Brodie's work is one of the sources cited in the annotated screenplay of Stone's movie, *Nixon* (1995). The film presents an image of the president as heroic failure: illuminated with obvious references to pop-psychology, notably in its constant use of flashbacks to relate the mature Nixon's conduct to memories of his fractured childhood. As he observes the shipwreck of his presidency on the mounting tide of Watergate revelations, Nixon at one point confesses to Haldeman that he had come to the presidency 'over the bodies . . . four bodies'. The film suggests that although his political triumph may have come in the aftermath of the Kennedy assassinations, his drive for power was fuelled by the loss of his siblings in childhood. And in a line that is clearly reminiscent of Brodie's speculation as to whether Nixon considered the accidents of fate that led him to his goal were benign or malevolent, Stone's president asks 'who's helping us? Is it God? Or is it . . . Death?'[54]

In keeping with the image of a beleagured president maddened by the burdens of the office, like Johnson prowling the corridors in search of portraits of his predecessors, the film also has Nixon talking to the pictures of presidents past. As he listens to the tape of his conversation with Haldeman, where he has revealed his belief that the price of his election has been the death of his brothers and the Kennedys, Nixon is seen in the Lincoln sitting room. Drunk, he looks up at the portrait of Abraham Lincoln to interrogate him about death: 'how many did you have? Hundreds of thousands . . . Where would we be without death, hunh Abe?'[55] The president who had saved the nation through the catharsis of civil war had done so with his reputation and his sanity intact, and is now to be counted among the audience: silent witnesses to the mental disintegration of his successor in the White House.

Later, as Nixon is about to resign, he is shown, alone, and talking to another portrait, this time of JFK. In an echo of de Gaulle's remark about Johnson, Nixon tells his assassinated predecessor: 'when they look at you, they see what they want to be. When they look at me, they see what they are'.[56] Three sources are given as the inspiration for this scene: Bob Woodward and Carl Bernstein's book, *Final Days*, Fred Emery's *Watergate*, and Jonathan Aitken's *Nixon*. Given the fact that Nixon, as in his conversation with Lincoln's portrait, is alone in this encounter with the painting, some dramatic licence necessarily may have been taken with the historical record. In Nixon's memoirs, such incidents do not appear, although he does recall walking the darkened corridors of the executive mansion at this time, claiming 'I was not afraid of knocking into anything in the dark'. Emery uses this remark to suggest that it is an 'evident rebuttal to stories that had him wandering around talking to pictures'.[57] It seems a curious connection to make: why should the ability to navigate the corridors of power with the lights out have anything to do with a tendency to interrogate the pictures on the walls?

Once more, though, it is the image which is important. If Nixon's psychological health has suffered through Watergate, then suggestions of a distracted president conversing with the ghosts of his predecessors do not seem misplaced. The film's borrowings from Freud makes its view of a psychologically afflicted president instantly recognisable to audiences familiar already with the vernacular of pop culture psycho-analysis. Stone's portrait of Nixon thus resonates with what Ray Price himself terms 'symbolic truth' which is 'hailed as true by those who want to believe it true'.[58]

CONCLUSION: THE GAMES PRESIDENTS PLAY

The pressures of leadership during the Vietnam war created tensions within the presidency that made the mental health of the incumbents – both Johnson and Nixon – a matter of concern to their critics. The reason for this is that they were stuck with their support for a version of American history, and its consequences in terms of the nation's mission in Vietnam, at a time when for many, neither history nor mission any longer made sense. The 'credibility gap' was not simply that which opened up between what the president said about Vietnam, and what people came to believe was the reality of the situation there. It was also, and more fundamentally, related to the capacity of consensus history, and its celebratory version of America's past, to convince the nation that it indeed represented the 'last best hope for mankind'.

The Watergate scandal again was the product of the problem of presidential credibility. For Kim McQuaid, as the events of Watergate unravelled, 'the growing controversy in Washington even filled the emotional and political void left by America's blunder in Vietnam. Government had failed. Leadership had failed. Something was wrong in Washington. Watergate, therefore, was a lightening rod for frustra- tion'.[59] The fracturing of political consensus occurred at the fault-line in American politics that emerged with a growing realisation that perhaps America's missionary zeal and military activism in support of the doctrine of containment and the threat of falling dominoes was misplaced. The interior logic of the cold war made sense to those who promulgated such theories. But the 'mission impossible' of Vietnam reflected an exterior reality on to presidential rhetoric. The 'imperial presidency' cracked under the strain.

In discussing the cultural connotations of games in American frontier society, Christian Messenger points out that two different images of the hero have been built around those who succeed on the one hand in the realm of competition, and those who triumph on the other in the realm of chance. The exaggerated legends surrounding heroes of the first kind 'centered on their strength and victories' in competitive games. The other version of the hero, however, was 'the trickster, the sly wagerer whose games made him a survivor in a hostile society as he created illusions through ingenuity'. These two popular figures were thus either 'heroes of physical skill' or 'heroes of chicanery'.[60] Cold war presidents might be an amalgam of both. For inspirational leadership can be connected with definitions of a world in which winning sports-teams seize hold of the popular imagination. In this context, far more than baseball or basketball, football is the competitive sport which sits easiest with the militaristic mindset of the cold war years. Presidents, then, have sometimes attempted to profit from an interest in football as the sport for the American 'hero of physical skill': none more so than John Kennedy and Richard Nixon. And if to live in a contingent world is to take part in a game of chance, where nuclear strategy itself is analogous to a card game, it may follow too that the nation's political leaders needed to be good at poker. Some were. For Franklin Roosevelt, Harry Truman, Dwight Eisenhower and again Nixon, at various times in their lives, poker was an important recreation.

Poker, as Stephen Ambrose points out, teaches a player an invaluable political lesson, 'to know when to fold his hand, and quietly withdraw from the game'. It also is an appropriate game to play in the cultural context of the nuclear age. Poker is about 'brinkmanship'. And Ambrose also argues that 'bluffing is poker's great art form'. Indeed,

> bluffing has nothing to do with gambling. The gambler puts his money into the pot on the basis of his belief (his gamble) that he has the best hand at the table. The bluffer *knows* his hand is inferior, that if his bet is called he will lose. He is not gambling – he is making a psychological attack on his opponent.[61]

The game of poker is an apt metaphorical construction, useful for making sense of cold war confrontations: Nixon's account of his meeting with Khrushchev in *Six Crises* is written in terms of a confrontation between two skilled players of the game.

Just before the Second World War broke out in Europe, Johan Huizinga wrote of 'the supreme importance to civilization of the play-factor'. He argued that

> civilization will, in a sense, always be played according to certain rules, and true civilization will always demand fair play. Fair play is nothing less than good faith expressed in play terms. Hence, the cheat or the spoil-sport shatters civilization itself. To be a sound culture-creating force this play-

element must be pure. It must not consist in the darkening or debasing of standards set up by reason, faith or humanity. It must not be a false seeming, a masking of political purposes behind the illusion of genuine play-forms.[62]

If the predilections of presidents for certain games – and notably in cold war America for football and poker – thus may give some insight by analogy into various styles of political leadership, then his comments also provide a clear warning for a civilised society should the player-politician try to bend the rules of the game.

The three presidents elected in the 1960s – Kennedy, Johnson and Nixon – occupied the White House as America's self-belief, imbued in the rhetoric of historical exceptionalism, was pitched against the realities of war in Vietnam. If Kennedy represented the existentialist as hero, and Johnson symbolised the values of cold war consensus culture, Nixon was the trickster who dispelled finally the illusion of heroic leadership embodied in the presidency. For he turned out to be Johan Huizinga's cheat, the spoil-sport who ruined the play element in American political life. He hid political purposes behind the illusion of genuine play forms. Nixon's actions over Watergate finally dispelled the myth of heroic leadership embodied in the presidency. He destroyed the political credibility of the chief executive and in so doing, like Kennedy before him but in a different manner, changed the rules of the game for those who subsequently were to hold the office.

For Walter Hickel, therefore, 'Watergate was the Vietnam of the so-called silent majority'.[63] And as Theodore White observed,

the true crime of Richard Nixon was simple: he destroyed the myth that binds America together, and for this he was driven from power. The myth he broke was critical – that somewhere in American life there is at least one man who stands for law, the President.

So,

of all the political myths out of which the republic was born, . . . none was more powerful than the crowning myth of the Presidency – that the people, in their shared wisdom, would be able to choose the best man to lead them. From this came the derivative myth – that the Presidency, the supreme office, would make noble any man who held its responsibility.

Watergate shattered those myths. 'Richard Nixon behaved otherwise. His lawlessness exploded the legends'.[64]

Philip Roth's satirical view of the Nixon presidency, *Our Gang*

(1971), was written prior to the revelations of Watergate. At one point, his president, Tricky Dixon, is faced with an absurd crisis – a revolution by the boy scouts of America. He makes a decision, and immediately congratulates himself.

> There, *that's* the way to be in a crisis: decisive! Just as I wrote in my book, summarizing what I learned during General Poppapower's heart attacks, 'Decisive action relieves the tension which builds up in a crisis. When the situation requires that an individual restrain himself from acting decisively over a long period, this can be the most wearing of all crises'.

Here Roth is quoting directly from *Six Crises*. Tricky continues:

> You see, it isn't even what you decide – it's *that* you decide. Otherwise there's that darn tension; too much, and, I tell you, a person could probably crack up. And I for one will not crack up while I am President of the United States. I want that to be perfectly clear. If you read my book, you'll see that my entire career has been devoted to not cracking up, as much as to anything. And I don't intend to start now.[65]

By the end of the book, Dixon, having been assassinated, is on the come-back trail, challenging Satan for the presidency of hell.

Like Johnson before him, there was a sense in which Nixon did indeed 'crack up' as Vietnam and Watergate defined the progress of the 'imperial presidency' from the optimism of the New Frontier to defeat in Southeast Asia. If the distinctive personalities of both proved insufficient to tackle the political tasks with which they were confronted, however, the blame can be laid at the dysfunctional tensions created by cold war convictions. Characterisations of LBJ as 'psychologically afflicted' or Nixon as obsessively and increasingly paranoid deflect attention from fundamental issues raised by America's pursuit of its 'mission impossible'. For as Vietnam demonstrated increasingly the hollowness of ideological posturing and cold war rhetoric, the temptation nevertheless was to blame the messengers – those presidents to whom, following JFK, the nation had looked for heroic leadership – rather than to re-examine the message. And when Nixon's unelected successor, Gerald Ford, proclaimed that 'our long national nightmare is over', the implication was still that America's dream of its rendezvous with destiny would emerge from the political twilight of Vietnam and Watergate intact. As future presidents would find, however, it was rather the problem of political credibility that both Johnson and Nixon had exposed – and which had ultimately eroded their careers – that would continue to define the course of American public life.

NOTES

1. Quoted in Kraus, *The Great Debates*, p. 430.
2. Nixon, *Six Crises*, p. xxiii.
3. Schlesinger, *A Thousand Days*, p. 584.
4. Wills, *Nixon Agonistes*, p. 147.
5. Ambrose, *Nixon: The Education*, p. 63.
6. Nixon, *Six Crises*, p. xxviii.
7. Ibid. p. xxviii.
8. Wills, *Nixon Agonistes*, p. 147.
9. Nixon, *Six Crises*, pp. xxv–xxvi.
10. Ibid. p. 2.
11. Ibid. pp. 8–9.
12. Ibid. pp. 10–12. This view, which Nixon emphasises in *Six Crises*, dramatises his role in relation to the rest of the Committee. There is no doubt, moreover, that the prevailing interpretation at the time was that Nixon alone had stood firm while the rest of the Committee had expressed doubts about the wisdom of pursuing Hiss. See Tanenhaus, *Whittaker Chambers*, for a further exploration of this.
13. Nixon, *Six Crises*, p. 12.
14. Wills, *Nixon Agonistes*, pp. 26 and 28.
15. Nixon, *Six Crises*, p. 219.
16. Ibid. p. 223.
17. Ibid. pp. 223 and 246.
18. Ibid. pp. 253 and 265.
19. Ibid. pp. 270, 292 and 294.
20. Ibid. p. 294.
21. Ibid. p. 439. Bradlee, in *Conversations with Kennedy*, reports Kennedy's reaction to this, (p. 75): 'I can't stand the way he puts everything in Tricia's mouth. It makes me sick. He's a cheap bastard; that's all there is to it.'
22. Tuchman, *The March of Folly*, p. 465.
23. Nixon, *Memoirs*, p. 783.
24. Ambrose, *Nixon:The Triumph*, p. 654.
25. Schlesinger, *The Imperial Presidency*, pp. 254–5.
26. Ibid. p. 428.
27. Turner, *Max Weber*, pp. 188 and 222.
28. McQuaid, *The Anxious Years*, p. 169; Haldeman, *The Ends of Power*, p. 79; McCarthy, *The Mask of State*, p. 24.
29. Nixon, *Memoirs*, pp. 762–4, passim.
30. Ibid. p. 337.
31. Quoted in Crowley, *Nixon in Winter*, p. 257.

32. Maraniss, *First in His Class*, p. 187.
33. Nixon, *Memoirs*, pp. 403 and 408.
34. Quoted in Crowley, *Nixon in Winter*, p. 252.
35. See *Public Papers of the Presidents: Richard Nixon (1969)*, pp. 901–9.
36. Nixon, *Memoirs,* p. 411.
37. Quoted in Crowley, *Nixon in Winter*, pp. 250 and 352–3.
38. Nixon, *Memoirs*, p. 400.
39. Engelhardt, *The End of Victory Culture*, p. 202.
40. Ellsberg to Seymour Hersh, quoted in ibid. pp. 203–4.
41. Haldeman, *The Ends of Power*, p. 83. See also Engelhardt, *The End of Victory Culture*, p. 203.
42. Engelhardt, *The End of Victory Culture*, p. 204.
43. Nixon, *Memoirs*, p. 385.
44. Kissinger, *White House Years*, p. 305.
45. Brodie, *War and Politics*, p. 188. Brodie was, he wrote, aware of this because of the work of his wife, Fawn Brodie, who was then writing her psychobiography of Thomas Jefferson, before going on to tackle Nixon.
46. Brodie, *Richard Nixon*, pp. 25 and 507.
47. Ibid. pp. 392–3 and 543.
48. Ibid. pp. 144 and 528.
49. Nixon, *Memoirs*, p. 9.
50. Brodie, *Richard Nixon*, pp. 331 and 332.
51. Wicker, *One of Us*, p. 234.
52. Mazlish, *The Leader*, p. 200.
53. Price, *With Nixon*, pp. 19–20.
54. Hamburg, *Nixon*, pp. 183–4.
55. Ibid. p. 184.
56. Ibid p. 303.
57. Nixon, *Memoirs*, p. 1086; & Emery, *Watergate*, p. 479.
58. Price, *With Nixon,* p. 356.
59. McQuaid, *The Anxious Years*, pp. 214–15.
60. Messenger, *Sport and the Spirit of Play in American Fiction*, pp. 61–2.
61. Ambrose, *Nixon: The Education*, pp. 112–14.
62. Huizinga, *Homo Ludens*, p. 211.
63. Quoted in Sorensen, *Watchmen in the Night*, p. 20.
64. White, *Breach of Faith*, pp. 322 and 323–4.
65. Roth, *Our Gang*, pp. 41–2.

CHAPTER SIX

Gerald Ford and Jimmy Carter:
Faith Healers

INTRODUCTION: STRATEGIES OF HEALING

If John F. Kennedy had refined a style of heroic presidential leadership, characterised by the need to combat crises and confront challenges in order to define the nation's sense of purpose and mission during the cold war, his immediate successors, Lyndon Johnson and Richard Nixon, in grappling with his legacy, had been overwhelmed by events directly related to such historical hubris. Vietnam had exposed the 'credibility gap' between cold war rhetoric and the reality of the impossible mission in Southeast Asia. Watergate had become a short-hand expression for the web of corruption that determined Nixon's 'breach of faith', undermining popular confidence in American leadership.

The two presidents in power for the remainder of the 1970s – one unelected, the other a self-proclaimed 'outsider' in terms of the national political establishment – could not attempt to emulate the heroic style of JFK: instead they had to come to terms with the political and cultural dislocations they inherited from both Johnson and Nixon. It was Gerald Ford's misfortune not only to pardon his predecessor (an act of political courage, rather than political self-interest) but also to be in office when the struggle to prevent a unified and communist Vietnam was finally lost. Jimmy Carter was politically astute in surfing a mood of national disillusionment all the way to the White House. But his attempt to lead by moral example promised much but delivered little in the way of restoring self-confidence. It would instead be a new president in a new decade who, combining Carter's populism with rhetorical magic, would prove to be, in an echo of Theodore Roosevelt, 'the master therapist of the middle class'.

The collapse of the imperial presidency as a combined outcome of the nation's adventure in Vietnam (abroad) and the Watergate scandal (at home) appeared to be a physical and psychological shock to America's body politic. As such, it would be described in an appropriate metaphor. Following Nixon's resignation it was, in the title of Gerald Ford's memoirs, *A Time to Heal*. Following his short presidency, and failure to win election in his own right, Ford gave way to Jimmy Carter who came to the White House as 'the Vietnam syndrome' entered the political vocabulary of the country: a condition which became part of the perceived 'malaise' that characterised the time. Both presidents, then, took office when the United States seemed chastened by its past and uncertain of its future. What price now the heroic president as leader?

Ford and Carter had several things in common. Neither sought to match the grandiose ambitions of Kennedy, Johnson or Nixon. They could not. The nation had lost stomach for the challenges suggested by an exceptional destiny, and indeed the rhetoric of the 1960s seemed irrelevant to the immediate concerns of the post-Vietnam era. Both presidents stressed integrity rather than vision: to try to restore public confidence in the institution of chief executive rather than aspire to the position of heroic leader that had been coveted by those who had gone before them.

Instead they pursued similar strategies aimed at reclaiming the moral highground for the presidency, and refocusing political attention away from the perceived divisions caused by war and Watergate. As far as 'Mr. Johnson's war' and Nixon's crimes and misdemeanours were concerned, both the Republican president and his Democrat successor aimed to forgive and forget. Ford's rhetorical attempts to do this owed much to the example of one of his heroes, Abraham Lincoln. Carter, on the other hand, brought a spiritual dimension to the moral dilemmas that faced the nation: insisting on repentance as a pre-requisite for forgiveness and as a prelude to the process of forgetting. But the nation did not heal. Attempting to move beyond the cultural dislocations of the 1960s and 1970s through encouraging a process of historical amnesia was ultimately to prove a strategy that was politically flawed. For Ford and Carter also share the distinction of being the first two incumbent presidents since Herbert Hoover to have been defeated at the polls.

'A FORD NOT A LINCOLN'

When Gerald Ford became Nixon's unelected vice-president, following the resignation of Spiro Agnew, following corruption charges ironically unconnected to the Watergate scandal, he proclaimed himself 'a Ford not a Lincoln'. A neat pun, it encapsulated the fact that the new vice-president came from Michigan, the home of the Ford motor company, whose production of cheap automobiles had pioneered the democracy of car ownership in America, (it was Ford's subsidiary company that produced the more expensive Lincoln continental), and the idea that here was an ordinary leader, not one who might assume the historic heroic status of Whitman's 'redeemer president' from Illinois. At the same time, however, when he took over from Nixon, Ford seemed to see the situation of the nation as analogous to that which had confronted it during and after the Civil War. He thus appropriated the rhetoric of Lincoln in many of his key public statements as he tried to deal with the political, social and cultural fallout from the Vietnam war and Watergate.

Ford, indeed, initially represented Watergate as more divisive even than Vietnam, and with the capacity to do more damage to the well-being of the country. His remarks on taking the oath of office – 'just a little straight talk among friends' – resembled in places a prayer: 'As we bind up the internal wounds of Watergate, more painful and more poisonous than those of foreign wars, let us restore the golden rule to our political process, and let brotherly love purge our hearts of suspicion and hate.' Ford talked of 'the lonely burdens of the White House', and appeared to sense the inheritance of a dubious legacy. 'I can only guess at those burdens, although I have witnessed at close hand the tragedies that befell three Presidents and the lesser trials of others'.[1] So JFK's assassination, Lyndon Johnson's war in Vietnam and Richard Nixon's resignation of office are linked as reminders of the wreckage of the desire for heroic leadership. Ford had been a member of the Warren Commission which had investigated the death of a president, House minority leader while Johnson was president and had eventually become Nixon's unelected deputy as vice-president. His career had progressed while the imperial presidency crumbled.

Now the new president set about breaking with that past. His immediate actions with respect first to Vietnam and then to Watergate were related. In August 1974, Ford was scheduled to speak at the seventy-fifth annual convention of Veterans of Foreign Wars. In his memoirs, he wrote that his secretary of defence, James Schlesinger, suggested that 'one way to hasten the healing process and draw a real distinction between the Nixon and Ford Administrations would be to do something about the fifty thousand draft evaders and deserters from the Vietnam War'. In deciding what gesture to make, Ford recalled that:

> after the Civil War, Lincoln had offered deserters restoration of their rights if they withdrew support from the enemy and swore allegiance to the Union. He was criticized for being too lenient, but his was probably the right decision at the time.[2]

During the Civil War, it had indeed been the case that some Union soldiers had deserted and had gone to fight for the Confederacy – the so-called 'galvanized Yankees'. Lincoln's decision offered them a way to reclaim their citizenship, as now, a little over a century later, Ford tried to do for those who had, for various reasons, avoided service in Vietnam.

So at the convention, Ford talked about the fifty thousand or so Americans charged with 'offenses loosely described as desertion and draft dodging' because of their refusal to participate in the war. 'I am throwing the weight of my presidency into the scales of justice on the side of leniency. I foresee their earned reentry . . . into a new atmosphere of hope, hard work and mutual trust.' By opting for a policy of clemency rather than amnesty, however, – 'as I reject amnesty, so I reject revenge' – Ford was making a gesture of reconciliation rather than forgiveness. As John Greene observes, 'with amnesty, the punishment is terminated; with clemency, the punishment is made less severe'.[3] But there was no such fine distinction in dealing with his predecessor. In September 1974, the month after he had taken office, Ford pardoned Nixon.

Five months earlier, in a televised address announcing that he was giving up the transcripts of tapes requested by the House Judiciary Committee as they advanced the constitutional process of presidential impeachment, Richard Nixon had used an image that he too had borrowed from Lincoln. Anxious to claim what was left of the moral and political high-ground in the face of the erosion of his public credibility, the president confessed that: 'ten angels swearing I was right would make no difference' as to whether his word was sufficient to be taken on trust. Now, in the most critical speech of his presidency, Ford used the same Lincoln-inspired sentiment. 'I do believe that right makes might, and that if I am wrong, ten angels swearing I was right would make no difference'. The juxtaposition of such rhetoric has been taken to suggest complicity between Nixon and Ford: a Faustian bargain that had led the one to resign and the other to assume office.[4] It is a charge that blighted Ford's presidency.

For the new president, however, Richard Nixon and his family had suffered 'an American tragedy in which we have all played a part. It could go on and on, or someone must write the end to it. I have concluded that only I can do that, and if I can, I must'. Ford was convinced that while Nixon was threatened with Watergate litigation, the national nightmare would in fact continue.

> My conscience tells me clearly and certainly that I cannot prolong the bad dreams that continue to reopen a chapter that is closed. My conscience tells me that only I, as President, have the constitutional power to firmly shut and seal this book. My conscience tells me it is my duty, not merely to proclaim domestic tranquillity but to use every means that I have to insure it.[5]

With Watergate as with Vietnam, it made sense to try to seek new beginnings.

He had 'intended to convince my fellow citizens' that the pardon was 'necessary surgery – essential if we were to heal our wounded nation'.[6] Ford was convinced that the prospect of a former president being dragged through the courts as a result of a continuing obsession with the Watergate scandal was not simply self-defeating but also symptomatic of the nation's contemporary 'sickness'. In his memoirs, he records his pre-eminent concern over 'the precipitous decline in the faith that Americans traditionally placed in their nation, their institutions and their leaders. In the fall of 1974 they even seemed to have lost faith in themselves'. He goes on to quote from an editorial in the *Daily Telegraph*, where Americans had been taken to task by the British newspaper: 'for too long you have been beating your breasts in self-flagellation in the traumas over Watergate and Vietnam . . . The self-criticism and self-destructive tendencies are running mad'.[7] The act of healing could thus only occur if the wounds were cauterised, through clemency for those who had deserted from the mission in Southeast Asia, and through a complete pardon for Richard Nixon.

Yet as Myra MacPherson observes 'when Ford's limited clemency program went into effect, it was roundly – and accurately – denounced as "shamnesty" by amnesty activists'.[8] Vernon Jordan, later to become a pivotal figure in Bill Clinton's impeachment struggle, resigned as a member of the Clemency Board in protest at its ineffectual operation. Such criticisms were nothing compared to those that Ford faced over the issue of Nixon's pardon. The contrast between the treatment of the former president and that of those who had disagreed with the Vietnam war and who had voted with their feet seemed clear. Indeed, Jerry terHorst, Ford's press secretary, made this the central issue over which he resigned. In his letter to Ford explaining his decision he wrote of his opposition to the pardon: 'as your spokesman I do not know how I could credibly defend that action in the absence of a like decision to grant absolute pardons to the young men who evaded Vietnam military service as a matter of conscience . . .'.[9] As Ford's approval ratings sank from 71 per cent to 49 per cent, Nixon telephoned him. During their conversation, Ford confessed that 'I expected an adverse reaction. It's been worse than I thought, but I've done it, and I'm convinced that it was the right decision, and I think history will prove my point'.[10] And yet, undoubtedly, 'the hour, the timing in his presidency, and its relationship to clemency extended to Vietnam-era draft evaders undermined the pardon as rhetoric'[11], and had continuing repercussions upon popular perceptions of Nixon's successor in the White House.

It was difficult for Ford to avoid the impression that in attempting to lead the nation away from the wreckage of the immediate past, he was adopting a dual standard of forgiveness. Indeed, he was asked at a press conference on 16 September 1974, given that his 'intention was to heal the wounds of the Nation', why he had granted 'only a conditional amnesty to the Vietnam war draft evaders while granting a full pardon to President Nixon'.[12] The question itself shows how the two issues were to become firmly linked in the popular mind. The answer was of course political: Ford alone had the constitutional right, and therefore the ability to pardon his predecessor. How to deal with draft evaders was an issue that was bitterly contested. Yet had Ford managed to finesse it in such a way that a single standard of mercy – and justice – could be applied to those considered to have suffered through war and Watergate, his political credibility might have been preserved.

In an effort to mollify congressional Democrats who were convinced that Nixon had struck a bargain over the pardon with Ford before agreeing to resign, the new president took the unusual step of agreeing to testify before a subcommittee of the House Judiciary committee. He observes in his memoirs that this had not occurred since Washington's time, although there was a precedent which impressed him: 'there were unsubstantiated reports that Lincoln had done so informally in order to deny reports that his wife was a Confederate spy'. Ford's appearance before the partisan subcommittee gave him an opportunity to claim that 'there was no deal, period, under no circumstances'.[13] But the doubts remained.

The pardon was an attempt – however clumsy – to end the corrosive impact of the Watergate scandal upon American domestic politics.

Through an act of forgiving – the pardon – it was hoped that a process of forgetting could take place. By consigning Nixon's administration to history, Ford might start to rebuild the institution of the presidency. A similar pattern of thinking appeared to influence the president's view of Vietnam. Here again, and moving beyond his initial gesture of reconciliation in the announcement of the clemency programme, Ford invited the nation simply to forget the humiliation of its defeat in Southeast Asia.

In his speech at Tulane University on 23 April 1975, Ford argued that: 'today, America can regain the sense of pride that existed before Vietnam. But it cannot be achieved by refighting a war that is finished as far as America is concerned'. And then the president used the same imagery to characterise the impact of the war on American society as he had in describing the affect of Watergate in his remarks on taking office. 'As I see it, the time has come to look forward to an agenda for the future, to unify, to bind up the Nation's wounds, and to restore its health and its optimistic self-confidence.' This would involve avoiding recriminations. And the long-term repercussions of the war in Vietnam would, for Ford, be trivial. 'We, of course, are saddened indeed by the events in Indochina. But these events, tragic as they are, portend neither the end of the world nor of America's leadership in the world'.[14] So defeat was a setback, and indeed, like the constitutional crimes and misdemeanours of Watergate, was a wound that would be healed only if the nation forgot its past and concentrated on the future.

The metaphor of the wounded nation that needed time to recuperate without recriminations was one which Abraham Lincoln had played with in his second inaugural address, and his rhetoric continued to resonate in Ford's speeches. Thus Lincoln in 1865 elegantly expressed the sentiments that seemed similarly compelling to Ford over a century later:

> with malice toward none, with charity for all, with firmness in the right as God gives us to see the right, let us strive on to finish the work we are in, to bind up the nation's wounds, to care for him who shall have borne the battle and for his widow and his orphan, to do all which may achieve and cherish a just and lasting peace among ourselves and with all nations.[15]

Reconstruction was necessary once more.

Two days before Ford made his speech at Tulane, President Thieu of South Vietnam had resigned. Five days after the president had effectively drawn a line under America's failed mission in Southeast Asia,

North Vietnamese forces reached Saigon, and nineteen hours later the final helicopter evacuation from the roof of the American embassy in the city took place. Yet if the evacuation of Saigon, according to Ford, closed 'a chapter in the American experience', as Myra MacPherson suggests, 'for many Americans, by inference, this meant "Forget the veteran" ', an attitude which would 're-inforce silence'.[16] In such an atmosphere, the reconstruction which Ford attempted made little sense if it excluded those most directly involved in the nation's 'mission impossible'. Here, then, is the flaw in Ford's attempt to heal. The assumption that after forgiveness could come forgetting is misplaced. That much is clear if the analogy of reconstruction after the Civil War is explored. For the former Confederate States, the conflict was not forgotten – indeed it became defined as a noble and heroic 'lost cause'. Even though the South was, for many years, treated – and sometimes mistreated – as a maverick region within the United States, within the former confederacy itself, memories of the war between the states, and its significance in the creation of a cultural identity were not repressed. It was only in the 1980s that a process of historical revisionism would reinterpret the Vietnam war similarly as a 'noble cause'.

In the immediate aftermath of the reunification of Vietnam, however, Ford was able to attempt a rehabilitation of America's sense of self-worth as a military power, if not claiming for himself the mantle of heroic leadership. On 12 May 1975, the American merchant ship *Mayaguez* was seized by the Cambodian government and its crew held hostage. As John Greene observes 'the crisis afforded an opportunity for Ford to look presidential':[17] ordering the first use of military force since the end of the Vietnam war. The action was successful, although luck may have played a greater part than judgement.

Ford's critics go further. For Richard Slotkin, it was

> a rescue operation in which 41 Marines died to save 39 sailors aboard a ship seized by Cambodian or Vietnamese troops – a trivial and perhaps unnecessary skirmish which the administration described as a 'symbolic victory' demonstrating that the United States was not a 'paper tiger'. The recapture of a single ship was thus said to outweigh and offset the consequences and significance of the defeat of a national government whose independence we had helped to establish and whose integrity we had supported through nearly twenty years of diplomatic, economic, and military aid and for whose sake we had fought a long and costly war.[18]

Nevertheless, Ford was able to claim in his memoirs that 'all of a sudden, the gloomy national mood began to fade' and his public approval ratings similarly began to improve.[19] The pattern for post-Vietnam military adventurism had been set: temporary boosts to the image of heroic presidential leadership might be gained through rapid, and sometimes symbolic, gestures designed to 'prove' the nation's resolve when faced with a self-defined international 'crisis'.

In his State of the Union address in 1976, Ford took stock of the achievements of his first full year in office.

> As you recall, the year 1975 opened with rancor and bitterness. Political misdeeds of the past had neither been forgotten nor forgiven. The longest, most divisive war in our history was winding towards an unhappy conclusion. Many feared that the end of that foreign war of men and machines meant the beginning of a domestic war of recrimination and reprisal. Friends and adversaries abroad were asking whether America had lost its nerve . . . Ours was a troubled land.

And yet,

> I see America today crossing a threshold, not just because it is our Bicentennial but because we have been tested in adversity. We have taken a new look at what we want to be and what we want our Nation to become . . . I have heard many inspiring Presidential speeches, but the words I remember best were spoken by Dwight D. Eisenhower. 'America is not good because it is great,' the President said, 'America is great because it is good'.

So America had come through its rite of passage – 'tested in adversity' it had survived and had learnt that its achievements as a nation had to be rooted in an adherence to moral principles. It could only be 'great' if it was 'good'. The implication is that those who had led the nation through Vietnam and Watergate had failed because of lack of the same kind of moral – and indeed religious – commitment that had been at the core of their predecessor's philosophy. Indeed, Ford ended his speech by connecting the hero as president – Eisenhower – with other towering figures from America's past:

> President Eisenhower was raised in a poor but religious home in the heart of America. His simple words echoed President Lincoln's eloquent testament that 'right makes might'. And Lincoln in turn evoked the silent image of George Washington kneeling in prayer at Valley Forge.[20]

The immediate past is an aberration: Ford is claiming that America has now moved beyond the divisions it caused by rediscovering the animating religious and moral principles which had historically sustained its democratic republic. It was a big claim to make. If true, the president had indeed been a successful healer.

In accepting the Republican presidential nomination in 1976, Ford argued that he had achieved this aim, and this time linked his claim with the historical drama of Independence Day in the year of the Bicentennial:

> Something wonderful happened to this country of ours the past two years. We all came to realize it on the Fourth of July. Together, out of years of turmoil and tragedy, wars and riots, assassinations and wrongdoing in high places, Americans recaptured the spirit of 1776. We saw again the pioneer vision of our revolutionary founders and our immigrant ancestors.[21]

For John Greene, then, 'as a moral leader, Ford surpassed the examples of every president since 1960'. Yet his conclusion that the president was successful in 'healing the scars of the spirit caused by Watergate and Vietnam' is at least questionable.[22] Ford's decision to offer clemency to those who had avoided the draft proved insufficient to bury the memory of resistance to the Vietnam war, and his pardon for his predecessor aroused discordant popular suspicions of an insider trading a political deal.

If it was 'a time to heal', Ford's short tenure as physician for the national psyche proved to be but a palliative. Jimmy Carter was able to exploit a continuing sense of popular mistrust with the traditional rhetoric of American exceptionalism in order to defeat Ford at the polls. But he too was to find that in the aftermath of Vietnam and Watergate, the restoration of American morale was more difficult than either he or many of his contemporaries might imagine.

JIMMY CARTER: 'WHEELER-HEALER'

In *The Coup* (1978), John Updike's novel set in the fictionalised African country of Kush, President Ellellou and his interior minister Michaelis Ezana discuss the problems that confront them. In addition to drought, 'world geopolitics has added economic distress'. It is 1973, and 'now that the Americans are no longer vexed by Vietnam and the Watergate imbroglio promises to remove from their chests the incubus of Nixon', they have realised that 'as a race they are morbidly fat'. As a consequence, less peanut butter is being eaten, and 'the peanut growers of their notoriously *apartheid* South are compelled to export'. For the marxists of Kush, 'nothing more clearly advertises the American decline and coming collapse than this imperative need, contrary to all imperialist principles, to export raw materials'.[23] But the immediate consequence is that Kush's peanuts are being undersold on the world market in Marseilles, and a crisis looms.

Updike's satire is both subtle and compelling. In the wake of Vietnam and Watergate, Americans had turned in on themselves – an obsession with appearance is a reflection of a culture of narcissism – and the nation's attempts to project itself as a world power, politically and economically, might be regarded elsewhere as self-parody. Such a sense of America as an 'ordinary country' would apparently be confirmed as the 1970s drew to a close: a real rather than a fictional *coup* in Iran, which replaced the Shah with the Ayatollah, would lead to challenges that would ultimately wreck the administration of a president, himself a peanut grower from the American South: Jimmy Carter.

'He was elected to redeem the country, not to govern it'.[24] In his presidential memoirs, Jimmy Carter explains the reasons for the success of his 1976 election campaign:

> to me . . . the most significant factors were the disillusionment of the American people following the national defeat suffered in Vietnam, the Watergate scandals, and my success in convincing supporters that we should keep our faith in America and that I would never permit any repetition of such embarrassments.[25]

What Carter aspired to be – and what the American people wanted – was a populist hero who could be trusted. Such trust, however, had to be grounded in absolute moral principle. Indeed, it was Carter's conviction that the nation would respond to the candidacy – and the presidency – of 'a man of God who promised moral leadership after having mistakenly trusted a decade and a half of amoral leaders'. But that style of leadership came at a price: 'the whole nation would have to share the guilt for the sins of Vietnam and Watergate' as in return 'Jimmy Carter promised to help purge the nation of its sins'.[26] The new president 'believed completely Reinhold Niebuhr's dictum that 'the sad duty of politics is to establish justice in a sinful world" '.[27] And in that world, the traumas of the 1960s and 1970s were clear evidence of sin.

Vietnam and Watergate thus have been characterised as 'symbolic failures, the first of America's "mission", the second of America's democracy'.[28] Carter, the first president elected after these separate but related debacles of foreign policy and domestic politics, attempted to project himself as a Whitmanesque 'redeemer president' rather than a Nietzschean hero in the White House: an ordinary citizen who would restore the faith of his fellow Americans in their country, and rebuild their trust in their government. Although he diagnosed the problem of post-Vietnam 'malaise', however, he failed to supply an adequate answer to it. Instead he established a mood of repentance rather than revival. It was left to his successor, Ronald Reagan, to try to regenerate the nation's spirit, through refashioning Vietnam from an 'embarrassment' to a 'noble cause'.

It was significant, however, and in keeping with the temper of the times, that both Carter and then Reagan would emphasise as part of their political characters the fact of being 'born again'. As Richard Reeves observes , 'Carter's secret' in 1976 was his realisation 'that what national leaders and other candidates perceive as a political crisis is actually a spiritual crisis'.[29] Thus, even while accepting the Democrats' nomination, in Peter Meyer's words, 'somehow, Jimmy Carter seemed to say, *we* must repent for *our* sins – for the tragic war, our imperfections, mistakes, the moral decay, the absence of goals and values – and place our trust, like children, in a leader who is moral, religious, who himself has repented and been saved'.[30]

In 1966, having served in Georgia's Senate, Carter had been tempted to enter federal politics by running for congressional office. Instead he chose to campaign to become governor of his home state. He lost the election. While his fellow southerner Lyndon Johnson presided over the debacle of Vietnam, Carter, out of politics, underwent a religious conversion. He 'experienced a religious quickening . . . his religious faith became an essential part of his life. Carter went on lay evangelism missions and committed himself to a life of service unprecedented in American life'.[31] In 1972, he ran a successful campaign to become Georgia's governor: his spring-board to the White House four years later.

The significance of this is twofold. Carter's first electoral defeat removed him from the political arena at a critical time for his party. The divisions within the Democrats caused by the Vietnam war had led to Nixon's success in 1968. And when Carter returned to office in Georgia, it was to observe the president's entanglement in the web of Watergate. Thus, Carter could simultaneously distance himself from the politics of Vietnam, while positioning himself as the 'outsider' who would run for the presidency against the corrupt political establishment in Washington. In his infamous interview with *Playboy* magazine during his 1976 campaign, Carter thus confessed that he 'never spoke out publicly about withdrawing from Vietnam until March of 1971', because prior to that he had been a peanut farmer and he 'wasn't asked about the war' until he took office. He continued: 'if I had known in the sixties what I knew in the early seventies, I think I would have spoken out more strongly. I was not in public office'.[32] When he did come to address the subject of Vietnam, however, the further significance of his early political experience is apparent.

Carter's reaction to electoral defeat – his 'born again' religious conversion, involved a process of confession, forgiveness and spiritual healing that enabled him to re-enter the political arena with renewed moral conviction and sense of purpose. And what had worked for him as an individual could also work for the nation as a whole. In order to overcome the sense of failure and defeat caused by Vietnam, if the nation were to understand its guilt, its sins might be forgiven, and its morale could be recovered. Jimmy Carter's analysis of the spiritual dimension of the nation's 'sickness' determined his political strategy of forgiving and forgetting. 'Being firmly grounded morally, Carter knew, allowed one to deal with disappointment in a positive way'.[33] It was an analysis defined by personal experience, and it convinced him that the recovery of absolute standards of moral principle – the adherence to 'human rights' as the basis of foreign policy, for example – was necessary to redeem the soul of the nation.

As John Dumbrell observes, 'Carter was, in political commentator Eric Severaid's phrase, a "wheeler-healer", riding to power on the promise of national reconciliation'.[34] This much was apparent in his inaugural address, where Carter paid tribute to his predecessor, thanking him 'for all he has done to heal our land', and at the same time promising more. In a number of careful circumlocutions, he alluded to the continuing impact of Vietnam and Watergate upon American politics and society. So, 'let our recent mistakes bring a resurgent commitment to the basic principles of our Nation, for we know that if we despise our own government we have no future'. And 'we will not behave in foreign places so as to violate our rules and standards here at home, for we know that the trust which our Nation earns is essential to our strength'.[35] The new president had made reference to a reading from the Old Testament prophet Micah, promising a renewal of America's search for humility, mercy and justice. 'These words', wrote Carter in his memoirs, 'did not seem overly critical of our nation, but still held the reminder of the need to seek God's help and guidance as we sought to improve our commitment to justice and mercy'.[36]

Carter's first action as president was to declare a 'blanket pardon' for those who had resisted the draft during the Vietnam war. The wording was seen, at the time, to be important. An amnesty would have implied forgetting: a pardon symbolised forgiveness. It was a fine distinction, but one made by, among others, Fritz Efaw, the draft resister whom Ron Kovic had nominated for vice-president at Carter's convention, in order to publicise this issue.[37] And therein would lie the essential ambiguity of Carter's political message. For the relevance of the claim to be 'born again' was that it might allow both individuals, and by extension the nation, a fresh start. And new beginnings allowed former sins to be forgotten. Yet at the same time, the president as preacher continued to remind America of its immediate past mistakes, insisting that the nation be held accountable before attempting to expurgate its 'guilt'.

In his speech at Notre Dame University on 22 May 1977, Carter thus offered his explanation for the outcome of American policy in Southeast Asia.

> For too many years, we've been willing to adopt the flawed and erroneous principles and tactics of our adversaries, sometimes abandoning our own values for theirs. We've fought fire with fire, never thinking that fire is better quenched with water. This approach failed, with Vietnam the best example of its intellectual and moral poverty. But through failure we have now found our way back to our own principles and values, and we have regained our lost confidence.[38]

He was wrong. To explain America's defeat in Vietnam purely as a consequence of the nation being traduced from its traditional high moral values, of being forced to step down into the political gutter to slug it out with its ideological opponents, proved politically unconvincing. Confidence, far from being restored, was still shaken.

For Carter, religion underpinned politics. Key aspects of his administration's agenda, such as the human rights policy and a concern with moral probity in public life and international conduct, flowed naturally from his Southern baptist beliefs. On the issue of human rights, it was as if, in Richard Barnet's words, 'the sin of Vietnam . . . would be expunged by working for redemption in the rest of the world'.[39] What Jimmy Carter failed to do, however, was to link his born-again conviction with any of the nation's cultural or historical myths, although as Richard Slotkin observes, in finally recognising the nation's 'malaise', he 'was astute in identifying the *cultural* character of the crisis'.[40] It was as if the president's sense of religiosity existed in the abstract, remote from any historical or cultural context that could reinforce its political appeal.

As Donald Spencer argues in *The Carter Implosion* (1988), Robert Altman's film *Nashville* (1975), released the year before Carter beat Ford, summed up the mood of its times. 'That ambitious spectacle, billed as a bicentennial portrait of America, chronicled the psychic processes of a nation going mad, exhausted by its own mindless materialism and corrupted heroes.' The sole voice of sanity is that of the presidential candidate, whose response to such cultural disintegration is to proclaim that 'what this country needs is some one syllable answers'. In his election campaign , Carter seemed to embody that message – 'I will never lie to you'- and indeed as Spencer suggests 'it was that enduring, naive determination to view all political issues in essentially moralistic terms that transformed the presidential campaign of 1976 from an intellectual debate, much needed in that troubled year, into a spiritual crusade'.[41] What worked in the campaign, however, could not be translated into an effective political message in the White House. For Carter as president was no longer the outsider. Confronted with the realities of governing, he appeared to lack the clarity and simplicity of vision which had characterised his campaign.

Three years into his administration, then, Carter was still wrestling with the complexities of the post-Vietnam loss of national confidence. Facing re-election, unpopular, with his style of leadership criticised by members of his own party, in April 1979 he read what Theodore White records as the 'Apocalypse Now' memorandum – itself a reference to Francis Ford Coppola's movie about Vietnam – produced by Pat Caddell, his private pollster. Caddell wrote: 'America is a nation deep in crisis. Unlike civil war or depression, this crisis, nearly invisible, is unique from those that previously have engaged Americans in their history.' It was 'a psychological crisis of the first order', and one which in turn would prompt Carter to try to 'understand what was wrong with the country'.[42] If Caddell's analysis, based on his polling data was right, then Carter was faced with a problem that transcended even those that had confronted Abraham Lincoln and Franklin Roosevelt: a crisis of national confidence that could not be traced directly to the divisions caused by civil war or economic depression, yet one which seemed as tangible and as threatening, not least to Carter's own chances of re-election.

As a result of this, the president began a process of analysing the nation's contemporary mood. Indeed, for White, 'perhaps no President since Lincoln has probed so deeply into the metaphysics of spirit that makes America a nation as Jimmy Carter tried to do'.[43] Although ostensibly linked with his concern to develop a coherent energy policy, therefore, his address to the nation on 15 July 1979 followed this much publicised process of consultation and soul-searching, and tackled wider issues. Thus, the president addressed

> a fundamental threat to American democracy . . . nearly invisible in ordin-ary ways. It is a crisis of confidence. It is a crisis that strikes at the very heart and soul and spirit of our national will. We can see this crisis in the growing doubt about the meaning of our own lives and in the loss of a unity of purpose for our Nation.

Yet if Carter was attempting to revitalise his own leadership through creating an atmosphere of crisis to which his administration would respond, his was not a tangible threat, rather it was an analysis of spiritual unrest and psychological disturbance. His speech identified the causes of America's contemporary 'malaise' – the epithet which would characterise his words, even though he himself did not use it on that occasion. The erosion of national self-confidence was suggested by changing attitudes towards society, government, and the 'idea of America' itself. 'These changes did not happen overnight. They've come upon us gradually over the last generation, years that were filled with shocks and tragedy.' This sense of paralysis flowed from the past to the present, in a nation traumatised by the assassination of its political leaders in the 1960s, by Vietnam, Watergate, and now by inflation and dependence upon foreign oil.

In Carter's words,

> we were taught that our armies were always invincible and our causes always just, only to suffer the agony of Vietnam. We respected the Presidency as a place of honor until the shock of Watergate . . . These wounds are still very deep. They have never been healed.[44]

Again, for Theodore White, 'no President since Abraham Lincoln had spoken to the American people with such sincerity about matters of spirit'.[45] Yet however acute his diagnosis, Carter nevertheless could not supply the cure: his 'born-again' religiosity helped him to the White House, but his presidency still personified the nation's doubts over its mission in the immediate aftermath of intervention in Vietnam.

As Richard Polenberg argued, 'the war in Vietnam produced . . . fragmentation, alienation, confrontation, what the editors of *Time* would call "the loss of a working consensus, for the first time in our lives, as to what we think America means" '.[46] Yet any attempt to rebuild that consensus necessarily had to discuss, at some level, the significance of the Vietnam experience in American history. Carter's analysis of the moral and spiritual crisis in American life, and loss of national self-confidence was itself an acknowledgement that defeat in Southeast Asia was an event which had a profound psychological impact upon American society and culture. And at the heart of the 'malaise' was a popular mistrust of foreign adventurism: the 'Vietnam syndrome'.

It made its debut in American political debate during Carter's presidency. It was a simple idea. As Michael Klare summarised, the 'Vietnam Syndrome' represented 'the American public's disinclination to engage in further military interventions in internal Third World conflicts'.[47] In this sense it was then a self-denying ordinance, in keeping with the prevailing mood of Jimmy Carter's administration. Yet the implications of the 'Vietnam syndrome' as a restraint upon an activist foreign policy soon became clear. The consequence of a reluctance to re-emphasise the military commitment which would need to accompany a policy of containment, to preserve American influence abroad, was easily characterised as international impotence. This was further dramatised by events in the Middle East. Four months after Carter's 'malaise' speech, the nation itself was taken hostage along with the staff of its embassy, imprisoned in Teheran. That crisis in Iran, coupled with the ineffective military response to it – the failed risk of a rescue attempt – effectively ejected Carter from the White House. The simple non-interventionism prescribed by the 'Vietnam syndrome' was not a salutary reminder of the dangers of international activism. Rather it rapidly became an inhibition on the preservation and pursuit of vital interests overseas.

From a restraint, the 'syndrome' became a constraint. It was an obstacle that was placed in the way of the projection of American military power abroad. Public support for any such enterprise, once guaranteed, was now conditional. Particularly among conservative analysts of Carter's malaise, therefore, there was the assumption that the nation was still traumatised by its experience in Vietnam. The fact of failure and the experience of defeat eroded America's sense of purpose. To restore self-confidence, the 'syndrome' had necessarily to be overcome.

Yet the 1970s, and Carter's own tenure of the White House, represented a time when, in William Gibson's words, 'it is necessary to remember the *repression* of the war . . . its strange absence from national life'.[48] Such a denial of the events of the recent past could even be extrapolated into a rejection of the relevance of American history in its entirety. The mythic assurances that had failed to work their customary political and military magic in Southeast Asia – the failure of pioneer heroes on the new frontier and the consequent questioning of the nation's providential purpose – apparently served only to modify Henry Ford's notorious aphorism. American history was bunk.

CONCLUSION: FORGIVING AND FORGETTING

Gerald Ford and Jimmy Carter shared a common approach to the problem of attempting to recover national morale: they believed that the legacy of both Vietnam and Watergate might be confronted through a process of forgiveness and forgetting. Indeed it was through forgiveness that forgetting was rationalised as a legitimate response to such national traumas. Ford's adoption of this strategy backfired: his limited programme of clemency for those who had rejected the nation's mission in Southeast Asia stood in stark contrast to his absolute pardon of Nixon for any high crimes or misdemeanours related to the Watergate scandal. Similarly, while Jimmy Carter also tried to recapture the moral highground of American politics, his insistence on collective repentance for the sins of the immediate past, coupled with his inability to inspire a coherent vision for the future, meant that he remained more an analyst of the national condition than – as Ford had seen himself – a therapist.

Forgiving and forgetting was a flawed strategy. As Christopher Lasch put it in *The Culture of Narcissism* (1978), 'Americans seem to wish to forget not only the sixties, the riots, the new left, the disruptions on college campuses, Vietnam, Watergate, and the Nixon presidency, but their entire collective past, even in the antiseptic form in which it was celebrated during the Bicentennial'. But, he argued, 'a denial of the past, superficially progressive and optimistic, proves on closer analysis to embody the despair of a society that cannot face the future'.[49] On the other hand, there were those who tried to address this contemporary problem, not by walking away from the quarrel, but by re-emphasising the importance of history in the understanding of national character and purpose.

In his foreword to the third edition of *The Roots of American Order* (1992), therefore, Russell Kirk claims that 'this book, the first edition of which was published in 1974, is an endeavour to help in the restoring of historical consciousness among Americans'. Kirk was adamant, then, that

> lacking a knowledge of how we arrived where we stand today, lacking that deeper love of country which is nurtured by a knowledge of the past, lacking the apprehension that we all take part in a great historical continuity – why, a people so deprived will not dare much, sacrifice much, or take long views. With them, creature comforts will be everything; yet, historical consciousness wanting, in the long run they must lose their creature comforts too.

In this way 'no study could be more relevant to our present discontents' than to trace the religious, secular and cultural roots of America's political order.[50] Where Lasch had seen American liberalism as intellectually exhausted, and devoid of political ideas, Kirk, emphasised the necessity to conserve in order to replenish the American spirit: 'this book is meant to water roots, for the renewing of order and the betterment of justice and freedom'.[51] He sought to revitalise America's confidence in its history by reminding his readers of the way in which the nation's public philosophy, grounded in a diaspora of religious and secular influences, was by implication the crowning achievement of Western culture and civilisation itself.

In his concluding chapter, significantly called 'Contending against American Disorder', Kirk indeed draws an explicit parallel between the Civil War, after which one section of America – the South – had experienced for the first time the shock and the reality of military defeat, and what was, by implication, the contemporary post-Vietnam malaise. He quotes Orestes Brownson, writing in 1865: 'the nation has suddenly been compelled to study itself, and henceforth must act out of reflection, understanding, science, statesmanship, not from instinct, impulse, passion, or caprice, knowing well what it does, and wherefore it does it'. 'That sentence', suggests Kirk, 'applies equally well to the circumstances of the United States in our present decade, when domestic and foreign troubles have induced many Americans to inquire into the order to which they belong'.[52] So if liberals – among them Carter – would endeavour to repress the recent history of overseas adventurism, conservatives like Kirk would call now for a re-emphasis upon the past as a means of regenerating confidence in the future. But there was still the unspoken problem of providing a satisfactory history that would account for America's experience in Vietnam. Even the language used avoided the bitter word itself: Vietnam. Instead circumlocutions such as 'domestic and foreign troubles' were deemed to have caused present 'discontents'. But this kind of conservative analysis, which recognised the importance of historical interpretation in the establishment of national beliefs, and indeed in the re-establishment of national self-confidence, did set a stage. Enter, from the right, Ronald Reagan.

NOTES

1. Ford, 'Remarks upon Taking the Oath of Office as President', 9 August 1974 (see Website: Gerald Ford Library and Museum).
2. Ford, *A Time to Heal*, p.141. The index to Ford's memoirs refers to his proposed 'amnesty for draft evaders and deserters', p. 453. For him, clemency represented the opportunity to earn amnesty. In such a politically charged arena, such semantics were significant.
3. Greene, *The Presidency of Gerald R. Ford*, p. 40.
4. See the discussion in Campbell and Jamieson, *Deeds Done in Words*, chapter 9.
5. Ford, 'Remarks on Signing a Proclamation Granting Pardon to Richard Nixon', 8 September 1974 (see Website: Gerald Ford Library and Museum).
6. Ford, *A Time to Heal*, p. 179.
7. Ibid. p. 181.
8. MacPherson, *Long Time Passing*, p. 410.
9. Quoted in Ford, *A Time to Heal*, pp. 175–6.
10. Ibid. p. 181.
11. Campbell and Jamieson, *Deeds Done in Words*, p. 180.
12. Quoted ibid. p. 179.
13. Ford, *A Time to Heal*, pp. 197–9.
14. Ford, 'Address at a Tulane University Convocation', 23 April 1975 (see Website: Gerald Ford Library and Museum).
15. Lincoln, 'Second Inaugural Address', Saturday, 4 March 1865 (see Website: Presidential Inaugural Addresses).
16. MacPherson, *Long Time Passing*, p. 217.
17. Greene, *The Presidency of Gerald R. Ford* p. 150.
18. Slotkin, *Gunfighter Nation,* p. 622.
19. Ford, *A Time to Heal*, p. 284.
20. Ford, 'Annual Message to Congress on the State of the Union' (see Website: Annual Messages to Congress on the State of the Union).
21. Ford, 'Remarks upon Accepting the Republican Presidential Nomination', 19 August 1976 (see Website: Gerald Ford Library and Museum).
22. Greene, *The Presidency of Gerald R. Ford*, p. 193.

23. Updike, *The Coup*, pp. 85–6.
24. Meyer, *James Earl Carter*, p. 60.
25. Carter, *Keeping Faith*, p. 125.
26. Meyer, *James Earl Carter,* p. 104.
27. Quoted in Bussey, 'Jimmy Carter', p. 94.
28. Roelofs, *Ideology and Myth in American Politics*, p. 254.
29. Meyer, *James Earl Carter: The Man & The Myth*, p. 59.
30. Ibid. p. 105.
31. Bussey, 'Jimmy Carter', p. 92.
32. Quoted in Meyer, *James Earl Carter,* p. 134.
33. Bussey, 'Jimmy Carter', p. 99.
34. Dumbrell, *The Carter Presidency*, p. 2.
35. Carter, 'Inaugural Address', Thursday, 20 January 1977 (see Website: Presidential Inaugural Addresses).
36. Carter, *Keeping Faith*, p. 20.
37. Although Efaw referred to the 'pseudo-debate over the terms "amnesty" . . . and . . . pardon', there was no doubt which he preferred. For him, if Carter 'genuinely wishes to have Vietnam removed as a bone of intra-party contention . . . he would be wise to proclaim a total amnesty'. Efaw, 'Amnesty', pp. 589 and 591.
38. McMahon, *Major Problems in the History of the Vietnam War*, p. 600.
39. Quoted in Meyer, *James Earl Carter*, p. 83.
40. Slotkin, *Gunfighter Nation*, p. 624.
41. Spencer, *The Carter Implosion*, p. 19.
42. White, *America in Search of Itself*, p. 258.
43. Ibid. p. 260.
44. Carter, *Keeping Faith*, p. 120.
45. White, *America in Search of Itself*, p. 268.
46. Polenberg, *One Nation Divisible*, p. 208.
47. Klare, *Beyond the Vietnam Syndrome*, p. 1.
48. Gibson, 'The Return of Rambo' p. 378.
49. Lasch, *The Culture of Narcissism*, pp. 5 and xviii. In keeping with the mood of the times, Lasch's work was sub-titled 'American Life in an Age of Diminishing Expectations'.
50. Kirk, *The Roots of American Order*, pp. xvii and 5.
51. Ibid. p. 10.
52. Ibid. p. 470.

CHAPTER SEVEN

Ronald Reagan: Star

INTRODUCTION: BACK TO THE FUTURE

Reflecting on the 1964 election, Richard Nixon wrote:

> one Republican winner was not on the ballot. The week before the end of the campaign, Ronald Reagan made a nationwide television broadcast on Goldwater's behalf. Reagan's views were as conservative as Goldwater's but he had what Goldwater lacked: the ability to present his views in a reasonable and eloquent manner. The broadcast started a groundswell of support that swept Reagan into the California governor's office in 1966 and into the race for the presidential nomination in 1968.[1]

His pursuit of the presidency was tenacious. After losing out to Nixon in 1968, in 1976 he challenged the incumbent Gerald Ford unsuccessfully for the Republican nomination. Four years later, Ronald Reagan finally became the party's candidate and won the election. Writing about Reagan while he was still president, Garry Wills observed that

> he spans our lives, culturally and chronologically. Born in the year the first studio opened in Hollywood, he reached that town just two years after Technicolor did. His second term as President runs through 1988, the two-hundredth anniversary of the ratification of the United States Constitution, and his life spans over a third of that history of constitutional government . . . Born eleven years into the twentieth, he is scheduled to leave the White House eleven years from the twenty-first century.[2]

So the former movie star whom Nixon identified as a potential president – and who proved indeed to be the 'great communicator' – becomes, in Wills' portrait, the embodiment of the 'American century', a politician able to assume a unique role in national political life: an everyman as mythic hero.

Reagan was not a major movie star. If he had not become president it is unlikely that many of his films would be remembered. But his Hollywood career is significant because it connected him, in his own mind and in popular imagination, with screen versions of America's mythic past. Thus, as Wills argues,

> he is an icon, but not a frail one put away in the dark . . . He is a durable daylight 'bundle of meanings,' as Roland Barthes called myth. Reagan does not argue for American values; he embodies them. To explain his appeal, one must explore the different Americas of which he is made up. He renews our past by resuming it. His approach is not discursive, setting up sequences of time or thought, but associative; not a tracking shot but montage. We make the connections. It is our movie.[3]

Ronald Reagan's presidency can be defined through the language and images of Hollywood. He brought to the office something that it had lacked since the days of JFK: star quality.

On 8 June 1982 in the speech to the British House of Commons where he referred to the Soviet Union as an 'evil empire', Ronald Reagan also observed: 'if history teaches anything, it teaches self-delusion in the face of unpleasant facts is folly'.[4] But equally, as Harold Evans suggests, 'Reagan was firmly in the saddle of American exceptionalism . . . His imaginative powers were strong but selective'.[5] So American history, for Reagan, was a narrative of unparalleled success, based upon selective interpretations which avoided difficult and controversial issues. For him, the historical drama of the nation's past was based upon vignettes of heroes and heroic incidents, all of which confirmed ideas of exceptionalism, destiny, and the unrelenting optimism of the American dream. His second inaugural address illustrates this view and this vision. So

> history is a ribbon, always unfurling; history is a journey. And as we continue our journey, we think of those who traveled before us . . . A general falls to his knees in the hard snow of Valley Forge; a lonely President paces the darkened halls and ponders his struggle to preserve the union; the men of the Alamo call out encouragement to each other; a settler pushes west and sings a song, and the song echoes out forever and fills the unknowing air. It is the American sound. It is hopeful, big-hearted, idealistic, daring, decent, fair. That's our heritage, that's our song. We sing it still.[6]

It is a carefully crafted script: scenes from America's past form a classic Reagan montage.

Yet as Garry Wills points out, 'what happens if, when we look into our historical rearview mirror, all we can see is a movie?'.[7] For James Combs, 'Ronald Reagan presided over the celebration of an imaginary country . . . He offered us an "improved" past that originated in popular culture as an idealization of what the country was supposed to remain to be forever'.[8] In other words, Reagan's approach to history meant that it was possible to escape into a past where memories of traumatic events such as the assassination of JFK, or defeats like Vietnam could be sublimated. Indeed, if the past was a problem, it could be fixed through reinvention and revisionism. The movie which encapsulated this idea was *Back to the Future* (1985), where the hero was able to travel back from the 1980s to the 1950s to influence the course of history for the better, and coincidentally find a Ronald Reagan western being shown at the local cinema. Reagan reached into America's mythological past to try to recall the driving optimism of the American dream which had been dislocated by the assassination of JFK, the Vietnam war and Watergate. His explicit connection of the past and popular culture, history and Hollywood, meant that the 1980s became a decade of revisionism, as the president who dominated its politics aimed to convince a receptive audience that the past indeed had another pattern.

ASSASSINATION

During the 1980s, Dallas was reinvented in American popular culture. From being the city where Kennedy had been shot, it became through its eponymous soap-opera a place where, as Haynes Johnson observes a new hero, J. R. Ewing symbolised 'the American dream gone haywire, but it was, on the viewing evidence, an American dream millions wished to pursue'.[9] It was the most popular show on television, not only in America, but in other countries as well. And the storyline which defined *Dallas* in the mind of its audience was one revolving around 'who shot J.R.'? Following a botched attempt to kill him, J.R.'s assassin was finally revealed following weeks of anticipation and speculation. The fantasy life of *Dallas* in the 1980s was far removed from the reality of 22 November 1963.

Like Kennedy, Reagan was the victim of an assassination attempt. Unlike JFK he survived. It was an event which, for Haynes Johnson, helped to transform the new president 'from a politician of dubious credentials and public achievements into a mythic figure in American life'. It happened a mere nine weeks into his first term in office.

His survival from a bullet wound lodged an inch from his heart was taken as an augury of a national turn for the better; it signaled the breaking of the skein of bad luck that had plagued the nation and its leaders for nearly twenty years.[10]

But it was not simply the fact of the failed attempt on his life that confirmed Reagan in the position of mythic hero. His reaction, showing both courage and self-deprecating humour, at once dramatised his ordeal and reassured his audience. And at the same time, the event itself – captured this time by ever vigilant television cameras – and the personal narrative of the assassin, John Hinckley, seemed to become part of the complex relationship between Reagan's life in the movies and his political persona.

'Honey, I forgot to duck'. His comment to Nancy Reagan, a line taken from Jack Dempsey after he had lost the world heavyweight boxing championship to Gene Tunney in 1926, became a classic Reagan quote, along with his remark to the doctors about to operate on him: 'I hope you're all Republicans'. As Haynes Johnson suggests,

the subsequent cheerfulness and grace that Reagan displayed during his long recovery in hospital and White House, his ritual waves and smiles given during the long-range photo opportunities, also contributed strongly in reassuring the public. They all conveyed a sense to the public that Reagan possessed larger-than-life qualities . . . Reagan's survival alone was proof enough that the country's luck had turned for the better.[11]

And as if to bury the traumatic memory of Kennedy's death further, Reagan would go to the Republican convention in Dallas in 1984 to be renominated for a second term as president.

For Ronald Reagan, living with the past meant living in the past. But his American dream could not have imagined the scenario of 30 March 1981, the day he was shot, not as an actor in a movie western, but in a real-life drama played out on the streets of Washington DC. It was as if politics, history and the movies had momentarily coalesced. Fascinated by the film *Taxi Driver* (1976), and fixated by one of its stars (Jodie Foster), John Hinckley, his assassin, thought that he could demonstrate his love for her by killing a political celebrity. Prior to his attempt on Reagan's life, he had also stalked Jimmy Carter. As Garry Wills suggests, in *Taxi Driver*, when Robert De Niro as Travis Bickle, the psychologically disturbed Vietnam veteran, bought his small arsenal of guns from a hustler in a hotel room, he trained the long barrel of one down through a window at cars moving towards an underpass. The washed-out colours seen through the window, the angle of the barrel, the look of the road are all arranged to suggest black-and-white photographs from the windows of the Dallas Book Depository. Bickle is seen making himself an Oswald . . . And after Bickle turned himself into Oswald, John Hinckley turned himself into Bickle . . . It was a movie-driven man who tried to murder our first movie-actor President'.[12]

Reagan's assassin appeared as a character from Nathanael West's *The Day of the Locust* (1939): someone who was alienated from American society, and who found a vicarious identity through a movie-fuelled fantasy life.[13] The attempt to assassinate Ronald Reagan, symbolically the most significant moment of his presidency, fused memories of the death of Kennedy with the image of an assassin inspired by a movie that portrayed a contemporary popular perception of one cultural conse-quence of the Vietnam war – the unstable veteran taking revenge upon American society. Reagan survived and in so doing transcended that narrative. And he achieved the mythic status and political authority to mould the contemporary mood.

REVISIONISM AND REVIVAL

In an article published in *Foreign Affairs* in 1982, William McNeill argued that

> a people without a full quiver of relevant agreed upon statements, accepted in advance through education or less formalized acculturation, soon finds itself in deep trouble, for in the absence of believable myths, coherent public action becomes very difficult to improvise or sustain.

He went on to suggest that 'what is needed is a suitably charismatic figure with a vision of past and future that millions will find so compelling as to make them eager to join in common action to achieve newly articulated purposes'.[14] The argument, indeed, appears as much an elegy for Kennedy and the New Frontier in the post-Vietnam era as it is a eulogy for Ronald Reagan and the attempt to rewrite the history of America's war in Vietnam that was to characterise the 1980s.

Carter had proved neither the hero nor the leader America required. His emphasis on both personal and political morality had limited appeal, notably in relation to the setting of a post-Vietnam foreign policy agenda, since, as Robert McKeever suggests, 'for most Americans the Vietnam War exploded the myth of American invincibility rather than the myths of innocence or moral superiority'.[15] What the nation required was not repentance but a restoration of that myth.

It was this that Carter's successor as president promised. Indeed, as Richard Slotkin argues, 'if Ronald Reagan or any of his handlers had read McNeill's diagnosis of the disease of "public myth" they would have wondered why McNeill failed to recognize their administration as the prescribed cure'.[16] But the 'care and repair of public myth' that was McNeill's theme takes time. Two years into Reagan's administration, despite the fact of the attempted assassination and its aftermath, the revisionism upon which it depended was still at an early stage.

Slotkin goes on to suggest that Reagan's intent was to rehabilitate the myth of the frontier as the energizing source of American activism. Yet it can be argued that his success in regenerating a sense of national purpose – although transient in that it depended largely on the fact of his incumbency – was founded also upon his ability to communicate once more the missionary message that was rooted in the spirit of American religious persuasion. This was Reagan's version of Carter's 'born-again' promise. And inspirational rhetoric couched in the language of historical myth was a talent which the oldest elected postwar president shared with one of his younger predecessors: John Kennedy.

Reagan, then, 'paid more attention to rhetoric than any president since John Kennedy'.[17] Both manipulated national myth in pursuit of a political purpose. Robert Osgood, writing in *Foreign Affairs* in 1981, suggested that

> in the 1980 presidential campaign Governor Ronald Reagan emerged as the rallying point for, and articulator of, the pent-up reaction to the 'Vietnam syndrome'. Like President Kennedy, he interpreted his political mandate as, above all, the restoration of the nation's power and prestige in response to a heightened and neglected Soviet threat.[18]

Kennedy and Reagan in this context seem politically and rhetorically, if not ideologically or mythologically, symbiotic, their presidencies the parentheses that would enclose the American involvement in Vietnam. Common to both was an ability to articulate their political message through connecting contemporary concerns with historical myths. If Kennedy had Frederick Jackson Turner and the frontier on his side, then Reagan set out America's mission in language redolent of John Winthrop and the Puritan 'errand'. And if Kennedy had set the nation on course for its war in Vietnam, it was Reagan who would preside over the reinvention of that experience as an attempt to overcome the 'Vietnam syndrome', the self-imposed obstacle to future interventions engendered by failure and defeat.

Carter's one-term presidency was in this sense transitional. Like his predecessor, Reagan exploited the desire to create a spirit of national regeneration in the aftermath of Vietnam and Watergate. But the new president connected the idea of being 'born again' with the rhetorical resonances of American history, and in particular the legacy of Puritan settlement. A recurrent image in Reagan's rhetoric was the idea of America as John Winthrop's 'city on a hill'. His 1980 campaign for the Republican nomination thus has been described as 'another test of American greatness, of whether we will again dream grand dreams or settle for the smaller dreams of lesser candidates'.[19] Reagan plundered American history for comforting images of a celebratory past: the touchstones for his mythic interpretations of the nation's triumphant progress. His speeches encompassed the broad sweep of Puritan origins, revolutionary idealism (Tom Paine's 'we have it in our power to begin the world over again' – itself a image of rebirth in an historical context), Lincoln's nationalism and the emergence of the United States into the twentieth century as the most powerful nation in the world.

Among the faithful of the Republican party, Reagan sometimes appeared as an evangelical preacher at a revivalist gathering. In his acceptance speech at the Republican National Convention in August 1980, he had confessed that 'more than anything else, I want my candidacy to unify our country; to renew the American spirit and sense of purpose' and had ended his speech with an appeal to 'begin our crusade joined together in a moment of silent prayer'.[20] Right-wing evangelists flourished in the Reagan era, none more than the president himself: missionary fervour was once more in fashion.

Reagan's election itself thus symbolised the frustration engendered by the Carter years. In his inaugural address, Carter had warned that 'we cannot afford to drift'. But that is precisely what, four years later, Reagan would accuse him of doing. America had become an 'ordinary country', whose president agonised over the complexities of international relations and America's place in them after its defeat in Vietnam. Reagan's own first inaugural address made his alternative message clear. 'So, with all the creative energy at our command, let us begin an era of national renewal. Let us renew our determination, our courage and our strength. Let us renew our faith and our hope. We have every right to dream heroic dreams'.[21] He might have added, 'and let us thus reconstruct our memory of Vietnam'.

Looking back on Reagan's tenure of the White House in 1989, Robert Tucker noted that

> there is no reason to question the importance of Vietnam for Mr. Reagan, just as there is no reason to question his conviction that until the nation overcame its Vietnam syndrome the erosion of America's power and position would continue. For that syndrome made impossible the reconstitution of the domestic consensus required for the reassertion of the nation's power.[22]

Jeff Bass has suggested that 'Reagan entered office determined to prove that Vietnam was an "aberration" '.[23] So, for Stephen Vlastos, 'explaining why America lost the Vietnam War (but need not lose the next time around)' became 'central to the revisionist project' undertaken during Reagan's presidency. The president himself set the agenda. 'With his uncanny sense of the lowest common denominator in the popular culture', Reagan realised the necessity of providing a simple and straightforward account of America's 'mission impossible'.[24] Once that message was accepted, it could be used as a spring-board for regenerating national self-confidence. The idea that America had been defeated in Vietnam thus began to be rationalised and amended.

The political message of revisionism was clear. 'Never again', declared Ronald Reagan in 1981, would the United States 'send an active fighting force to a country to fight unless it is for a cause that we are prepared to win'.[25] America, he implied, had faltered in Vietnam merely because of a lack of national political will. In the same year, Colonel Harry Summers, in a book suffused with Clausewitzean analysis, argued that had the military been able to fight a war free from political constraints and uncontaminated by contemporary theories of counter-insurgency, the outcome would have been different. This work, published by the US Army War College, has been described subsequently as 'the semi-official US Army view of the war'.[26] America's failure was America's fault. Vietnam had been a problem of political attitude and a question of military strategy, rather than a reversal of fortune at the hands of a resolute and defiant enemy.

Central to the revisionist message was the changing historiography of the war. As Nietzsche observed, 'the war is not even over before it is transformed into a hundred thousand printed pages and set before the tired palates of the history-hungry as the latest delicacy'.[27] So it was with Vietnam. According to Summers, however, writing in 1985, early works had been influenced by a 'tyranny of fashion'. The war was presented as 'patently illegal, immoral, and unjust, and woe betide anyone who had the audacity to challenge this received truth'. But as he noted approvingly, 'the literature on the war in Vietnam has undergone significant improvement in the past several years. Once dominated by emotional, one-sided, and in some cases deliberately distorted accounts, now at long last evenhanded and objective works are finding their way into publication'.[28] And yet it can be argued that the historiography of the war was subject to the contemporary style of what Carl Degler termed, in his 1980 address to the Organization of American Historians, 'advocacy history'.[29]

Stanley Karnow's Pulitzer Prize-winning *Vietnam: A History* was first published in 1983. It rapidly became one of the most popular accounts of the war, selling over a million copies. On the back cover of the 1991 revised and updated edition of this book its publishers claimed that

> this monumental narrative clarifies, analyzes, and demystifies the tragic ordeal of the Vietnam war. Free of ideological bias, profound in its understanding, and compassionate in its human portrayals, it is filled with fresh revelations drawn from secret documents and from exclusive interviews with the participants. . . .

Reviewers thought the work 'dispassionate', 'extraordinarily objective' and 'a seminal work'.

Karnow thus opens with a vignette of the Vietnam War Memorial in Washington. The names on it, he writes,

> represent a sacrifice to a failed crusade, however noble or illusory its motives. They bear witness to the end of America's absolute confidence in its moral exclusivity, its military invincibility, its manifest destiny. They are the price, paid in blood and sorrow, for America's awakening to maturity, to the recognition of its limitations. With the young men who died in Vietnam died the dream of an 'American century'.[30]

The language is revealing. It advances the idea of the mission – a 'crusade' – which may be viewed, in equal measure, from the political right as 'noble' or from the left as 'illusory'. Karnow takes no hostages to political fortune. Moreover, the American casualties of the war did not die, as at Gettysburg, in the cause of regenerating America's democratic purpose. Rather they are now the silent witnesses to the nation's new 'maturity', as if Vietnam becomes its childhood or adolescent adventure. The unstated, or understated, idea is of the mission as something naive, or undertaken in innocence of its inevitable outcome. Later Karnow quotes Clark Clifford: 'we made an honest mistake. I feel no sense of shame . . . We felt that we were doing what was necessary. It proved to be unsound'.[31]

As John Pilger has pointed out,

> all the conservative and liberal myths are paraded arm in arm in Karnow's history. His readers are told that the war was a 'failed crusade' conducted for the 'loftiest of intentions', that the communists were 'terrorists' who were 'merciless' and 'brutal' in contrast to the Americans who were 'sincere' and 'earnest' and whose 'instincts were liberal'.[32]

Karnow provided not only an explanation but also a perspective from which his American readers could take some comfort. If the war had resulted in defeat, the failure had been in some senses an aberration. The opening chapter of *Vietnam* characterises the experience. It was 'the war nobody won' – not even, so it appeared, the Vietnamese.

It was not only the historiography of the war that was influenced, whether unconsciously or by design, by a desire to resurrect national self-esteem. Pilger continues: 'at the level of popular culture, always the vanguard in matters of national redemption, the post-war propaganda has worked assiduously to celebrate the invader and to reduce the invaded to their wartime status of commie stick figures on celluloid'.[33] Reagan's nostrum, Vietnam as a 'noble cause' which had been imperfectly executed, re-echoed in Hollywood's representations of American involvement in Southeast Asia, again from those ostensibly at opposite ends of a political spectrum. Thus Rambo's plaintive 'do we get to win this time' as he prepares for yet another mission to Vietnam is hardly less predictable than the hero of Oliver Stone's *Platoon* (1986) discovering that the real enemy there had been the Americans who had fought themselves.

It was as though the pursuit of happiness and, indeed, the restoration of faith in the nation's imperialist mission, involved a sense of being unencumbered by historical embarrassment rather than of remaining haunted by the past. Here presidential rhetoric colluded with the cinematic versions of history that, in the pre-Vietnam era, informed the public persona of Ronald Reagan himself. And,

> by transmuting the rhetoric of the presidency into ceremonial discourse, sustained by an infrastructure of Hollywood entertainment values and Madison Avenue market-research techniques, Reagan enacted what other

politicians had only attempted: a vision of the public sphere belonging more to Steven Spielberg than Thomas Jefferson, a long-running movie designed to make audiences laugh and cry, rather than a political space in which they might actively participate.[34]

Reagan retained the presidency in 1984, the first incumbent to win re-election since the ill-fated Nixon in 1972. The rhetorical strategy seemed to work.

Reagan's own ability to proselytise a revisionist message in turn rested on the malleability of his audience: its receptiveness to a reassertion of traditional myths and messages. As Nietzsche had fore-seen:

> to determine . . . the boundary at which the past has to be forgotten if it is not to become the gravedigger of the present, one would have to know exactly how great the *plastic power* of a man, a people, a culture is: I mean by plastic power the capacity to develop out of oneself in one's own way, to transform and incorporate into oneself what is past and foreign, to heal wounds, to replace what has been lost, to recreate broken moulds.[35]

The revisionist project was to explore the 'plastic power' inherent in American myth and political culture.

The president maintained the revisionist mood throughout his tenure of the White House. In 1980 he had announced that 'we must rid ourselves of the "Vietnam syndrome". It has dominated our thinking for too long'.[36] Speaking to Bobby Muller, a founder of the Vietnam Veterans of America Foundation, Reagan summarised his version of America's involvement in Southeast Asia. 'Bob, the trouble with Vietnam was that we never let you guys fight the war you could have done, so we denied you the victory all the other veterans enjoyed. It won't happen like that again, Bob . . .'.[37] No longer scapegoats, Vietnam veterans were now victims of America's error. As Muller commented elsewhere: 'it's a changing dynamic . . . That's what revisionism is all about'.[38]

The political and military explanations of America's failure in Vietnam allowed the war to be discussed, but the fact of the Vietnamese victory to be dismissed. The revisionist interpretation of America's mission in Southeast Asia was accompanied by a refusal to accept that the opposition had won. Instead, during the Reagan years, alternative versions of American involvement continued to be advanced. Some strained credulity. John Pilger recounts one of the president's own manipulations of the historical record. In drawing a distinction between

America's action in Vietnam, and his administration's activities in Central America, Reagan argued that

> the comparison was 'totally unjustified' because 'North and South Vietnam had been, previous to colonisation, two separate countries'. He said that at the 1954 Geneva conference provisions had been made that 'these two countries could by a vote of all their people decide together whether they wanted to be one country or not'. He said that Ho Chi Minh, 'refused to participate in such an election'. He added that American military advisers were sent to South Vietnam to work in civilian clothing and without weapons until they were attacked with 'pipe bombs'. Ultimately, said the president, John Kennedy had authorised the 'sending of a division of marines'.

As Pilger comments, 'he was wrong on every score':[39] and yet such an assessment allowed Reagan to pursue the political purpose of revisionism in attempting once again to legitimise American adventurism abroad.

In written accounts of America's experience in Vietnam, Karnow's apparently even-handed historiography became part of what, by the end of the 1980s, was increasingly characterised as the 'Vietnam Debate'. A number of books began to present anthologies of both sides of the 'argument' as to the causes of America's involvement, the nature of the war, the failure of the mission, and the lessons to be drawn. Objectivity might be maintained through the assumption that 'truth' would lie somewhere in a synthesis of the views included in such analyses.[40] Summers' 'emotional one-sided accounts' could now be balanced, and occasionally over-balanced, by alternative views. Thus for Leslie Gelb and Richard Betts, 'the irony of Vietnam' was that 'the system worked'. In their book of that title, they argued that until Congress finally refused to bankroll the South Vietnamese government, the objective of a non-communist government there was sustained. William Sullivan, moreover, went further and managed to identify some 'positive consequences' of the American involvement. Referring to the 'Vietnam operation' as 'one of the master strategic strokes of the century', he argued that the outcome of the failed intervention was that 'we've now got an equilibrium in the Pacific which is probably the best that has prevailed there since the sixteenth century'.[41]

Revisionism thus reopened the debate over Vietnam which, as Norman Podhoretz in his influential work *Why We Were in Vietnam* (1982) argued, had 'already been settled in favor of the moral and political position of the antiwar movement' by the time that North and South Vietnam were unified in 1975.[42] Fifteen years later, in 1990, the introductory remarks in a book which took 'a fresh look at the arguments' in that debate were unequivocal in promoting the alternative view. 'The United States entered the war in Indochina with the highest of moral objectives: to protect the right of self-determination of the people of the republic of Viet Nam (RVN) and to maintain world order by deterring aggression.' Furthermore 'no amount of historical reexamination or introspection will alter the high moral purpose of the United States or the reality that North Vietnam has militarily conquered South Vietnam and subjugated Cambodia and Laos'.[43] So in swift succession, Carter's claim that American foreign policy had been characterised by its 'moral and intellectual poverty' is set aside and the nation's role in 'deterring aggression' is once again rationalised and legitimised: the fact that the North 'conquered' the South and 'subjugated' the neighbouring states of Cambodia and Laos is evidence of where the true source of aggression lay.

Such accounts strip away the arguments that might cause America to doubt the morality and the purpose of its mission. In Norman Podhoretz's view, contrasting Carter's assessment of the bankruptcy of American foreign policy with the attitude of his successor, the lesson to be drawn from American intervention in Southeast Asia is clear.

> When Ronald Reagan . . . called the war 'a noble cause' . . . he was accused of having made a 'gaffe' . . . I believe the story shows that Reagan's 'gaffe' was closer to the truth of why we were in Vietnam and what we did there . . . than Carter's denigration of an act of imprudent idealism whose moral soundness has been so overwhelmingly vindicated by the hideous consequences of our defeat.[44]

But any account of American involvement, in the highly charged atmosphere of revisionism, might remain, indeed, only as Podhoretz styles it, a 'story'.

Throughout the 1980s, then, the 'Vietnam syndrome' proved to be resilient to the revisionist campaign. Domestic doubts endured about America's capacity to remain committed to its imperialist persuasion and the projection of its political will abroad through the use of military power. Revisionism preached that failure in Vietnam had been due to America's own shortcomings. But it begged the questions: if these 'faults' were remedied, would future adventures work? And in Nietzschean terms, how 'plastic' was America's historical memory and political culture? As one Vietnamese refugee, assimilated in America, pointed out in the *Nation* in 1990:

but Vietnam – well, Vietnam is special. What Henry Kissinger described as a 'fourth-rate power' has cracked our ivory tower and plagued the American psyche; that hell in a small place devastated the bright and shiny citadel. For the first time in American history, we are caught in the past, haunted by unanswerable questions, confronted with a tragic ending.[45]

The mechanics of failure might be addressed by revisionist argument, some of it from the 'ivory tower' of academic analysis. But there remained a psychological dimension to the failure of America's mission that characterised the nature of the 'syndrome' itself.

As long as the 'Vietnam syndrome' remained either as restraint or constraint, it implied that an obstacle existed which would have to be cleared every time foreign interventionism was suggested. Revisionism might provide comforting explanations for the failure of former actions: it could not anticipate that future international adventures would be successful. For those still anxious to promote further activism abroad, the 'syndrome' took on a medical meaning. It became an illness to be cured. In effect, it was regarded as a symptom of the collective post-traumatic stress of a nation that, in the Reagan years, was being persuaded by some to reinvent its experience in Southeast Asia. Indeed in 1980, and coincidentally with Ronald Reagan winning election to the presidency, in William Gibson's words, 'after years of lobbying efforts by veteran's groups and affiliated therapists, the American Psychiatric Association listed Post-Traumatic Stress disorder (PTSD) as a medical diagnosis in the third edition of its official Diagnostic and Statistical Manual'. Thus, he suggests. 'through the diagnosis of PTSD, the veteran in essence was transformed into a patient for therapy and ritually reincorporated back into American society in exchange for depoliticizing his or her knowledge of the war'.[46] In similar fashion, the nation became a suitable case for treatment.

To carry the revisionist argument to its intended conclusion, the psychological dimension of the 'syndrome' thus needed to be addressed. Mary Kaldor, criticising America's bombing raid on Libya in 1986, argued that military power, 'if it is to remain popular domestically, . . . has to stay at the level of psychological spectacle . . . But so long as military power remains in the psychological realm, its effectiveness depends on its psychological success'.[47] Vietnam too had demonstrated that. And as Jeff Bass observes, 'for the official mind of Washington in the early 1980s, the Vietnam syndrome manifested itself in the form of anxiety over a perceived erosion of U.S. power and influence in the world'.[48] So beating or overcoming the

'Vietnam syndrome' meant rehabilitating America's sense of invincibility, reflected in its confidence in its military superiority over others.

Throughout the 1980s, then, fear of further failure confronted a wish to redress defeat. Reluctance to assert power was accompanied by a psychological desire to demonstrate that American military force could still be used successfully abroad. And in so far as it continued to inhibit complete freedom of foreign policy action, the 'Vietnam syndrome' could be described in the language of psychological illness as readily as it could be expressed in the rhetoric of a failed political commitment and in the analysis of past military mistakes. The comments of General William Westmoreland, the former commander of American forces in Vietnam, are relevant: in 1990 he suggested that

> Vietnam was a war that continues to have an impact on politics. I fear that one of the big losses, in fact, probably the most serious loss of that war, is what I refer to as the Vietnam psychosis. Any time anybody brings up the thought that military forces might be needed, you hear the old hue and cry 'another Vietnam, another Vietnam'. That can be a real liability to us as we look to the future.[49]

In Westmoreland's world, the 'syndrome' had become a synonym for a national 'psychosis'.

Yet Westmoreland's remarks encapsulate the dilemma of revisionists. The idea of the 'Vietnam syndrome' as a constraint upon an activist foreign policy, as something to be overcome if the rhetoric of exceptionalist destiny and mission was to recover its power over the nation's imagination, was the creation of the Reagan years. Revisionism argued that the Vietnam experience, the 'mission impossible' had been exceptional. America's frustration had been its fault. Failure could be fixed. That case, however, could be proven only by the evidence of future military success: overcoming the 'syndrome' meant challenging the psychology which underpinned it. And at a practical level doubt remained. If the commitment of military resources to an interventionist adventure seemed likely, the Reagan administration still confronted the realities of public opinion. Westmoreland's 'psychosis' reached beyond the blandishments of revisionist persuasion.

CONCLUSION: REAGAN AND HISTORY

What, then, had Reagan achieved? As he launched his 'crusade', he maintained his faith in the fact that 'I have always believed that this

— 150 —

land was placed here between the two great oceans by some divine plan . . . We can meet our destiny and that destiny can build a land here that will be for all mankind a shining city on a hill'.[50] But in addition to the mythic rhetoric, he also played a populist chord that emphasised not simply future prospect but also historic achievement. In comparing the inaugural addresses of successive presidents, Barbara Hinckley indeed observes that 'just as Kennedy has struck the theme for a new generation of Americans, Reagan strikes the countertheme, reminding his listeners of the greatness of the nation's past'.[51] And whereas Kennedy had been presented as the model of American heroic leadership, Reagan reversed the imagery, finding such qualities, as Whitman had done, among the ordinary citizens of the American republic.

The existential hero had failed; indeed the traditional iconography of the western hero had been battered by the rupturing of confidence in the success story of America as it encountered resistance and defeat in Vietnam. Reagan rebuilt. In his first inaugural address, he included an important populist message.

> Those who say that we're in a time when there are no heroes, they just don't know where to look. You can see heroes every day going in and out of factory gates . . . You meet heroes across a counter. And they're on both sides of that counter . . . They're individuals and families whose taxes support the government . . . Their patriotism is quiet but deep.[52]

Where Kennedy had demanded volunteers for heroic sacrifice, Reagan finds his heroes within a democratic landscape of America such as Norman Rockwell might have imagined. Kennedy's heroes needed to be extra-ordinary: Reagan's are just ordinary citizens, going about their everyday business. This is the constituency which would re-elect him in 1984, when, as one of his aides put it, a vote for Ronald Reagan was a vote for a mythic America.[53] And these are the heroes that would be sorry to see him leave office in 1989, in their view having gained what Kennedy himself had hoped for but had been unable to achieve: victory in the cold war.

Reagan emphasised celebratory history as a way of regenerating national pride. He connected the spiritual and the secular roots of America's past. In his address to the National Association of Evangelicals in 1983, he argued that 'America is in the midst of a spiritual awakening and a moral renewal', and suggested that 'much of this new political and social consensus I've talked about is based on a positive view of American history, one that takes pride in our country's accomplishments and record'. For Reagan, America's triumph was a self-evident truth: 'any objective observer must hold a positive view of American history, a history that has been the story of hopes fulfilled and dreams made into reality'.[54] It was as if Reagan sought to achieve what Norman Mailer thought Kennedy might do in 1960: a reconciliation of politics and myth in the union of the visible and underground rivers of American history. The difference was, however, that whereas the current in Mailer's subterranean river was one which flowed with 'that concentration of ecstasy and violence' that defined for him the American dream, Reagan's nostalgic appeal was to the evangelical inspiration of New England and to the successes celebrated in Hollywood-style reconstructions of America's past: a story which always had a happy ending.

Reagan, though, could not rely even on his supporters to endorse fully a resurgence of America's imperial persuasion. The Vietnam war had encouraged President Nixon to embark upon the covert policies which escalated into the crimes and misdemeanours of Watergate. Fear of the reaction to overseas adventurism – the 'Vietnam syndrome' – similarly persuaded the Reagan administration to privatise American foreign policy. Revisionism, although successful at a rhetorical level, could not build the consensus necessary to achieve some of its purposes. The consequences unravelled in political scandal: the revelations of Irangate. When Congress, sensitive to public opinion, prevented the executive from implementing its explicit policy of containing communism in Nicaragua, the encouragement was given to Oliver North's 'neat idea': trading arms for hostages with Iran, and using the proceeds to fund the Contras against the Sandanista government in Central America.

In 1987, Immanuel Wallerstein made the point that

> if Reagan has not been able to invade Nicaragua, the reason seems clear enough. The US public seems ready to tolerate maximally the loss of a handful of lives in an action over three days (Grenada), but not the loss of 200 lives in a situation of indefinite further loss (Beirut), and surely not the prospective loss of tens of thousands of lives in a far-off warfare zone (Nicaragua). Call it the Vietnam syndrome, or what you will, but the fact is that it has become a political reality so clear that *even* Reagan has not dared go against it directly. This is the simplest explanation of the inefficacious convolutions of the Iran-Contra fiasco.[55]

Reagan's revisionist rhetoric had been frustrated by a different form of containment: America's desire to contain itself. 'Another Vietnam' still acted as a powerful counter-weight to the desire to overcome the self-imposed restraint of the 'syndrome'.

Sigmund Freud, writing in *Civilization and Its Discontents*, suggested that

> it is said, however, that each one of us behaves like the paranoic, substituting a wish-fulfilment for some aspect of the world which is unbearable to him, and carrying this delusion through into reality. When a large number of people make this attempt together and try to obtain assurance of happiness and protection from suffering by a delusional transformation of reality it acquires special significance . . . Needless to say, no one who shares a delusion recognizes it as such.[56]

Reagan's revisionist project of the 1980s was designed to regenerate national self-confidence and commitment to an activist foreign policy after the failure of mission in Vietnam. The political and military explanations of defeat appeared to have a populist resonance, as the president tied them to the discourse of celebratory history that once again took pride in the nation's mythic past. For many in America, wish-fulfilment – Vietnam as a 'noble cause'- was a comfortable psychological device that avoided the need to confront difficult and challenging historical truths.

At the same time, the revisionist interpretations of America's experience in Southeast Asia, which aimed to confront the self-imposed obstacle of the 'Vietnam syndrome', were part of the wider foreign policy concerns of the Reagan administration. The president's own 'paranoid style' moreover, has been analysed, particularly in relation to his view of the contemporary political process in both El Salvador and Nicaragua.[57] For Reagan, the threat was self-evident. In his speech to a joint session of Congress in 1983 he warned that

> El Salvador is nearer to Texas than Texas is to Massachusetts. Nicaragua is just as close to Miami, San Antonio, San Diego, and Tucson as those cities are to Washington where we're gathered tonight . . . The goal of the professional guerilla movements in Central America is as simple as it is sinister – to destabilize the entire region from the Panama Canal to Mexico . . . We cannot be certain that the Marxist-Leninist bands who believe war is an instrument of politics will be readily discouraged. It's crucial that we not become discouraged before they do. Otherwise the region's freedom will be lost and our security damaged in ways that can hardly be calculated.[58]

The president appears here as a suitable case for Freud's analysis. For Norman Mailer, our country was built upon the expansive imaginations of people who kept dreaming about the lands to the west – many Americans moved into the wild with no more personal wealth than the strength of their imaginations. When the frontier was finally closed, imagination inevitably turned into paranoia (which can be described, after all, as the enforced enclosure of imagination – its artistic form is a scenario) and, lo, there where the westward expansion stopped on the shores of the Pacific grew Hollywood. It would send its reels of film back to the rest of America, where imagination, now landlocked, had need of scenarios. By the late Fifties and early Sixties, a good many of these scenarios had chosen anti-Communism for their theme – the American imagination saw a Red menace under every bed . . .[59]

Ronald Reagan's world-view was a product of his Hollywood experience. His political career began in the 1950s when he became president of the Screen Actors Guild during the McCarthy era, and was instrumental in introducing a loyalty oath for new members.[60] His attitude towards communism was formed. He believed in the conspiracy. In 1961, speaking of his experience in Hollywood, he observed that 'ugly reality came to our town on direct orders of the Kremlin'.[61] It was a conviction which accompanied him to the White House.

The reality of the self-delusion that guerillas in El Salvador and the Sandanista government in Nicaragua were agents of a world-wide communist conspiracy, bent on overturning the US government and subverting its democratic inheritance, thus informed the Reagan administration's attitude towards Central America. Yet when that reality ran up against the alternative reality of the 'Vietnam syndrome' as a constraint, the limitations of a paranoid style were exposed. For at that point, constitutional processes were ignored in a way potentially as damaging, if not more so, as had been the case with Watergate. But when the president admitted that he 'told the American people I did not trade arms for hostages' and subsequently found out that he had done so, Freud's 'delusional transformation of reality' seemed complete. 'My heart and my best intentions still tell me that is true, but the facts and the evidence tell me it is not'.[62] The 'plastic capacity' for wish-fulfilment among his audience was sufficient for him to escape any threat of impeachment, and leave office with a reputation more or less intact.

For Haynes Johnson, Reagan 'succeeded in achieving what the philosopher Joseph Campbell had described as the ability to reacquaint Americans with "the literature of the spirit" and to rekindle a powerful national mythology'. By the 1980s and following the unsuccessful attempt on his life, moreover, Americans were in a mood for the resurrection of old myths. In the survival and good luck of Ronald Reagan, they found what they were seeking. 'The era of self-doubt is over,' Reagan had said in his inaugural address, and the nation cheered. In believing him, they were reaffirming a belief in their nation and in themselves. It was an irresistibly powerful combination.[63]

And so the 'teflon president' proved impervious to the consequences of the Irangate scandal, even though such a privatisation of American foreign policy was potentially a more impeachable offence than those which had led to Nixon's resignation or would result in Bill Clinton's trial and acquittal.

For Richard Slotkin,

the iconography, symbolism, and public ritual associated with American patriotism were indeed given new currency and credibility by Reagan's performance of his role. But his repair of public myth was partial and incomplete. He did not (could not) wholly succeed in effacing either the material consequences of our historical experience or its registration in memory.[64]

Nevertheless, he had the knack of connecting contemporary issues with images from the movies, and an ability to define ideas in terms of popular culture. So on 30 June 1985, after the release of American hostages held in Beirut, the president remarked: 'Boy, I'm glad I saw *Rambo* last night. Now I know what to do next time'.[65] And in his 1986 State of the Union speech, talking about the space programme, he was convinced that 'never has there been a more exciting time to be alive – a time of rousing wonder and heroic achievement. As they said in the film, Back to the Future, "*Where we are going, we don't need roads*" '.[66] Similarly his reference to the Soviet Union as an 'evil empire' conjured an image of the movie *Star Wars* (1977). And in turn this became a populist description of his strategic defence initiative, designed to return America to the security of a pre-atomic age by making the country safe from the threat of nuclear attack. Reagan offered such reassurance, as well as self-belief, optimistic rhetoric and indeed, for many of his fans, star quality.

In his farewell address to the nation, he took stock of his achievements. He claimed credit for 'two great triumphs'. One was economic recovery. The other was 'the recovery of our morale'. The 'Reagan Revolution' appeared to him as 'The Great Rediscovery; a rediscovery of our values and our common sense'. But the address also contained a warning, that the 'new patriotism' he had inspired should be 'grounded in thoughtfulness and knowledge'. The retiring president then outlined his version of contemporary history. 'Those of us who are over 35 or so years of age grew up in a different America'. So things had changed in 1954: after Eisenhower, JFK had come and gone and Lyndon Johnson had obtained the Tonkin Gulf resolution as a 'blank cheque' for war in Vietnam, before defeating Barry Goldwater at the polls. In 'different America' citizens absorbed patriotic values from family, community, and school. 'And if all else failed, you could get a sense of patriotism from the popular culture. The movies celebrated democratic values and implicitly reinforced the idea that America was special. TV was like that, too, through the mid Sixties'.

To 'reinstitutionalize' America's replenished spirit,

> we've got to teach history based not on what is in fashion but what's important . . . If we forget what we did, we won't know who we are. I am warning of an eradication of the American memory that could result, ultimately, in an erosion of the American spirit.

For Reagan, therefore, celebratory history with its attendant symbolic myths was the driving force of American patriotism and pride. He exited from political life with a final reference to the 'shining city'. Confident that 'after 200 years, two centuries, she still stands strong and true on the granite ridge, and her glow has held steady no matter what the storm', the credits of the presidential movie of America's pageant begin to roll. His final script had contained the rhetorical references and influences that had inspired his presidency. Its hero – Reagan – is seen to 'walk off into the city streets' with the satisfaction that he and his political allies 'for eight years did the work that brought America back'.[67] Back from where, and to what, remained, however, an open question.

NOTES

1. Nixon, *Memoirs*, p. 263.
2. Wills, *Reagan's America*, p. 1.
3. Ibid. p. 4.
4. Reagan, 'Speech to the House of Commons', 8 June 1982, (see Website: Ronald Reagan Speeches).
5. Evans, *The American Century*, p. 614.
6. Reagan, 'Second Inaugural Address', Monday, 21 January 1985 (see Website: Presidential Inaugural Addresses).
7. Wills, *Reagan's America*, p. 388.

8. Combs, *The Reagan Range*, p. 133.
9. Johnson, *Sleepwalking through History*, p. 145.
10. Ibid. p. 153.
11. Ibid. p. 161.
12. Wills, *Reagan's America*, pp. 209–10.
13. See ibid. p. 210; Hinckley, who lived in Hollywood in 1976, 'was drawn like one of Nathanael West's locusts to Southern California'.
14. McNeill, 'The Care and Repair of Public Myth', pp. 1 and 5–6. See also Hellmann, *American Myth*, pp. 205–6.
15. McKeever, 'American Myths and the Impact of the Vietnam War', p. 49.
16. Slotkin, *Gunfighter Nation*, p. 643.
17. Kellerman and Barrilleaux, *The President as World Leader*, p. 177.
18. Osgood, 'The Revitalization of Containment', p. 471.
19. Blakenship and Muir, 'The Transformation of Actor to Scene', p. 140.
20. Reagan, 'First Inaugural Address', Tuesday, 20 January 1981, (see Website: Presidential Inaugural Addresses).
21. Quoted in Paul Boyer, *Reagan as President*, pp. 22 and 28.
22. Tucker, 'Reagan's Foreign Policy', p. 9.
23. Bass, 'The Paranoid Style in Foreign Policy', p. 188.
24. Vlastos 'America's "enemy"', pp. 67 and 69.
25. Quoted in Klare, *Beyond the Vietnam Syndrome*, p. 13.
26. Summers, *On Strategy*. The description is from Knockton, 'Vietnamese Social Conflict and the Vietnam War', p. 109.
27. Nietzsche, 'On the Uses and Disadvantages of History for Life', p. 60.
28. Summers, 'Palmer, Karnow and Herrington', pp. 4 and 9–10.
29. Degler, 'Remaking American History', p. 15, *passim*.
30. Karnow, *Vietnam*, p. 9.
31. Ibid. p. 25.
32. Pilger, 'A Noble Cause', pp. 267–8.
33. Ibid. p. 268.
34. Weiler and Pearce, 'Ceremonial Discourse', pp. 12–13.
35. Nietzsche, 'On the Uses and Disadvantages of History for Life', p. 55.
36. Quoted in Johnston, 'Containment and Vietnam', p. 238.
37. Quoted in Pilger, 'New Age Imperialism', p. 107.
38. Quoted in MacPherson, *Long Time Passing*, p. 725.
39. Pilger, 'A Noble Cause', p. 273.
40. Examples of such works include: Moore, *The Vietnam Debate*; McMahon, *Major Problems in the History of the Vietnam War*; and monographs such as Levy, *The Debate over Vietnam*.
41. Quoted in McMahon, *Major Problems in the History of the Vietnam War*, pp. 604–5.
42. Podhoretz, *Why We Were in Vietnam*, p. 14.
43. Friedman and Moore, 'Introduction', p. xii.
44. Podhoretz, *Why We Were in Vietnam*, p. 210.

45. Lam, 'My Vietnam, My America', p. 724.
46. Gibson, 'The Return of Rambo', pp. 383 and 385.
47. Kaldor, 'Introduction', p. 10.
48. Bass, 'The Paranoid Style in Foreign Policy', p. 187.
49. Westmoreland, 'Vietnam in Perspective', p. 45.
50. Quoted in Smith, 'Symbol and Idea in *Virgin Land*', p. 26.
51. Hinckley, *The Symbolic Presidency*, p. 61.
52. Reagan, 'First Inaugural Address', Tuesday 20 January 1981 (see Website: Presidential Inaugural Addresses).
53. Cited in Blankenship and Muir, 'The Transformation of Actor to Scene', p. 155.
54. Quoted in Boyer, *Reagan as President*, p. 167.
55. Wallerstein, 'The Reagan Non-Revolution', p. 472.
56. Freud, *Civilization and Its Discontents* p. 36.
57. See Bass, 'The Paranoid Style in Foreign Policy', p. 184, *passim*.
58. Quoted in Boyer, *Reagan as President*, pp. 236 and 239.
59. Mailer, *Oswald's Tale*, p. 722.
60. See Caute, *The Great Fear*, p. 505.
61. Quoted in Wills, *Reagan's America*, p. 376.
62. Quoted in Boyer, *Reagan as President*, p. 222.
63. Johnson, *Sleepwalking through History*, pp. 154 and 166–7.
64. Slotkin, *Gunfighter Nation*, p. 653.
65. Quoted in Schneider, ' "Rambo" and Reality', p. 41.
66. Reagan, 'Annual Message to Congress on the State of the Union', 4 February 1986 (see Website: Annual Messages to Congress on the State of the Union). Reagan's speech was scheduled originally for 28 January but was postponed when, earlier that day, the *Challenger* space shuttle exploded shortly after lift-off.
67. Reagan, 'Farewell Address to the American People', 11 January 1989, in pp. 262–7, *passim* (see Website: Ronald Reagan Speeches).

CHAPTER EIGHT

George Bush: Deputy

INTRODUCTION: 'FIGHTING THE WIMP FACTOR'

Ronald Reagan had cast him in the role of deputy. His presidency would be defined by his attempts to transcend his popular image as a pallid imitation of his predecessor. Once more, the hero as president was succeeded by his vice-president. Unlike Lyndon Johnson, however, George Bush could claim Texas only as his adoptive state. And Ronald Reagan, populist leader, was hard to follow. The revisionist rhetoric, which had contributed to his appeal, remained convincing to those who wished to believe it in part because he retained the ability to sell his message of unrelenting optimism in the American dream. He was the 'great communicator'. Bush did not have the same talents. Despite a political career which, for an aspiring chief executive, was both unique and remarkable: representing Texas in Congress and later the representative of the United States in China; ambassador to the United Nations and chair of the Republican National Committee during Watergate; then head of the CIA under Gerald Ford, nevertheless he came to the presidency very much as Reagan's understudy. His first political task as leader, therefore, was to emerge from Reagan's shadow.

He had failed to do this when he had run against Reagan for the Republican nomination in 1980. Then, for Jack Germond and Jules Witcover, 'he was one of those candidates who is like a sheet of plate glass, undeniably there, but not always visible to the naked eye'.[1] It was at this time that Bush's harsher critics had described him as a 'wimp': a characterisation which was to re-emerge during the run-up to the 1988 presidential campaign. On 19 October 1987, during the week when Bush announced his candidacy, *Newsweek*'s cover story was headlined 'Fighting the Wimp Factor'. Bush's image was a 'potentially crippling handicap'. He had been 'emasculated by the office of vice-president' and, according to the magazine, in a poll, 51 per cent of those canvassed had agreed that being perceived as a 'wimp' was a 'serious problem' for him.[2] As *Newsweek*'s publisher Katherine Graham recalls: 'the "wimp" label had been a thorn in the Bush campaign flesh since that time. The profile of Bush had been fair and complete, but the effect of the word "wimp" crying out from the cover on the newsstands everywhere was hard to overcome'.[3]

So Bush had an image problem. In May 1988, a Gallup poll showed him trailing the likely Democrat nominee, Michael Dukakis, by 16 percentage points. And as Haynes Johnson observes, 'more ominously, more than 40 percent of the voters held an unfavorable opinion of Bush . . . Bush's negative rating at that point was the highest recorded for a presidential candidate before the fall campaign'. He was more unpopular than Goldwater had been in 1964, McGovern in 1972, Carter in 1980 and Mondale in 1984, all of whom had emphatically lost the election in those years.[4] His solution would be to run a negative campaign which effectively villified his opponent.

The Bush campaign learnt from the tactic which Lyndon Johnson had used against Barry Goldwater in 1964. Rumours circulated about Dukakis's mental health. One 'suggested that Dukakis had twice undergone psychiatric treatment for depression', and a question about his 'fitness to govern' surfaced at a presidential press conference two weeks after he had secured the Democratic nomination. Ronald Reagan responded by saying that he would not 'pick on an invalid' – a 'joke' which nevertheless 'lent credence to the rumours about Dukakis's mental health and stability'.[5] Dukakis was able to disprove the allegations but could not prevent the damage done to his campaign.

The issue of leadership did surface briefly as a theme in the campaign. If Dukakis, defeated by the negative campaigning, was unable to exploit it effectively in relation to Bush – as governor of Massachusetts his own credentials appeared less than impressive when contrasted with those of the incumbent vice-president – it affected the candidacy of Bush's running mate, Senator Dan Quayle. In the campaign debate between the vice-presidential candidates, the issue of Quayle's youth – he was 41 – and inexperience was confronted directly. Finally, after being asked repeatedly about his qualifications to take over as president should the occasion arise, Quayle let down his guard. As a Republican, he might have suggested that an apt precedent for his candidacy would be Richard Nixon, who had also had limited experience in the Senate before being selected on the Eisenhower ticket – aged 39 – in 1952. But after Watergate, Nixon could not be counted a good role model. Instead Quayle infamously tried to compare himself to John F. Kennedy, only 43 when he became president. Lloyd Bentsen, who had defeated George Bush in his attempt to be elected to the Senate in 1970, and now Quayle's Democrat opponent, delivered the knock-out: 'Senator, I served with Jack Kennedy, I knew Jack Kennedy, Jack Kennedy was a friend of mine. Senator, you are no Jack Kennedy'.[6] If Bentsen, from Texas, was himself no Lyndon Johnson, then Quayle indeed could not lay claim to the mantle of Kennedy's heroic leadership, any more than could Michael Dukakis or George Bush.

As president, however, Bush's wish to bury the 'wimp' factor appeared to converge with a similar desire to complete Reagan's revisionist project, and finally to overcome the 'Vietnam syndrome' through a decisive and successful use of American military power. He would be helped by the two events which defined his presidency: the end of the cold war, and Iraq's invasion of Kuwait. By capitalising upon both, Bush could emerge not simply as a heroic leader in his own right – in the Kennedy rather than the Reagan mould – but also as the president who had managed to move the nation beyond the social and cultural dislocations caused by the failed mission in Vietnam. Yet for all his efforts, George Bush's achievement was brittle. The political capital accumulated from victory in the Gulf was not sufficient to secure him a second term in the White House. If, by 1992, the 'wimp factor' had disappeared, it had been replaced by the sense that the president had problems with 'the vision thing': an inability to articulate his 'idea of America' in a contemporary context. And despite victory in the Gulf, doubts soon emerged as to whether the 'Vietnam syndrome' had indeed been overcome.

THE END OF HISTORY
AND THE NEW WORLD ORDER

In his inaugural address, George Bush made specific reference to America's war in Southeast Asia. For the new president, Vietnam

> cleaves us still. But, friends, that war began in earnest a quarter of a century ago; and surely the statute of limitations has been reached. This is a fact: the final lesson of Vietnam is that no great nation can long afford to be sundered by a memory.[7]

Bush had succeeded to the White House with first-hand experience of the way in which the revisionist assessment of the 'Vietnam syndrome' as an obstacle to international activism could corrupt American foreign policy: limiting options to the point where conspiratorial choices appeared preferable to legal actions. A member of the administration that had been caught out in the Iran-Contra scandal, he would not risk another foreign policy short-cut that went beyond the bounds of constitutional propriety. Instead, his objective was to complete the revisionist project, so that the 'syndrome' no longer limited America's freedom of action in world affairs. If the Gulf War would provide a tactical opportunity to achieve this aim, the strategic context in which it was framed was also significant.

In 1989, a year and a day after George Bush was elected president, the symbolic event occurred which marked the end of the cold war in the popular imagination. The Berlin Wall was demolished. It had been constructed in the divided city as an act of communist containment – to keep the population of East Germany free from the contagions of capitalism and democracy. And yet, as George Bush's Secretary of State, James Baker, put it in a speech to the Berlin Press Club a month after the event, 'on November 9, the wall became a gateway'. In an echo of John Kennedy's famous speech in the city, Baker continued 'and all of us who watched these scenes felt, once again: We are all Berliners'.[8] Earlier in the same year, Francis Fukuyama had published an article in *The National Interest* that asked whether, as the cold war drew to a close, the world was witnessing the 'end of history'.

The tearing down of the Berlin Wall gave dramatic substance to Fukuyama's thesis, the essence of which was that resistance to the 'idea of America' – expressed politically as democracy and economically as free markets – had also collapsed. The 'end of history' became a popular, if transient catchphrase of the time. According to this view then, 'the twentieth century saw the developed world descend into a paroxysm of ideological violence, as liberalism contended first with the remnants of absolutism, then bolshevism and fascism, and finally an up-dated Marxism that threatened to lead to the ultimate apocalypse of nuclear war'.[9] What had been the outcome of that ideological conflict? As 'up-dated Marxism' became out-dated Marxism, liberalism had finally triumphed. So if history is the record of such ideological conflict – effectively a contest over differing conceptions of how society should be organised and individuals should live – then with conflict over, history too is at an end. Fukuyama suggests that 'what we may be witnessing is . . . the end of history as such: that is, the end point of mankind's ideological evolution and the universalization of Western liberal democracy as the final form of human government'.[10] Furthermore, 'are there, . . . any fundamental "contradictions" in human life that cannot be resolved in the context of modern liberalism, that would be resolvable by an alternative political-economic structure?'[11] The implied answer is, of course, no.

The two greatest ideological challenges to twentieth-century liberalism have failed. The first of these, fascism, did not survive as a viable ideology after the Second World War, and the second, communism, would not survive the ending of the cold war. Fukuyama claims that it is the United States which has demonstrated the essential redundancy of Marxist aspirations, as, 'the egalitarianism of modern America represents the essential achievement of the classless society envisioned by Marx'. This broad generalisation implies that liberal democracy has achieved in practice what Marxists can only argue about among themselves. And indeed, the intellectual left is essentially a thing of the past. For Fukuyama, 'those who believe that the future must inevitably be socialist tend to be very old, or very marginal to the real political discourse of their societies'.[12]

So liberalism is the undisputed champion of the ideological world. Are there any other challengers it needs to confront? What about religion and nationalism, waiting in the wings for their tilt at the title? Take religion first. Fukuyama argues that

in the contemporary world only Islam has offered a theocratic state as a political alternative to both liberalism and communism. But the doctrine has little appeal for non-Muslims, and it is hard to believe that the movement will take on any universal significance.

Islam thus remains in its ghetto of fundamentalist religious persuasion. Nationalism, similarly, cannot represent itself as a positive and universally appealing force. Thus, 'the vast majority of the world's nationalist movements do not have a political program beyond the negative desire of independence *from* some other group or people, and do not offer anything like a comprehensive agenda for socio-economic organization'.[13] Religion and nationalism as potentially worthy opponents for liberalism thus turn out to be not the threats they might appear to be. And yet, as the balkanisation of Yugoslavia and indeed the disintegration of the Soviet Union itself were to show, nationalism, often fuelled by religious fundamentalism, was to prove increasingly resistant to the blandishments of liberal democratic and capitalist ideology.

So what happens at the 'end of history'? There is peace. The underlying assumption of liberalism is that democracies do not go to war unless provoked. If every country is now embracing democracy and markets, war is a thing of the past. As Fukuyama puts it, 'large scale conflict must involve larger states still caught in the grip of history, and they are what appear to be passing from the scene'. Wars, then, will still be fought, but essentially these will be small-scale skirmishes between those nations still in the grip of history – nations which organise according to islamic or nationalist principles – or between those states which seek to challenge still the primacy of liberal-democratic, capitalist organisation. But as each nation becomes convinced that there is no ideological alternative to liberalism, then wars will die out. Does this mean utopia achieved in international relations? The world as a marketplace where democracies trade with each other peaceably? Fukuyama ended with two warnings. First, he suggests, 'the end of history will be a very sad time . . . In the post-historical period there will be neither art nor philosophy, just the perpetual caretaking of the museum of human history'. It is as if Louis Hartz's 'liberal tradition', with its lack of ideological argument and debate has taken over the world. And, as Fukuyama also observes, 'perhaps this very prospect of centuries of boredom at the end of history will serve to get history moving again'.[14]

But until then, what can be extracted from this thesis? The idea of 'the end of history' puts the United States very much on the right side of the ideological argument, and indeed allows it to claim not simply a pragmatic victory in the cold war, but also a philosophical, intellectual and indeed a moral victory as well. The past forty-five years could be seen as an essential part of a struggle that has now been won. Setbacks, such as Vietnam, become incidental to the main message: democracy and capitalism have triumphed over other ideologies, and it is sometimes the case that battles are lost in the course of winning a war. Fukuyama's thesis would naturally appeal to those who supported America's actions during the cold war. The end – victory – justified the means: containment. And in keeping with George Bush's wish, Vietnam could finally be relegated to a cold war footnote.

Fukuyama's article was the product of a euphoria, brought about as the Soviet Union collapsed, and reform movements in eastern Europe rejected the ideals of communism. Talk was of the 'peace dividend': resources that had previously been devoted to fighting communism could now be diverted back to other uses. If the 'end of history' would allow the United States to move beyond containment, it was still left to the president to 'play the hand for America' in the post-cold war era.

Bush, then, argued that America could now influence and shape a 'new world order'.

The president joined in the self-congratulatory mood. In his 1990 State of the Union address, he spoke of

> America, not just the nation but an idea, alive in the minds of people everywhere. As this new world takes shape, America stands at the center of a widening circle of freedom – today, tomorrow, and into the next century . . . This nation, this idea called America, was and always will be a new world – our new world.

He went on to recount a scene played out near Prague, presumably where history was indeed coming to an end. 'A worker, dressed in grimy overalls, rises to speak at the factory gates.' But this is no bolshevik: instead the worker intones the opening words of America's Declaration of Independence. It is Bush's attempt to imitate Reagan's populist style. Later in the speech he spoke of playing catch with children in Poland, 'little leaguers' who could now dream of playing in the world series.[15] The world seemed poised to be remade in the American image. Contained in this rhetoric is a sense too of what the New World Order should look like. For the word 'order' implies not only stability but also rank. There was to be no doubt, then, as to who would stand at the apex of the world order: the model to which all should aspire.

But Saddam Hussein, still caught in the vice of history, did not understand the rules of this new game. On 31 August 1990 Iraq invaded Kuwait. Having confronted Manuel Noriega in Panama the previous year, now George Bush's leadership would be tested in a crisis in which his opponent, if not a Khrushchev, a Mao or even a Ho Chi Minh, would be portrayed initially as worse than all three: a re-incarnation of the epitome of twentieth-century evil, Adolf Hitler. Indeed, the reaction to Saddam's invasion of Kuwait demonstrated that the 'Munich mentality' – the conviction that 'aggression unchallenged is aggression unleashed'- had not, as Donald Spencer argues, 'collapsed simultaneously with the humiliations of Vietnam'.[16] Rather, it still counted for a great deal in the thinking of the last American president to fight in the Second World War, and one who was determined to bury finally the memory of failure in Vietnam.

MR BUSH'S WAR

Once more, an international crisis afforded the opportunity for the president to assume the role of heroic leader. On 11 September 1990, addressing a joint session of congress, Bush emphasised that, having defined the invasion of Kuwait as a threat too to the security of Saudi Arabia, 'it was then that I decided to act to check that aggression'. From the outset, then, this would be George Bush's challenge – in the end, his war. Yet the adventure in the Gulf was also to demonstrate America's intent to deal with threats to his new idea of world order and to prove the nation's military ability to overcome the Vietnam syndrome. Its sustaining rhetoric thus emphasised both aims. In his speech to congress, Bush claimed that

> we stand today at a unique and extraordinary moment. The crisis in the Persian Gulf . . . offers a rare opportunity to move toward a historic period of cooperation. Out of these troubled times . . . a new world order – can emerge; a new era – freer from the threat of terror, stronger in the pursuit of justice, and more secure in the quest for peace, an era in which the nations of the world, East and West, North and South, can prosper and live in harmony.

He appealed for 'political will and consensus at home' – the very things Vietnam had undermined – for America to realise this vision. In the Gulf, then, 'vital issues of principle are at stake'. Such aggression could not be tolerated, and the United States could not ignore it. Bush argued that 'recent events have surely proven that there is no substitute for American leadership' in the international response to Saddam Hussein's deliberate provocation.[17]

A couple of weeks later, in a speech at the United Nations, Bush's rhetoric was almost lyrical:

> two months ago, in the waning weeks of one of history's most hopeful summers, the vast, still beauty of the peaceful Kuwaiti desert was fouled by the stench of diesel and the roar of steel tanks. Once again the sound of distant thunder echoed across a cloudless sky, and once again the world awoke to face the guns of August . . . Iraq's unprovoked aggression is a throwback to another era, a dark relic from a dark time.

Telescoping history, the president went on to take a broader view of the world in the post-cold war era, linking the outcome of that ideological struggle to the crisis in the Gulf. Now, far from history being at an end, there had been the 'resumption of history'. So, 'Communism held history captive for years. It suspended ancient disputes; and it suppressed ethnic rivalries, nationalist aspirations and old prejudices . . . The revival of history ushers in a new era, teeming with opportunities and perils'. In other words, and in places like the former Yugoslavia, before the 'end of history' could be approached, the tensions that had been suppressed or frozen during the period of communist hegemony would have to be worked out. In similar fashion, Saddam Hussein's invasion of Kuwait represented 'the first assault on the new world that we seek, the first test of our mettle'.[18] Not only the world, but also the president himself was being challenged. For the Gulf War would dramatise Bush's own image as the nation's heroic leader.

Bush's rhetoric in the early stages of the Gulf crisis drew explicit parallels between Iraq's annexation of Kuwait and Germany's invasion of Poland which led to the outbreak of the Second World War. Saddam became Hitler. At a Republican campaign rally in Massachusetts on 1 November the president claimed that the Iraqis had: 'tried to silence Kuwaiti dissent and courage with firing squads, much as Hitler did when he invaded Poland'. In a further link to Nazi wartime atrocities he continued: 'they have committed outrageous acts of barbarism. In one hospital, they pulled 22 premature babies from their incubators, sent the machines back to Baghdad, and all those little ones died'.[19] At a subsequent news conference, Bush was asked if he was comparing seriously Saddam Hussein's treatment of Kuwaitis with Hitler and the Holocaust. The president's rambling reply came as close as possible to confirming that impression, without drawing the explicit connection.

> I didn't say the Holocaust. I mean, that is outrageous. But I think brutalizing young kids in a square in Kuwait is outrageous, too. And I think if you go back and look at what happened when the Death's Head regiments went into Poland, you'll find an awful similarity. I was told – and we've got to check this carefully – that Hitler did not stake people out against potential military targets and that he did, indeed, respect – not much else, but he did, indeed, respect the legitimacy of the Embassies. So, we've got some differences here. But I'm talking – when I'm talking about – I see many similarities, incidentally. I see many similarities by the way the Iraqi forces behaved in Kuwait and the Death's Head regiments behaved in Poland. Go back and take a look at your history, and you'll see why I'm as concerned as I am.[20]

Yet although in George Bush's view, this was a confrontation of epic proportions such as that which had faced Roosevelt in the Second World War, the war in the Gulf would be fought too with the legacy of the more recent past in mind.

As George Herring put it: 'such was the lingering impact of the Vietnam War that the Persian Gulf conflict appeared at times as much a struggle with its ghosts as with Saddam Hussein's Iraq'.[21] With the crisis continuing, speculation increased that the United States might be drawn into 'another Vietnam'. In a statement at his news conference on 30 November, the president tackled the question head on:

> In our country, I know that there are fears about another Vietnam. Let me assure you, should military action be required, this will not be another Vietnam. This will not be a protracted, drawn-out war. The forces arrayed are different. The opposition is different. The resupply of Saddam's military would be very different. The countries united against him in the United Nations are different. The topography of Kuwait is different. And the motivation of our all-volunteer force is superb. I want peace. I want peace, not war. But if there must be war, we will not permit our troops to have their hands tied behind their backs. And I pledge to you: There will not be any murky ending. If one American soldier has to go into battle, that soldier will have enough force behind him to win and then get out as soon as possible, as soon as the U.N. objectives have been achieved. I will never – ever – agree to a halfway effort.[22]

Contained within George Bush's remarks are several revisionist assumptions about the Vietnam war. That failure had thus been because Vietnam was a protracted war against a well-motivated enemy, with the advantage of favourable terrain, and the capacity for limitless resupply. The implicit criticism of America's actions in Vietnam are made. The conscript army had lacked motivation, and had been forced to fight with its hands tied. The war had been inconclusive, fought to a 'murky ending', indeed it had been a 'halfway effort'. The Gulf War thus would be fought mindful of such revisionist 'errors'.

In a radio address on the Gulf crisis in January 1991, the president was even more forthright:

> I've seen the hideous face of war and counted the costs of conflict in friends lost. I remember this all too well, and have no greater concern than the well-being of our men and women stationed in the Persian Gulf. True, their morale is sky-high. True, if they are called upon to fight the aggressors, they will do their job courageously, professionally and, in the end, decisively. There will be no more Vietnams.

Here, then, the reference to Vietnam appears almost as a stock refrain, but given what Bush had just said, the implied criticisms are self-evident. If the Gulf is not another Vietnam, it will be because the morale of the troops in Southeast Asia was so low that they could not fight 'courageously, professionally and, in the end, decisively'.[23] The juxtaposition of the president's comments appears to denigrate the nation's approach to Vietnam as a way of boosting confidence in the new mission about to be undertaken in the Gulf.

Again, in announcing the commencement of military action in the Gulf, Bush made explicit reference to the conflict in Southeast Asia.

> I've told the American people before that this will not be another Vietnam, and I repeat this here tonight. Our troops will have the best possible support in the entire world, and they will not be asked to fight with one hand tied behind their back. I'm hopeful that this fighting will not go on for long and that casualties will be held to an absolute minimum.[24]

As John Pilger points out: 'if seven-and-a-half million tons of bombs dropped on a peasant land and two-and-a-half million people killed is the result of such constraint, the prospect of both hands free ought to bring pause to those who believe the end justifies the means'.[25] The president went on to link the Gulf War with an earlier, more successful conflict: 'Thomas Paine wrote many years ago: "These are the times that try men's souls". Those well-known words are so very true today'.[26] Once again, then, America was involved in a war for its independence, this time from the constraints of the Vietnam syndrome.

So the pre-conditions for the successful projection of power abroad finally had been met. The confrontation in the Gulf presented Bush with his opportunity. It would not be 'another Vietnam'. For, as Stephen Vlastos points out, revisionists believed that in their assessment of America's mistakes in Southeast Asia, they had found some answers. 'In the final analysis, the cause of failure is easily remedied: to win the next one, send packing the unmanly Washington bureaucrats and politicians who chose the path of gradual escalation; put real men in charge who will go in big, hard and fast'.[27] That was what had happened by the time that 'Desert Shield' became 'Desert Storm'.

THE GULF WAR AND VIETNAM

The crisis in the Gulf became George Bush's opportunity to stage what he imagined would be a final confrontation with the legacy he had inherited from the nation's failure in Southeast Asia. In these terms, Ronald Reagan's interventions in Grenada and Libya and Bush's own action in Panama were sideshows: sparring matches before the main event. If the war against Iraq was a success, the 'Vietnam syndrome' might not only be overcome, it could also be cured. After a decade of revisionism, it was as if George Bush, and indeed many of those who tried to influence political and popular opinion in America, were spoiling for this fight.

In the same way that the critic John Aldridge had seen America's involvement in Vietnam as a reaction to the shock of Kennedy's assassination, and Norman Mailer had attempted to lay bare the psychological motivations behind the nation's impulse to war, so in March 1991, in a controversial article published in the *Nation*, the Gulf War was dramatised as the product of a collective national psychosis. Lloyd De Mause, a psychohistorian, addressed the possibility that 'the homicidal and suicidal acts of entire nations – wars – might . . . stem from mental disorders'. In this analysis, America media images of Saddam Hussein as a 'terrifying parent' figure, who during the crisis would actually take children hostage, conspired with feelings of guilt and depression among those suffering in the aftermath of Reagan's 'success binge' of the 1980s. This created an atmosphere in which support for war could be nurtured. So, 'right after Iraq invaded Kuwait, grateful comments appeared in the media'. Even liberal publications were not immune from such bellicosity. '*The New Republic*, for example, said, "Saddam Hussein did the world a favor by invading Kuwait", and Ben Wattenberg headlined his column, "Thanks, Saddam, We Needed That".'[28] In diagnosing this national pyschological disorder, moreover, De Mause argued that it was reminiscent of the condition made familiar by the Vietnam War.

'If a patient were to walk into a psychiatric clinic suffering from intrusive images of terrifying figures torturing children, severe depression unrelated to current life events, and suicidal wishes, a post-traumatic stress disorder (P.T.S.D.) would likely be suspected'. This, then, was 'the diagnostic category' which most closely coincided with 'the popular mood in America during the months leading up to the gulf crisis'.[29] In his attribution of such feelings to the post-traumatic stress of infancy, De Mause calls to mind Michael Herr's observation in *Dispatches*: 'I think that Vietnam was what we had instead of happy childhoods'.[30] It was as if a 'revisionist psychosis' had emerged as a counterpoint to General Westmoreland's analysis of the 'Vietnam syndrome' as a continuing and damaging psychological impediment on America's capacity to go to war.

If America was influenced by a collective predisposition that encouraged a war mentality at the beginning of the 1990s, then another important question is raised. How far did the United States collude, consciously or unconsciously, in the creation of the crisis in the Gulf?

There is no doubt that its policy in the region, which, during the 1980s, had 'tilted' towards Iraq in the hope of thereby containing Iran, was in retrospect optimistic if not opportunistic. Mark Hosenball, writing in *The New Republic* in June 1992 argued that 'in hindsight, the extent to which the Bush and Reagan administrations collaborated in Saddam's ruinous military delusion is appalling'. Furthermore, 'President Bush points to his conduct of Operation Desert Storm as proof of his mastery of international affairs, yet his files demonstrate how he helped to create his own nemesis'.[31] The way to remedy bad policy may be to fight a war, but at the same time, the desire for a conclusive military victory to purge the feeling of failure in Vietnam had influenced foreign policy for the previous decade.

Iraq's take-over of Kuwait was an accident that happened without too long a wait. According to John Pilger, for example, 'there is other evidence that Saddam Hussein was deliberately squeezed or "entrapped" into invading Kuwait. As a US client, he had become too powerful, too cocky and so – rather like Noriega – he had to go'.[32] A week before Iraq invaded Kuwait, a State Department cable had offered American embassies advice on 'US Reaction to Iraqi Threats in the Gulf'. It had suggested that America took 'no position on the border delineation issue raised by Iraq with respect to Kuwait, or on other bi-lateral isues' although it did express concern at Iraqi threats to resolve such issues by force.[33] When April Glaspie, the American ambassador in Baghdad, told Saddam that the president had instructed her that the USA was agnostic about the border disputes between the two countries she was thus 'operating within the Bush administration's policy framework'.[34] Yet when Ross Perot, the maverick Texan candidate for the presidency, in the third presidential debate of 1992, repeated the charge that the administration had told Saddam that 'we wouldn't get involved with this border dispute', George Bush was immediately defensive and vociferously denied the allegation that Iraq had thereby been encouraged to occupy a neighbouring state.[35]

In the event, the Gulf War presented the president with an opportunity to deal with what revisionists thought to be the pervasive psychological influence of the 'Vietnam syndrome' upon popular attitudes. He could confront too the popular reservations about his own capacity as 'commander in chief', which had emerged as he succeeded Ronald Reagan in the White House. In the immediate aftermath of the conflict, then, 'not only did Bush earn kudos for deftly orchestrating the allied success in driving the Iraqis from Kuwait, but he definitively quashed the "wimp factor" that dogged and annoyed him throughout his 1988 campaign'.[36]

The Gulf War thus promised to resolve the dilemma of post-Vietnam foreign policy and would become the defining event of Bush's presidency. If the 'syndrome' could be overcome, America itself would no longer be a 'wimp': self-confidence would replace self-doubt, and heroic leadership would once again be in fashion.

Strategy in the Gulf was framed in the context of a desire to apply the 'lessons' of Vietnam. For Bush's principal military adviser, Colin Powell,

> if force was to be used, it should be overwhelming, and its application should be decisive and preferably short. Military intervention should not be undertaken unless the outcome was all but guaranteed. The aims in using force needed to be precisely defined beforehand, and as soon as they were achieved American forces should be quickly extracted, lest the Pentagon risk sliding into a quagmire. American casualties had to be held to a minimum.[37]

In this sense the Gulf War would be planned and executed as a 'turkey shoot'.

In the moment of victory the Bush administration argued that success in the Gulf had exorcised defeat in Vietnam. The Gulf War thus became the concluding episode in the process of political and military revisionism, begun in the 1980s under the tutelage of Ronald Reagan, and aimed at transforming America's 'mission imposible' into a 'noble cause'. America had not simply beaten Iraq. In Bush's view, 1 March 1991 was 'a proud day for America. And, by God, we've kicked the Vietnam syndrome once and for all'[38]: later in a speech on 4 July, he welcomed home not only the veterans of the Gulf, but also, belatedly, the Vietnam veterans as well. The Americans who had been both victims and initially victimised as a result of the popular perceptions of defeat in Southeast Asia were now to be rehabilitated as they were swept up in the euphoria of success in the Gulf. Yet the rhetoric of victory confronted political reality. In the post-Gulf period, doubts soon surfaced over the nature of the president's proclaimed triumph.

POST-VICTORY BLUES

> All along I have said that the United States is not going to intervene militarily in Iraq's internal affairs and risk being drawn into a Vietnam-style quagmire. This remains the case. Nor will we become an occupying power with U.S. troops patrolling the streets of Baghdad.[39]

George Bush's comments, made just six weeks after his claim that the nation had finally 'kicked' the 'Vietnam syndrome' effectively devalued the political capital he had accumulated from the successful liberation of Kuwait. Two days after his admission, on 18 April, *The Washington Times* published an article by Frank Gaffney under the headline 'Return of the Syndrome'. So, 'even as Mr. Bush was triumphantly announcing the demise of this incapacitating legacy of America's last, wrenching war, he was falling prey to it'. Saddam Hussein remained in power. And as long as he did so, the president's victory was incomplete. 'If he wishes to lick the "Vietnam Syndrome" once and for all, Mr. Bush must bring to the liberation of Iraq the same determination, vision and unconstrained willingness to commit American resources that so brilliantly achieved the liberation of Kuwait'.[40] But the strategic consideration that such an action might result in a protracted war conflicted with the first priority of post-Vietnam military interventionism: that it should be rapidly executed rather than open-ended.

In the *Washington Post* on the following day, Charles Krauthammer argued that George Bush, far from kicking it, now had become the 'chief purveyor' of the syndrome. In his actions after Iraq's defeat, 'he simply raised the specter of Vietnam, an analogy without substance, and let its signal power, the power of fear and defeatism, do the rest. Bush did not just prove that the Vietnam syndrome lives. He gave it new life'.[41] The president was a victim of his own rhetoric: his reluctance to prolong the war an indication that his claim that the lasting impact of Vietnam upon the American psyche had been overcome was but another example of a delusional transformation of reality. Bush's dilemma was not lost on his political opponents.

Early in 1992 Strobe Talbott, one of Bill Clinton's principal foreign policy advisers, published an article in *Foreign Affairs* entitled 'Post-Victory Blues'. In it he aimed to undercut Bush's ability to use the political capital of 'Desert Storm' during the election year. He had an easy target. Talbott argued that

> when Americans fight, they want to see not just victory but virtue . . . In mobilizing his fellow citizens to go to war against Saddam Hussein, Bush had suggested that what was at stake were standards, championed by the United States but applicable to all humanity, about how governments should govern. But in the way he ended the war, he repudiated that principle.[42]

He repeated the argument that had been made soon after the war's conclusion. Having ejected Iraq from Kuwait, the American-led coalition forces had not pursued the war against Saddam. George Bush's demonised adversary, in the moment of military defeat, retained power through crushing the political opposition of the substantial Kurdish minority within Iraq.

Moreover, the liberation of Kuwait hardly represented a triumph for American values. Reservations were expressed about the nature of the regime that had been re-installed. As Thomas Omestad pointed out: 'Bush had appealed to Americans' idealism to win support for the war; afterward, he neglected the most basic ideal: democracy'. The regime that had been restored in Kuwait was autocratic rather than democratic. The triumph was transitory. So 'the glory of Bush's shining moment, the victory over Iraq, faded like a desert mirage. In its aftermath came serious doubts about his judgment and his credibility. And for that, the president had mostly himself to blame'.[43] Bush was facing, and shirking, some important political truths.

While asserting that the 'Vietnam syndrome' had been finally buried, Bush in effect demonstrated its continuing relevance to the conduct of American foreign policy. As Talbott pointed out, 'curing the "Vietnam Syndrome" was seen as an important benefit of Desert Storm, not to be jeopardized by over-reaching in the flush of victory'. The simple restraint remained. The president was unwilling to risk his military success by committing forces to an open-ended conflict against Iraq. In so doing, he called into question the principle upon which he insisted that the Gulf War had been fought. During 1991, 'administration spokesmen from the president down had cited the Gulf War as proof of the relevance and efficacy of American power'.[44] But Saddam Hussein's continuing survival exposed Bush's 'credibility gap'. The 'Vietnam syndrome' still existed as a constraint that counselled caution.

What, then, had America achieved? If the Gulf conflict was fought in part to redeem the failure of the nation's self-assigned mission in Southeast Asia, then the 'post-victory blues' suggested that the initial boast that the United States had overcome the 'Vietnam syndrome' might become more muted as time went by. As George Herring observed:

> it seems doubtful that military victory over a nation with a population less than one-third of Vietnam in a conflict fought under the most favorable circumstances could expunge deeply encrusted and still painful memories of an earlier and very different kind of war.[45]

The attempt at historical revisionism embarked upon in the 1980s, far from being sealed by success in the Gulf, was exposed by it.

The message of the 1980s had been that America could understand its failure in Vietnam if the depth of self-examination did not go beyond consideration of what it believed were its own political and military mistakes in Southeast Asia. Indeed, the identification of the 'Vietnam syndrome' itself effectively removed the need for foreign policy planners to analyse the reasons as to why and how the Vietnamese had successfully resisted the strategy of containment. Instead a domestic psychological block was thought to represent an obstacle to the further projection of military power abroad. If that 'syndrome' could be 'beaten', the coruscating impact of the Vietnam experience upon American society would end. The Gulf War promised revisionists such a cure. Yet the legacy of the conflict in Southeast Asia continued to have an impact upon American politics, and the fortunes of its leaders. For, less than two years after America's victory, the president who orchestrated it was defeated at the polls.

A 'KID' VERSUS A 'BUM'

The political omens seemed initially so promising. In March 1991, the president had an 89 per cent approval rating. The *Congressional Quarterly* wrote that

> Bush's successful gamble in the Gulf has given him a level of stature and popularity that presidents rarely achieve. In the war's afterglow, the immediate question is not whether he might be beaten in 1992 but whether he could establish a record-high winning percentage in a presidential election, surpassing the 61.1% rolled up by Lyndon B. Johnson in 1964.[46]

Leading Democrats were reluctant to confront an incumbent who appeared destined for a second term. What went wrong?

In his inaugural address, George Bush had invited Americans to forget the domestic political divisions caused by its greatest international embarrasment: the war in Vietnam. And yet, he would not take his own words seriously. In 1992, as his campaign for re-election faltered, Bush attempted to exploit rather than paper over the fault lines in America's political discourse that had been caused by Vietnam. He accused his opponent, Bill Clinton, of lack of patriotism for his involvement in anti-war demonstrations while he was a student overseas. Such youthful protest, it appeared, was not to be excused by the president's initial desire to move beyond recollections of the divisive impact of the war in Southeast Asia upon American society. It rendered his opponent unfit to hold a position of leadership.

Johnson's presidency had been destroyed by the war in Vietnam. George Bush eventually confronted a candidate from the same constituency that had repudiated LBJ in 1968, only for it to see Richard Nixon elected and the war continue for a further five years. In these terms, what was the nature of Clinton's challenge to Bush in 1992? For E. L. Doctorow it had a symbolic significance that stemmed from America's experience in Southeast Asia, and which could be couched in the familiar language of Freud.

> Mr.Clinton's dissenting actions during the Vietnam War place him at the head of the dark and threatening coalition of faux Americans. He is, finally, the treacherous son who dares oppose the father. As far as Mr. Bush and his backers are concerned, when the young people of this country rejected the war in Vietnam, they gave up their generational right of succession to primacy and power. They could no longer be trusted.[47]

So might the election campaign of 1992 be seen in this sense as another referendum on the Vietnam war?

On 1 May 1970, Richard Nixon, having authorised military operations in Cambodia, made some impromptu remarks at the Pentagon. Anti-war protestors were:

> these bums . . . blowing up campuses. Listen, the boys that are on the college campuses today are the luckiest people in the world, going to the greatest universities, and here they are burning up the books, I mean storming around about this issue . . .

On the other hand, in Vietnam, 'we've got kids who are just doing their duty . . . when it really comes down to it, they stand up and, boy, you have to talk up to those men'.[48] In that same year George Bush was running for election to the Senate from his adopted state of Texas. Nixon would campaign for him, and, after his protégé's defeat, would appoint him ambassador to the United Nations. Bill Clinton was then a Rhodes scholar at Oxford, and had become involved in demonstrations against the Vietnam war.

In Nixon's demonology, the 1992 presidential election pitted a 'kid' against a 'bum'. Bush had done his duty as the youngest American naval pilot in the Second World War. He would have been on the side of Nixon's angels in 1970. But Clinton had committed the generational heresy: he had doubted America's mission. In 1992, Bush disinterred those memories of conflict, not simply between generations but within 'the Vietnam generation' of which Clinton was a member. He tried to make personal conduct during the conflict in Southeast Asia a litmus test of presidential 'character'. If 'Desert Storm' truly had completed the revisionist process in reconstructing popular perceptions of the Vietnam war as a 'noble cause', he might have made the charge stick. But the lingering doubts about the nature of Bush's victory in the Gulf, and the superficiality of his analysis of anti-war feeling during America's involvement in Vietnam combined to undercut the political force of his accusation.

When George Bush seized upon the rhetoric of revisionism to attack Clinton's patriotism, his argument, like his earlier claim that the 'Vietnam syndrome' had been finally overcome by military success in the Gulf, was tested and found wanting. Already beset by domestic troubles during the re-election campaign, the president's attempt to reinvent the memories of the war that had sundered the nation seemed to be almost a final act of political despair. Clinton's conduct during the Vietnam war recalled the dilemmas faced by many of his generation, for whom the political and moral ambiguities of America's involvement in Southeast Asia were indeed divisive issues that subsequent revisionist arguments might not easily resolve. Bush's simplistic accusations made little impact on popular opinion.

CONCLUSION:
GEORGE BUSH AND THE VIETNAM GENERATION

As Doctorow also points out,

> all the Presidents since Vietnam, from Nixon to Bush, have been of the same World War II generation. They will not be moved. The thrust of their government has been, punitively, to teach us the error of our ways, to put things back to the time when people stayed in their place and owed their souls to the company store.[49]

In 1992, this conformist message no longer worked. Clinton managed to pre-empt the domestic political agenda – it was indeed 'the economy, stupid' which proved to be the issue. But Bush's electoral defeat also represented a transfer of power to one of the 'Vietnam generation'. It was a watershed not only for the liberal interventionist architects of cold war American foreign policy, but also for the conservative revisionists who had sought to excuse defeat in the aftermath of Vietnam.

Their cold war was already officially over. At the beginning of that era of sublime international tension, the Department of War had been renamed the Department of Defense. Such an alteration of title did not imply necessarily a change in purpose. But the use of different language does have an implication for the ways in which reality is perceived and expressed. During the 1960s and 1970s, that same Department of Defense prosecuted a war in Southeast Asia. What was the true nature of that conflict? The history of America's defeat in that war was manipulated by the language of revisionism. The need to overcome the 'Vietnam syndrome' was the expression of an agreement urged upon Americans in the 1980s that their failure had been their fault. The chance to confront that version of the past was presented to the nation after Iraq's invasion of Kuwait. Yet the Gulf War, in its own aftermath, revealed the contradiction between self-congratulatory rhetoric and political fact. Swift success brought ephemeral gains, as long as Saddam Hussein remained in power.

In 1991, therefore, George Bush made a claim for his victory over Iraq which, in the afterglow of 'Desert Storm', his policy effectively undermined. He would not commit America to an open-ended war against Saddam, much less involve the nation in Iraq's internal civil conflict. The metaphor of Vietnam, the country as 'quagmire', might have been re-invented in Iraq if America had become involved in a desert 'quicksand'. But the message would have remained the same. The 'syndrome' still counselled against prolonged overseas adventurism. While he was telling Americans that success in the Gulf atoned for America's failure in Vietnam, Bush's inaction was creating his 'credibility gap'. The following year, during his re-election campaign, he offered such a strained interpretation of American attitudes towards Vietnam in the 1960s that he failed to convince many with his argument that opposition to the war then had been an unpatriotic cause. Revisionist ideas must remain plausible. Taken too far, they can exhaust belief.

The extent to which revisionism thus embodied an inability to admit reality suggests why it was unable to cure its own creation: the complex psychological obstacle of the 'Vietnam syndrome'. Instead the earlier and more simple formulation of restraint, Vietnam as a reminder of the possible outcome of involvement overseas, remained as a political refrain. As George Herring observes, 'Vietnam should stand as an enduring testament to the pitfalls of interventionism and the limits of power, something to keep in mind after the deceptively easy military victory in the Persian Gulf'.[50] The revisionism of the Reagan and Bush years confronted a tortuous and complicated version of the 'Vietnam syndrome'. And yet, in his conduct after the conflict in the Middle-East, and in his comments on Clinton's 'character' during the 1992 campaign, it was Bush himself who finally gave the lie to the idea that the Gulf War had in some way erased fears of 'another Vietnam', and had transformed memories of American involvement in Southeast Asia.

George Bush might be excused his mistakes. For during the 1980s, revisionist political and military explanations of America's failure in Southeast Asia had retained a certain popular political resonance. Such ideas indulged the nation's capacity for self-delusion. And for many in America, wish-fulfilment was a comfortable psychological tactic for interpreting the nation's past. As the first member of the 'Vietnam generation' occupied the White House, the alternative became more challenging. To move beyond revisionism, to understand the legacy of the Vietnam war, rather than simply to try and overcome its surrogate 'syndrome', would be to accept the need for more strategic confrontations with history, reality and truth.

Just before he left office, Bush made some remarks at Texas A&M University in which he summarised his view of the post-cold war world and America's role in it. He said 'My thesis is a simple one: . . . America remains today what Lincoln said it was more than a century ago: the last best hope of man on earth'. Moreover,

> The Soviet Union did not simply lose the Cold War, the Western democracies won it. And I say this not to gloat but to make a key point. The qualities that enabled us to triumph in that struggle, faith, strength, unity and, above all, American leadership, are those we must call upon now to win the peace.

This was because, 'the end of the Cold War . . . has placed in our hands a unique opportunity to see the principles for which America has stood for two centuries – democracy, free enterprise, and the rule of law – spread more widely than ever before in human history'. 'History', concluded Bush, 'is summoning us once again to lead'.[51]

The Gulf War had tested the capacities of Bush as president, and America as a nation, to exercise leadership in the post-Vietnam and now post-cold war era. Far from proving America's ability to define a New World Order, the aftermath of the Gulf, as long as Saddam remained in power, continued to mean the verdict was open. In Bush's speech in Texas, therefore, there was perhaps a realism co-existing with the idealism: triumphalism tempered with an appreciation that new challenges from ethnic divisions and nationalisms are around to sabotage the stability of an American-led international order. At the same time, however, the underlying confidence in America's mission – Lincoln's last best hope – emerges as the continuing pulse of the 'idea of America' abroad. George Bush remained unrepentant. And yet, as he left office, he might reflect that kicking against the 'Vietnam syndrome' had proved a more complex and ultimately more self-defeating task than he might have imagined.

NOTES

1. Germond and Witcover, *Blue Smoke and Mirrors*, p. 118.
2. Warner, 'Bush battles the "Wimp Factor" ', pp. 29, 36 and 35.
3. Graham, *Personal History*, p. 613.
4. Johnson, *Sleepwalking through History*, p. 395.
5. Ibid. pp. 406–7.
6. Dan Quayle and Lloyd Bentsen, 'Vice-Presidential Debate', 5 October 1988 (see Website: Bensten–Quayle Vice-Presidential Debate, 1988).
7. George Bush, 'Inaugural Address', Friday, 20 January 1989 (see Website: Presidential Inaugural Addresses).
8. Baker, 'A New Europe, A New Atlanticism', p. 1.
9. Fukuyama, 'The End of History?', p. 3.
10. Ibid. p. 4.
11. Ibid. p. 8.
12. Ibid. p. 9 and 10.
13. Ibid. pp. 14–15.
14. Ibid. p. 18.
15. Bush, 'Annual Message to Congress on the State of the Union', 31 January 1990, (see Website: Annual Messages to Congress on the State of the Union).
16. Spencer, *The Carter Implosion*, p. 3 and 15. The quote 'aggression unchallenged . . .' is from Lyndon Johnson. See Kearns, *Lyndon Johnson and the American Dream*, p. 270.
17. Bush, 'Address before a Joint Session of the Congress on the Persian Gulf Crisis and the Federal Budget Deficit', 11 September 1990 (see Website: George Bush Digital Library).
18. Bush, 'Address before the 45th Session of the United Nations General Assembly in New York', New York 1 October 1990 (see Website: George Bush Digital Library).
19. Bush, 'Remarks at a Republican Campaign Rally in Mashpee, Massachusetts' 1 November 1990' (see Website: George Bush Digital Library).
20. Bush, 'The President's News Conference in Orlando, Florida', 1 November 1990, (see Website: George Bush Digital Library).

21. Herring, 'America and Vietnam', p. 104.
22. Bush, 'The President's News Conference', 30 November 1990, (see Website: George Bush Digital Library).
23. Bush, 'Radio Address to the Nation on the Persian Gulf Crisis', 5 January 1991 (see Website: George Bush Digital Library).
24. Bush, 'Address to the Nation Announcing Allied Military Action in the Persian Gulf , 16 January 1991, (see Website: George Bush Digital Library).
25. Pilger, 'Turkey Shoots', p. 105.
26. Bush, 'Address to the Nation, January 16, 1991'.
27. Vlastos, 'America's "Enemy" ', p. 69.
28. De Mause, 'The Gulf War as Mental Disorder', *passim.*
29. Ibid. p. 304.
30. Herr, *Dispatches*, p. 195.
31. Hosenball, 'The Odd Couple', pp. 27 and 35.
32. Pilger, 'Sins of Omission', p. 89.
33. Quoted in Gordon and Trainor, *The Generals' War*, p. 20.
34. Ibid. p. 22.
35. 'Third Presidential Debate' 19 October 1992, East Lansing, Michigan (see Website: George Bush Digital Library).
36. Omestad, 'Why Bush Lost', p. 71.
37. Gordon and Trainor, *The Generals' War*, preface p. viii.
38. Bush, 'Remarks to the American Legislative Exchange Council', 1 March 1991 (see Website: George Bush Digital Library).
39. Bush, 'Remarks on Assistance for Iraqi Refugees and a News Conference', 16 April 1991 (see Website: George Bush Digital Library).
40. Gaffney, 'Return of the Syndrome'.
41. Krauthammer, 'Good Morning Vietnam'.
42. Talbott, 'Post-Victory Blues', p. 69.
43. Omestad, 'Why Bush Lost', pp. 71–2.
44. Talbott, 'Post-Victory Blues', pp. 59 and 55.
45. Herring, 'America and Vietnam', p. 104.
46. *Congressional Quarterly Weekly Report,* vol. 49, no. 10, 9 March 1991, p. 584.
47. Doctorow, 'The Character of Presidents', p. 535.
48. Quoted in Ambrose, *Nixon: The Triumph*, p. 348.
49. Doctorow, 'The Character of Presidents', p. 535.
50. Herring, 'America and Vietnam', p. 119.
51. Bush, 'Remarks at Texas A & M University', 15 December 1992 College Station, Texas (see Website: George Bush Digital Library).

CHAPTER NINE

Bill Clinton: Survivor

INTRODUCTION: A QUESTION OF CHARACTER

In April 1969, just under six years after he had shaken hands with President Kennedy, Bill Clinton was drafted into the United States army. He faced the prospect of being sent to the place where JFK had staked America's cold war credibility: Vietnam. At the time, he was a Rhodes scholar at the University of Oxford. This, then, was how America's 'mission impossible' impinged directly on him, as it did on others of his generation. The difference was that Clinton went on to become president. And so his attitude to his draft notice, and to the war in Vietnam, would become a matter of public debate: for some a litmus test of presidential 'character'.

The controversy that surrounds Clinton's behaviour in relation to Vietnam – both in terms of the draft and with respect to his anti-war activities – is in itself suggestive of the war's continuing impact in American political discourse. George Bush's 'statute of limitations' has not been reached: the subject still worries the national conscience. So Clinton becomes representative of his generation: for his decisions – similar to those made by many of his contemporaries – highlight the sensitive personal and, in his case, controversial political choices that were forced by the war. Moreover, Clinton's behaviour remains an example which, because of the ambiguities of the war's legacy, is difficult to reconstruct, if not to understand.

Having been drafted, his choices were limited. He could resist it, obey it or avoid it. The clearest indication of his thinking about what he should do came in the now infamous letter he wrote to Colonel Eugene Holmes, the ROTC – Reserve Officer Training Corps – director at the University of Arkansas, after he had negotiated a way through the dilemmas that he faced. Resistance was ruled out for someone like

Clinton, who already had political ambitions, and who needed to 'maintain my political viability within the system'[1] . This was despite the fact that he was opposed not only to the war but also to the draft. Or rather he argued that if the war was wrong, then the draft too was a mistake: no democratic government 'should have the power to make its citizens fight and die in a war which, in any case, does not involve immediately the peace and freedom of the nation' .[2] If that was the case, then it might be assumed that Clinton should have had no principled objection to avoiding the draft. But the issue was more complex: his letter to Colonel Holmes was an attempt to explain his tortuous struggle, first to circumnavigate, and then to accept his draft status.

Among the alternatives to submitting to the draft were enlistment in alternative forms of military service. Like Dan Quayle, Bill Clinton could have chosen to go into the National Guard, but at that time, in Arkansas, it was not accepting any more recruits. Instead, 'the advanced ROTC program at the University of Arkansas did not have quotas and was open to law students. It had grown rapidly in size in the year since graduate deferments were eliminated, becoming a safe haven for students looking for a way around the draft'.[3] In the summer of 1969, Clinton enrolled in the law school and in the ROTC there, and his draft board granted him a deferment. Yet it was clear that if this was a course of action that he was forced into, it was one which he was reluctant to accept. Instead of taking up his place at his home state university, he returned to Oxford.

It was Richard Nixon who solved his problem. On 1 October 1969, the Nixon administration altered the draft rules for graduate students. Now they would be allowed to complete their academic year of study before having to report for military service. Wishing to avoid both the University of Arkansas law school and its ROTC, Clinton could now give up his deferment, become re-eligible for the draft, but stay in Oxford until the following July. During that time, Nixon's other policy changes, already announced, and which significantly affected his prospects of becoming involved in the war, would take effect. Besides beginning to reduce the number of troops in Vietnam, at the end of 1969, Nixon also effectively suspended the draft while designing its reform: the lottery. Once that was implemented, Clinton would be eligible for the draft only for a year, and his chances of being called up would be determined by the lottery number assigned to his birth date: the higher the number, the better his prospects of escaping military service. In David Maraniss's words 'luck would help determine the fate of a gambling town's favorite son'.[4] On 1 December, Clinton's number

– 311 – came up: sufficiently high for him no longer to worry about the ROTC in Arkansas. In the same week he wrote to Colonel Holmes from Oxford, he applied to Yale law school.

Bill Clinton survived the threat of going to fight in a war that he opposed with his political viability, if not his political credibility, intact: a feat of imagination and manipulation characteristic of his subsequent career. His actions over the draft can be read either as a genuine confrontation with the moral ambiguities of the time – a wrestling with a conscience which opposed Vietnam, but considered deferment as in a way as unprincipled as the war itself. Or as a sign of a sophisticated political intelligence weighing decisions with a sense both of the machiavellian moment and the future. Either way, Clinton managed to elevate the politics of ambiguity to fresh heights.

Coupled with the complexities of the draft, it was Clinton's active involvement in the anti-war movement that also detonated its political fallout some twenty-three years later, during the 1992 presidential election campaign. In fact, he was not actively involved in organising demonstrations against the war until after he returned to Oxford from Arkansas in September 1969. But he claimed that his opposition to the war had started earlier. In his letter to Colonel Holmes, Clinton wrote that while in a 'very minor position' on the Senate Foreign Relations Committee, – William J. Fulbright, its chair at the time, also from Arkansas, was one of Clinton's political mentors – he had

> the opportunity, however small, of working every day against a war I opposed and despised with a depth of feeling I had reserved solely for racism in America before Vietnam . . . I have written and spoken and marched against the war. One of the national organizers of the Vietnam Moratorium is a close friend of mine. After I left Arkansas last summer, I went to Washington to work in the national headquarters of the Moratorium, then to England to organize the Americans for the demonstrations Oct. 15 and Nov. 16.

For David Maraniss, 'Clinton rewrites his own history here'. In Washington, in 1966, when involved with the Fulbright committee, he had not been regarded as particularly opposed to the war. And rather than travelling to the UK as an emissary from the Moratorium headquarters to lead demonstrations overseas – a Che Guevara of the peace movement – Clinton had only helped 'organize the Americans at Oxford once he was there'. In explaining his actions over the draft, Clinton evidently felt it necessary to 'overstate his role' in the peace movement .[5] In the 1992 election campaign, the implications of his actions were similarly over-dramatised.

For George Bush, it was enough to disqualify Clinton from the presidency. Anti-war protest overseas was an issue both of judgement and character. At an election rally in Texas on 8 October the president claimed:

> my opponent has written that he once mobilized demonstrations in London against the Vietnam war. I simply for the life of me cannot understand how someone can go to London, another country, and mobilize demonstrations against the United States of America when our kids are dying halfway around the world. The issue here isn't patriotism. You can demonstrate all you want here at home . . . That's part of America. But I can't understand someone mobilizing demonstrations in a foreign county when poor kids, drafted out of the ghettos, are dying in a faraway land. You can call me old-fashioned, but that just does not make sense to me.[6]

The reference to the UK's capital city as 'another country' is in keeping with the fuzzy logic of the argument. Bush's objection to Clinton's behaviour is apparently based on the fact that he went overseas to protest. It isn't that he is unpatriotic, or that the act of demonstrating against the war is necessarily wrong, since it is fine to protest 'all you want here at home'. Rather, Clinton has broken with a fundamental American political tradition – that 'politics stops at the water's edge'. So the implication is that in making his protest abroad, Clinton was being 'un-American', indeed cowardly, and certainly rendering himself unfit for public service in the United States. If this behaviour did not make sense to George Bush, then his argument is similarly designed more for its emotional appeal than its rational rigour. Yet by suggesting that to demonstrate overseas is unacceptable, while protest at home is a constitutional right, the president at least avoids alienating a domestic constituency that had supported anti-war sentiment in America. Clinton belonged to that small minority which had demonstrated against the conflict abroad: politically a better target to attack.

Three days later, during the first presidential debate, and addressing a less partisan audience, Bush returned to this theme:

> I think it's wrong to demonstrate against your own country or organize demonstrations against your own country in foreign soil. I just think it's wrong. Maybe, they say, well, it was a youthful indiscretion. I was 19 or 20, flying off an aircraft carrier, and that shaped me to be Commander in Chief

of the Armed Forces. And I'm sorry, but demonstrating – it's not a question of patriotism. It's a question of character and judgment.[7]

Here the president merely asserts that demonstrating abroad is wrong. He doesn't justify or explain why that should be so. And he contrasts Clinton's 'youthful indiscretion' to his own behaviour at a younger age: service in the Second World War that had shaped his character, and given him the qualifications to become commander in chief.

In response, Clinton attempted to shift the grounds of the debate.

> You were wrong to attack my patriotism. I was opposed to the war, but I love my country. And we need a President who will bring this country together, not divide it. We've had enough division. I want to lead a unified country.[8]

So the issue here is loyalty to the nation, not character, and by referring to the need to unite the country, Clinton makes both a subtle reference to the continuing fault-lines in American society and culture caused by the nation's failed involvement in Vietnam, and makes an implicit criticism of the president's attempt to exploit them.

George Bush was nevertheless successful in creating a campaign issue. In the third presidential debate, the question of character, linked to Clinton's stance on the draft and the war, re-emerged. After suggesting that his 'credibility has come into question because of your different responses on the Vietnam draft', Clinton was asked: 'if you had to do it over again, would you put on the Nation's uniform? And, if elected, could you, in good conscience, send someone to war?' His reply did not address the central problem of credibility. Instead, he admitted only that

> if I had to do it over again, I might answer the questions a little better. You know, I had been in public life a long time and no one had ever questioned my role, and so I was asked a lot of questions about the things that happened a long time ago. I don't think I answered them as well as I could have. Going back 23 years, I don't know, . . . I was opposed to the war. I couldn't help that. I felt very strongly about it, and I didn't want to go at the time. It's easy to say in retrospect I would have done something differently.[9]

Then, focusing on whether he could become an effective commander in chief, he enlisted in support some powerful allies from the past.

> President Lincoln opposed the war, and there were people who said maybe he shouldn't be President. But I think he made us a pretty good President in

wartime. We've got a lot of other Presidents who didn't wear their country's uniform and had to order our young soldiers into battle, including President Wilson and President Roosevelt. So the answer is, I could do that. I wouldn't relish doing it, but I wouldn't shrink from it. I think that the President has to be prepared to use the power of the Nation when our vital interests are threatened, when our treaty commitments are at stake, when we know that something has to be done that is in the national interest. And that is a part of being President. Could I do it? Yes, I could.[10]

Such a prepared response reveals Clinton's political skill. First there is the admission of regret, not about what he had done or not done in the past, but in the fact that he had not been better able to respond to the questions raised during the campaign about his conduct. And then he argues convincingly that military service is not necessary for a president to be an effective wartime leader. Lincoln in the Civil War, and Wilson in the First along with Roosevelt in the Second World War had no direct experience of conflict prior to becoming president. Clinton puts himself in heroic company, and effectively defuses Vietnam as a test of presidential character.

The forensic investigation of Clinton's attitude and behaviour during the Vietnam war, of his actions, and of his subsequent responses to the issues it appeared to raise about his suitability to seek the presidency is an attempt to bring into focus a political persona at once elusive and enigmatic. It is also an early indication of the extent to which his public image was created around this and other issues of 'character' – possible drug use (he never inhaled), and infidelity (the so-called 'bimbo-eruptions' that threatened both his campaign and his presidency). Perhaps more than any of his predecessors, Clinton's presidency has been conducted in the glare of publicity that has investigated his personal morality in an effort to undermine his political agenda. Indeed, as Louis Liebovich suggests, 'perhaps no other president has ever been pursued by personal scandal so vigorously'.[11] The outcome would be the spectacle of presidential impeachment, a distinction that makes Clinton unique among twentieth century presidents, and only the second chief executive to haved faced – and won – a Senate trial in the history of the republic. Yet what also makes Clinton rare among presidents is the sense that, like Kennedy, he encapsulates the 'spirit of the age'. And he inspires admiration and intense antagonism alike through his intuitive grasp of a post-Vietnam phenomenon: the politics of relativity.

THE POLITICS OF RELATIVITY

Writing in the aftermath of the Civil War, Walt Whitman confessed, 'the fear of conflicting and irreconcilable interiors, and the lack of a common skeleton, knitting all close, continually haunts me'.[12] A similar concern had underlined the interpretations of the past advanced by the 'consensus historians' of the 1950s: if the cold war was at core an ideological struggle, then it was important to establish a 'meta-narrative' that could unify the nation in the face of communism: the perceived threat to its inherited values and principles. The 'common skeleton' was sketched in the language of exceptionalism and the rhetoric of mission. Then came Vietnam.

The war in Southeast Asia shattered faith in the meta-narrative of the cold war. It legitimised protest. When Clinton, as a student, took part in demonstrations against the war, he was among those for whom America's cold war mission was thrown in doubt because of the tenacity with which the Vietnamese opposed it. Indeed, in discussing 'Vietnam and the Revival of an Anti-imperial Mood?', the radical historian William Appleman Williams argued that there is an important interaction between foreign resistance to American intervention overseas and the 'generally latent but periodically consequential American opposition to an imperial foreign policy'.[13] In his view, the cold war was the product in part of a set of American assumptions and behaviour that were at the least questionable. The prevailing rhetoric of the Truman Doctrine and associated foreign policy pronouncements oversimplified the relationship between the USA and the USSR so that the reality of cold war confrontation provoked Soviet adventurism in response to it as much as it prevented it through containment. The resulting misallocation of moral, intellectual and material resources was the result of sublimating all other priorities to the waging of this ideological war. Furthermore, in the climate of the cold war, there was a constant temptation for the Executive to lie to the Congress and the public in the interests of 'national security'. Indeed, this effective violation of the Constitution by the Executive was condoned by what Williams suggested was the 'fear of the trauma of impeachment'.[14] The result was the temptation for the president to deploy the American military abroad to counter perceived threats: troops who then acted as an automatic trigger to confrontation and war.

All these things were in fact destabilising forces: all would eventually contribute to the 'credibility gap' that grew between official rhetoric and observable reality, and which the events of Vietnam served to heighten and to dramatise. For Williams, there had always been a popular domestic opposition to the assumptions which spurred the cold war on, and which existed alongside the general consensus of American society in deference to their leadership. This was slow to develop, but the Korean War called into question some of the cold war certainties. And ironically, these contributed to Eisenhower's election – Williams identifies Eisenhower as the most anti-imperial of America's cold war leaders, in the sense that he sensed the limits on the projection of American power abroad. Nevertheless, the president was still a product of his American times, and effectively his caution was not a denial of America's mission, merely a judicious insight into the possibilities of its pursuit.

It took Vietnam to release and to legitimise the domestic opposition to America's cold war mission. For Vietnamese resistance 'forced an ever increasing number of Americans to confront the truth that was destroying the very idea and reality of The City Upon a Hill'.[15] Moreover, the contemporary struggle for civil rights, which could be seen as a reaction against a form of domestic imperialism, interacted with the anti-war movement to crack the political, cultural and social consensus necessary to pursue the cold war. For Williams, therefore, it was 'the resistance by the Cubans, the Russians, the Chinese – and particularly the Vietnamese' which accelerated the anti-imperial mood within America and which 'confronted Americans with the need to re-examine and then change their traditional conception of America as a world unto itself'.[16] In other words, resistance abroad broke through the cocoon of exceptionalism by forcing some Americans – Clinton among them – to re-examine the cultural consensus upon which their society was based. Vietnamese resistance to the 'idea of America abroad' in particular might provide Americans with what Louis Hartz had called that 'spark of philosophy, that grain of relative insight' which would enable them to see the limitations inherent in their liberal consensus.[17]

America's failure in Vietnam thus challenged the assumptions of the historical meta-narrative which held together America's cold war consensus. After Gerald Ford's administration had witnessed the last helicopters clattering away from the roof of the American embassy in Saigon, it was left to his successors to pick up the pieces. For after Vietnam, the sense of cultural dislocation was complete. The initial reaction was to sublimate historical memory, and – Jimmy Carter's approach – to attempt to revitalise the nation with an appeal to moral absolutism: emphasising the universality of human rights. When that tactic proved ineffective, the strategy of reshaping historical memory, rhetorically during the Reagan administration, and pragmatically in the Gulf War during George Bush's presidency, seemed designed to reconstruct the cold war consensus and the meta-narrative which failure in Vietnam had symbolically ruptured. Indeed, the end of the cold war and victory in the Gulf constituted the high watermark of post-Vietnam revisionism.

Yet when George Bush lost the presidential election to candidate Clinton in 1992, and when Bob Dole lost to President Clinton in 1996, not only a generational shift in American politics took place. There was also an acceptance of the need to explore new 'ideas of America', for that is what Clinton represented. Bush and Dole were among those who had experienced economic depression and war, and had lived through the fears of the 1950s: the most traumatic of which was the prospect of nuclear war. In the culture of contingency, they were members of a different resistance. They, along with most Americans, would cling to the secure raft of a cold war meta-narrative which emphasised the reassuring nostrums of consensus history, telling and retelling the 'storybook truths' in which an exceptionalist belief was forged from mythologising the experience of the frontier. Bush and Dole encountered Vietnam with a sense of detachment which was the product of non-participation: they did not have to resolve the dilemmas which, as a 23-year-old student in Oxford, Bill Clinton had to face. But they did have to make sense of the dislocations which defeat in that war implied. The erosion of cultural meta-narrative was both real and potentially destructive of the image of America which had shaped their political beliefs and ideas. They were revisionists, and during his 1996 campaign Bob Dole in particular betrayed a Reagan-like nostalgia for the comforting American world of the postwar 'age of affluence' and the pre-Vietnam consensus in American society.

By then, however, the 'vital center' to which the resistance appealed had collapsed. On the one hand, the born-again fervour of the immediate post-Vietnam era, when a new beginning was a convenient tactic for avoiding confrontation with the immediate past, had hardened into the political energies of the fundamentalist right. On the other, the shockwaves of failure in Southeast Asia combined with the fragmentation of cultural and political consensus within America to legitimize the cacophony of voices raised in support of multi-culturalism: the need to retrieve heterogeneous histories – of blacks, of women, of native Americans, of Chicanos, of gays – and to value them equally in the market place of American ideas. The politician who understood this new *Zeitgeist*, since he was a product of it himself, was Bill Clinton.

For Fred Greenstein,

> it is as if the more cerebral side of John F. Kennedy's approach to leadership were writ large and amalgamated with Lyndon Johnson's proclivity to press the flesh, find ways to split the difference with his opponents, and otherwise practice the art of the possible.[18]

Clinton's politics of relativity recognised the need to navigate between the competing claims of the different and diverse elements of American society, and refused to privilege one at the expense of others. But as president he had to tread a difficult path between old rhetoric and new politics. For the distance between a fundamentalist vision (with its wholehearted acceptance of absolute standards of moral behaviour rooted in the intensity of its religious conviction) and a multi-culturalist ideal (with its accentuated promotion of 'political correctness') is as far as that which separated cold war warriors from anti-Vietnam protestors. During his campaign, Clinton may have expressed the hope that he could lead a unified country. As president, however, he had to face intense personal and political hostility, focused once more on the issue of 'character', convinced that instead of electing an amalgam of JFK and LBJ, America had opted for the Democrats' version of Richard Nixon: a leader both morally corrupt and politically bankrupt.

In his first inaugural address, the new president made a point of trying to reach out to the constituency that his election had left behind, struggling to make sense of the world in the absence of cold war convictions.

> Though we march to the music of time, our mission is timeless. Each generation of Americans must define what it means to be an American. On behalf of our nation, I salute my predecessor, President Bush, for his half-century of service to America, and I thank the millions of men and women whose steadfastness and sacrifice triumphed over depression, fascism and communism.

But now, in an echo of Kennedy, the torch had been passed: 'today, a generation raised in the shadows of the Cold War assumes new responsibilities in a world warmed by the sunshine of freedom . . .'. Moreover today we do more than celebrate America, we rededicate ourselves to the very idea of America . . . an idea ennobled by the faith that our nation can summon from its myriad diversity, the deepest measure of unity; an idea infused with the conviction that America's long, heroic journey must go forever upwards.[19]

Those are the sentiments of a traditionalist expressed in the familiar rhetoric of exceptionalism. Yet in his first days as president, Clinton, through attempting to promote the rights of a particular minority, threatened to undermine the morale of the institution which symbolised America's confidence in its position of international supremacy.

The issue was gays in the military. During his campaign, Clinton had made a commitment to help eliminate discrimination against gays who joined the military. As president, he was forced to retreat from this promise. Opposition within the military establishment meant that

Clinton settled on a policy of 'don't ask, don't tell' . . . The government could not actively search out gays, but military leaders had a right to weed out enlistees who were openly gay. The compromise satisfied no one and raised questions about Clinton's commitment to his stated policy objectives.[20]

What is interesting, however, is the president's rationale for his proposal. In his speech to the Annual Convention of the Newspaper Association of America in Boston, Clinton opened his remarks by saying:

'Today in Washington, many Americans came to demonstrate against discrimination based on their sexual orientation. A lot of people think that I did a terrible political thing – and I know I paid a terrible political price – for saying that I thought the time had come to end the categorical ban on gays and lesbians serving in our military service and that they should not be subject to other discrimination in governmental employment. Let me tell you what I think. This is not about embracing anybody's lifestyle. This is a question of whether if somebody is willing to live by the strict code of military conduct, if somebody is willing to die for their country, should they have the right to do it? I think the answer is yes . . . But in a larger sense, I want to say to you that I think the only way our country can make it is if we can find somehow strength out of our diversity, even with people with whom we profoundly disagree, as long as we can agree on how we're going to treat each other and how we're going to conduct ourselves in public forums. That is the real issue.[21]

This, then, encapsulates the new politics of relativity. Individual rights are paramount: no one code of behaviour should take moral precedence over others. And society should recognise and celebrate differences, America should look for 'strength' in its 'diversity', rather than condemn that which runs counter to the mainstream. In Bill Clinton's words:

> You are free to discriminate in your judgments about any of us – how we look, how we behave, what we are. Make your judgments. But if we are willing to live together according to certain rules of conduct, we should be able to do so. That is the issue for America.[22]

The issue of gays in the military is an instance of the politics of relativity clashing with entrenched beliefs in an institution that symbolised the values that lay at the heart of the nation's cold war consensus. Clinton recognised this. In July 1993, in his remarks at National Defense University, justifying his compromise policy, he observed that

> our military is a conservative institution, and I say that in the very best sense, for its purpose is to conserve the fighting spirit of our troops; to conserve the resources and the capacity of our troops; to conserve the military lessons acquired during our nation's existence; to conserve our very security; and yes, to conserve the liberties of the American people. Because it is a conservative institution, it is right for the military to be wary of sudden changes. Because it is an institution that embodies the best of America and must reflect the society in which it operates, it is also right for the military to make changes when the time for change is at hand.[23]

Navigating between the concerns of the military and the demands of those advocating gay rights necessarily involved compromise. Yet this, together with the president's acceptance of moral and political relativism could easily be construed as an inability to provide both direction and leadership, not only domestically but also in terms of the nation's post-cold war foreign policy. As John Hart suggests, then, Clinton was also 'faced with the immensely difficult problem of giving some meaning and substance to that hitherto vacuous phrase invented by his predecessor, "the new world order".'[24] In so doing, he again struck out in new and controversial directions

'FOREIGN POLICY AS SOCIAL WORK'
– EXCEPT FOR IRAQ

He has been portrayed as paying only reluctant attention to issues of international concern.

Clinton seemed for much of his first half-year in office to be almost oblivious to foreign policy. Neither his formative experiences as a Vietnam War protestor nor his dozen years as governor of a small southern state appear to have led him to address himself in any sustained way to the larger world . . . Clinton appears to have delegated the larger world to his foreign policy team for much of his first year. He stepped into the commander in chief role only in October, when events in Somalia and Haiti made it evident that, like it or not, as commander in chief and head of state he could not confine himself to leadership in the domestic sphere.[25]

In this view, perhaps no president since Franklin Roosevelt had been elected with such an overtly domestic political agenda. Yet like FDR, Clinton did have a sense of a bigger picture, and his leadership should not simply be defined and judged in terms of his initial focus on the domestic scene.

On 26 February 1993, only a third of the way into his first hundred days in office, Bill Clinton made a major speech on the global economy at American University in Washington DC. The symbolism of the occasion was significant, for as the new president observed:

thirty years ago in the last year of his short but brilliant life, John Kennedy came to this university to address the paramount challenge of that time: the imperative of pursuing peace in the face of nuclear confrontation. Many Americans still believe it was the finest speech he ever delivered.[26]

Now it was Clinton's turn to outline his vision of America's role in the world in the post-cold war era.

He emphasised the fact of global economic interdependence and the necessity for the United States to remain committed to the principles of free trade as it assumed its natural role of leadership as the most economically powerful nation within the world community. The 'great challenge of this day' is thus 'the imperative of American leadership in the face of global change'.

Through focusing on such economic issues, Clinton moves beyond the traditional rhetoric of exceptionalism. Rather,

the truth of our age is this – and must be this: Open and competitive commerce will enrich us as a nation. It spurs us to innovate. It forces us to compete. It connects us with new customers. It promotes global growth without which no rich country can hope to grow wealthier. It enables our producers who are themselves consumers of services and raw materials to prosper. And so I say to you in the face of all the pressures to do the reverse, we must compete, not retreat.

So 'in this global economy, there is no such thing as a purely domestic policy'.[27] America had to engage with the wider world, but its perspective should change from a cold war emphasis on military security. Its focus instead should be 'the economy, stupid' writ large and seen within a new global context.

At the same time, echoes of exceptionalist rhetoric remained. 'For the new world toward which we are moving actually favors us. We are better equipped than any other people on Earth by reason of our history, our culture and our disposition, to change, to lead and to prosper'. This was because 'we have always been a nation of pioneers', and

> here we are again, ready to accept a new challenge, ready to seek new change because we're curious and restless and bold. It flows out of our heritage. It's ingrained in the soul of Americans. It's no accident that our nation has steadily expanded the frontiers of democracy, of religious tolerance, of racial justice, of equality for all people, of environmental protection and technology and, indeed, the cosmos itself. For it is our nature to reach out.[28]

As the cold war ends, American pioneers should look for fresh challenges on the new frontier of the global economy.

Halfway through the president's first term, Strobe Talbott, who had become deputy secretary of state in the new administration, also sketched out the framework of Clinton's new world order. In October 1994, in a lecture delivered at Oxford University – where he had been a contemporary of Clinton's and himself a Rhodes scholar – Talbott analysed the cold war as not simply 'about land and power'. 'It was also a conflict, protracted, ruthless and in fact quite often rather hot – between competing concepts of how to organize the political and economic lives of individual human beings, of individual states, and of the planet as a whole'. Talbott then restated Fukuyama's 'end of history' argument. 'There's an increasingly universal sense . . . that democracy is the best form of political organization and the free market is the most successful form of economic organization.' Moreover, the idea that 'democracies don't go to war with one another' is now presented as an observation that is 'as close as we're likely to get in political science to an empirical truth'.[29]

What, then, is the administration's perspective on the wider world? Talbott claims that

> President Clinton believes that our generation has a historic opportunity to shape our world. And he believes that since it is, above all, the triumph of

> democracy and markets that has brought us victory in the Cold War, it must be, above all, the *defense* of democracy and markets that should guide us now.[30]

The question remains open, however, as to what should happen where democracy and markets do not exist.

Clinton had necessarily to grapple with some of the contradictions apparent in a world that had moved beyond the ideological rigidities of the cold war. In his Freedom House speech in October 1995, therefore, traditional executive rhetoric – 'we must stand for democracy and freedom' – was blended with the admission that, 'to use the popular analogy of the present day, there seems to be no mainframe explanation for the PC world in which we're living'. The president again denies the distinction between America's national and its international concerns. 'I would almost like to stop hearing people talk about foreign policy and domestic policy, and instead start discussing economic policy, security policy, environmental policy'.[31] In other words, Clinton consistently argues for the interdependence of America's conduct abroad and its policies at home, but still within the context of the assumption that the United States stands unchallenged as the leading nation in the world.

Clinton's shift in emphasis from the language of national defence and security to the language of economic and political interdependence is a clear departure from the revisionist rhetoric of his republican predecessors, Ronald Reagan and George Bush. At the same time, however, the president recognised that some international issues presented different challenges. As he had also observed in his speech at American University,

> the world clearly remains a dangerous place. Ethnic hatreds, religious strife, the proliferation of weapons of mass destruction, the violation of human rights flagrantly in altogether too many places around the world still call on us to have a sense of national security in which our national defense is an integral part.[32]

It was such concerns which defined the reality of American foreign policy early in his presidency, when the administration's desire to assert the traditional values of American moral leadership led to the use of military power in unfamiliar territory.

Michael Mandelbaum argued in *Foreign Affairs* in 1996 that it was 'foreign policy as social work'. So 'the seminal events of the foreign policy of the Clinton administration were three failed military interventions in its first nine months in office'. This was because in Bosnia, Somalia and Haiti, America had been unable to implement a 'distinctive vision of post-Cold War foreign policy' for a simple reason: 'it did not command public support' .[33] Thus, for Mandelbaum,

> historically the foreign policy of the United States has centered on American interests, defined as developments that could affect the lives of American citizens. Nothing occurred in these three countries fit that criterion. Instead, the Clinton interventions were intended to promote American values.[34]

In other words, the new administration tried to pursue a genuinely humanitarian foreign policy in areas of the world that were disconnected with America's strategic interests. But as soon as such actions threatened the lives of American military personnel, public opinion – the 'Vietnam syndrome' again – reacted against further intervention, and benevolent intentions collapsed.

Such a foreign policy was created, in Mandelbaum's view, in the absence of presidential leadership and popular support. There was a 'void'. A combination of circumstances arose in which 'a public and a president less interested in international affairs than at any time in the previous six decades combined with the disappearance of the familiar foreign policy guideposts of the Cold War'.[35] This situation was exploited by former Carter advisers who tried to re-invent his human rights agenda as the context within which foreign policy should be framed, and who once again failed to inspire the American public with a similar vision.

In essence, Mandelbaum attempted to do to Clinton what Strobe Talbott had done to Bush in the preceding presidential election year. This critical view of the administration's foreign policy was intended once more to undermine any political capital that the president had accrued from his achievements in the international arena. Moreover, his foreign policy record raised

> doubt about whether he measured up to the job of chief executive and commander in chief. The conduct of foreign policy was only one part of this problem, but it was likely to prove more convenient as a metaphor for issues of character and leadership than the details of his personal life.[36]

As with most critiques of Clinton, this once again linked the issues of character and leadership, although in his second term his personal life would render any metaphorical analysis of his foreign policy redundant.

If the administration's foreign policy was a form of international humanitarian relief, Iraq remained beyond its scope. Clinton's repeated threats and actions against Saddam Hussein began as apparent aftershocks from his predecessor's failure to bring the Gulf War to an effective political closure, and became a recurrent military motif of his presidency. In June 1993, having found 'compelling evidence' of an Iraqi plot to assassinate George Bush while he was on a visit to Kuwait city, the new president interpreted such action 'as an attack against our country and against all Americans'. In retaliation he authorised the launch of a cruise missile attack on the 'Iraqi Intelligence Service's principal command and control facility in Baghad'.[37] Thereafter, as sanctions against Iraq continued, and Saddam Hussein appeared to play a devious game of hide and seek with United Nation's weapons inspectors seeking details of 'weapons of mass destruction', the Iraqi dictator seemed to take on a similar significance for Clinton as Castro had for Kennedy in the early 1960s. Saddam's continued manoeuvrings led to 'Desert Fox': the sustained military offensive against Iraq in late 1998 – at a time when impeachment proceedings against the president in the House of Representatives were reaching a critical stage. Clinton's policy towards Iraq was hardly social work.

A HERO FOR THE TIMES?:
BILL CLINTON AS FORREST GUMP JR.

In an essay in *Time* magazine in February 1997, in an apt juxtaposition which links Clinton and Kennedy, Charles Krauthammer suggests that contemporary America is witnessing 'the end of heroism'. Heroic leadership is lacking, nowhere more than in American politics. So 'Clinton is the least consequential President in at least 60 years. But maybe it's not him. It's the times'. Whereas Kennedy's inaugural address dealt with fundamental issues facing cold war America, Clinton's end of year radio address forty-five years later 'was devoted to airbag safety. It featured the admonition "We must always wear our seat belts".' It was hardly a memorable mantra or indeed a heroic phrase. Krauthammer concludes that

> the 90s saw a real end to the wars of this century. And with that come fatigue, exhaustion, malaise – and loss of heroism. The romance of struggle is done. As Francis Fukuyama predicted, the West, triumphant, faces the sheer ennui of normal life, . . . Americans are living through Ulysses' nightmare. Our wars are done, our wishes granted. Now we suffer the consequences: the

quiet satisfactions, the banality, of normality. We made it through Scylla and Charybdis – and now what?[38]

The answer came two years later, with the spectacle of presidential impeachment: a meshing of political and constitutional processes that for a time threatened a popular president with removal from office by a Congress in which the vociferous opposition of the Republican right could not quite muster the political clout to realise its ambition.

Krauthammer's article drew attention to the examples of heroism that could be seen in contemporary Hollywood productions. In 1997, then, this was 'a sample of the historical figures currently being lionized at U.S. theaters: one fascist (*Evita*), one Nazi agent (*The English Patient*) and a pornographer with a penchant for sadistic misogyny (*The People vs. Larry Flint*)'. This was 'a reflection of how hard heroes are to come by today. When you are as estranged from the experience – the very idea – of heroism as Americans are, you improvise'.[39] Hollywood was, as usual, both tracking and reflecting the contemporary cultural mood just as earlier in the decade, during the new president's first term, it had also managed to capture the essence of the divide that Clinton tried to bridge.

If the award of an Oscar for best movie of the year has anything to do with the perceived contribution of a film as a commentary upon the cultural concerns of society, then what is to be made of the fact that the drama of the holocaust in *Schindler's List* in 1994 can be considered in the same context as the achievement of *Forrest Gump* in 1995? Is Gump a nostalgic lament for the loss of American innocence when, fifty years before, the United States inherited a world which was discovering in the holocaust the dimensions of the crimes against humanity which have defined much of the history of the twentieth century? In Schindler's story there is the graphic depiction of the human condition in the language of the philosopher Thomas Hobbes: life is 'nasty, brutish and short'. Contrast Gump's fantastic exploits: a portrayal of the possibilities of human enlightenment in a state of simplicity and *naïveté*. Loss of innocence can be avoided through a proper adherence to the terms of a social contract that deems each individual as being of equal worth: the enlightenment idealism which inspired America's Declaration of Independence, and a philosophy which, in contrast to that of Hobbes, is reminiscent of that of John Locke – the 'philosopher of the American revolution'.

Steven Spielberg's portrayal of the pivotal event in twentieth-century Jewish history focuses attention on a minority that could have been ignored as other groups within American society clamoured for attention, and sought too to retrieve their own narratives of betrayal as part of the recognition that multi-culturalism had a past as well as a future. If the history of discrimination is wrong, the film suggests, consider the most appalling case of persecution that had been inflicted upon the Jewish people. As other groups made similar claims – blacks and native Americans for example – and 'ethnic cleansing' became a euphemistic phrase for contemporary genocide, then it was still important not to lose sight of the history of the holocaust. Indeed, it was the president himself who would emphasise the point in his remarks when opening the United States Holocaust Memorial Museum in Washington in April 1993. The museum would thus 'bind one of the darkest lessons in history to the hopeful soul of America'. And for Clinton,

> the Holocaust, to be sure, transformed the entire 20th century, sweeping aside the enlightenment hope that evil somehow could be permanently vanished from the face of the earth; demonstrating there is no war to end all war; that the struggle against the basest tendencies of our nature must continue forever and ever . . . We learn again and again that the world has yet to run its course of animosity and violence. Ethnic cleansing in the former Yugoslavia is but the most brutal and blatant and ever-present manifestation of what we see also with the oppression of the Kurds in Iraq, the abusive treatment of the Baha'i in Iran, the endless race-based violence in South Africa. And in many other places we are reminded again and again how fragile are the safeguards of civilization.[40]

Steven Spielberg's film, then, would reflect the concerns of Clinton's multi-cultural society.

Yet if *Schindler's List* is a feel-good movie about a feel-bad subject, then *Forrest Gump* becomes a simple morality play in which history is a simple unambiguous narrative that has a successful, if not happy, resolution.[41] It is no less significant because of that. Its political message is contained in the central relationship of the film, between Forrest and his childhood sweetheart, Jenny. Like Clinton himself, both characters are children of the post-war, cold war generation – Jenny indeed was born in 1945, the year the war ended. Forrest symbolises the possibilities that would open up to those born into the 'age of affluence'. Although born with a back 'as crooked as a politician', he is able, literally, to run away from his disability. That talent – running – will sustain him throughout the movie. It brings him a college football scholarship and an education. On graduation, he finds a home in the army: his ability to take orders without question makes him an outstanding soldier.

In contrast, Jenny is brought up in poverty and sexually abused by her father. For her there is no escape into the myths and fantasies of the American dream. Instead she is attracted to the radicalism and counter-culture of the 1960s, ultimately to become a victim of its excesses. And embodied in her adult relationship with Forrest are the tensions that characterised America's society and culture caused by the fault-line of Vietnam.

Forrest and Jenny go their separate ways when he is sent to fight in Southeast Asia. On his return – as a hero – they meet again at an anti-war demonstration. When Forrest is invited to address the crowd, in the same place as Martin Luther King made his most famous speech ('I have a dream . . .') his views are never heard: significantly the microphone is sabotaged to make him temporarily one of Nixon's silent majority. Jenny is involved now with anti-war protest and the Black Power movement. They part company again. But when radical politics fail her she goes back to Forrest. They live together for a while, but once more she rejects him. Vietnam is now over, but its legacy lingers: she cannot accept his world of the American dream.

Gump's proposal of marriage comes as America celebrates its Bicentenary, but the reconciliation of dream and counter-culture is not possible at that time. Jenny leaves. Forrest starts running. In so doing he becomes a symbol of hope and unity for the entire country. The act of running becomes a force for healing: it enables the nation to 'put the past behind you'. In the timeframe of the film, Forrest runs until the fall of 1979, only then passing the metaphorical baton to the candidate who formally declared his intention to run for the presidency in November of that year: Ronald Reagan.

In his final reconciliation with Jenny, she apologises to him for her past. She was 'messed up a long time'. She will marry him; they already have a son and a hope for the future. At the wedding, Lieutenant Dan, the disabled veteran arrives with new legs to replace those he lost in the war and a new Vietnamese fiancée. So finally the trauma is in the past. The radical counter-culture of the 1960s – Jenny – has been absorbed back into the mainstream values of the American dream, even though the excesses of the time come back to haunt the present. But when Jenny dies, she has at least made her peace with Forrest.

It is a film which, as Clinton's first term in office drew to a close, provided a commentary on contemporary cultural concerns and a message which, with characteristic political skill, the president moulded to his advantage. Having seen the Democrat majority in Congress wiped out by Republican gains in the mid-term elections of 1994 –

which brough Newt Gingrich to power as speaker of the House of Representatives – Clinton, the 'come-back kid', reinvented himself as Forrest Gump junior, the 'smartest in his class' combining the best elements of a revitalised American dream. In drawing historical parentheses around the Vietnam war, *Forrest Gump* suggested it was time to move on: a theme that characterised Clinton's election campaign in 1996, which aimed at building a 'bridge to the future'.

In his second inaugural address, then, Clinton claimed that 'America stands alone as the world's indispensable nation'. And yet, 'the challenge of our past remains the challenge of our future'. Arguing for an end to racial and religious prejudice, and invoking the spirit of Martin Luther King, the president proclaimed that it was 'time to move on with America's mission', and with the solemnity of an Old Testament preacher, he ended with an exhortation.

> May those generations whose faces we cannot yet see, whose names we may never know, say of us here that we led our beloved land into a new century with the American dream alive for all her children, with the American promise of a more perfect union a reality for all her people, with America's bright flame of freedom spreading throughout all the world.[42]

Forrest Gump junior had come of age.

CONCLUSION:
THE TRIALS OF PRESIDENT CLINTON

'I did not have sexual relations with *that* woman'.[43] For all the lofty rhetoric of the second inaugural, the longest-serving Democrat president since Franklin Roosevelt would be remembered too for that short denial. The woman was Monica Lewinsky, but the remark recalls Lyndon Johnson's realisation that his presidency would be irredeemably tarnished by that 'bitch of a war' in Vietnam. If the war in Southeast Asia had been a test of Clinton's character, so now his relationship with a White House intern would become the defining standard by which his political opponents would seek to show him guilty of 'high crimes and misdemeanours' in the White House: the moral heir of the priapic John F. Kennedy would inherit the fate that should have been that of Richard Nixon.

When radical Republicans protested that the president should be held to account for his standards of moral behaviour in the White House and when Hillary Clinton suggested that there was a vast right-wing conspiracy against her husband, in a sense they were both right. Since Watergate, the issue of morality in American public life had been a recurrent theme. And throughout his presidency, opponents had doubted Clinton's moral and political integrity. His ability to reinvent himself politically – to win re-election after his repudiation at the mid-term elections of 1994 – fuelled their antagonism. Already under investigation for supposed ethical misconduct in the Whitewater case (involving land speculation in Arkansas that occurred prior to his becoming president), early in his first term Clinton was politically damaged by 'travelgate' (dismissing White House travel office employees and replacing them with political appointees), 'filegate' (procuring FBI files improperly) and the suicide of Vince Foster, a close friend who had become a high official in the administration.

Under pressure from Republicans who had gained control of Congress in 1994, Clinton appointed a special prosecutor, Robert Fiske jr., to investigate some of these issues. He was soon replaced by Kenneth Starr. In the same year Paula Jones filed a lawsuit against Clinton alleging sexual harassment while he was governor of Arkansas. The main props were now in place for the subsequent drama of Clinton's presidency. All that was left was to cast the remaining role, the White House intern who had an affair with the president: Monica Lewinsky.

In 1996, Kenneth Starr concluded Vince Foster's death was suicide, and not part of a sinister White House conspiracy to cover up murder. He continued to investigate Whitewater – which by then had led to the trial and conviction of some of Clinton's former associates, and other alleged abuses of power such as 'filegate'. Congress had meanwhile produced a report on the 'travelgate' affair that was critical of the president. But when Clinton was re-elected in November 1996, the many investigations had not found significant evidence of presidential misconduct.

That changed when, in 1997, Monica Lewinsky revealed details of her relationship with the president to Linda Tripp, who had been Foster's former secretary. Brought to the attention of Paula Jones's lawyers, Lewinsky subsequently gave them an affidavit denying the affair with Clinton. After Linda Tripp contacted Kenneth Starr to tell the special prosecutor about her taped conversations with Monica Lewinsky, he was able to pursue an investigation of possible obstruction of justice and perjury involving Clinton, and, when his report was finally delivered to the House judiciary committee, it triggered the impeachment process. In the mean time, there was the spectacle of Clinton's denials and subsequent confession to 'a relationship . . . that was not appropriate', and his philosophical discussion before the grand jury of the meaning of the word 'is'.[44] Meanwhile too the Paula Jones case had been thrown out of court.

The story of Clinton's impeachment, like that of his actions during the Vietnam war, can be approached only through a similar forensic investigation of the complex interactions of events, politics and personalities. It is as if, in the absence of larger crises, the president defined himself in terms of the personal challenges that he had to face and overcome. If Kennedy had the cold war to confront, Clinton had only Kenneth Starr, and the focus of the 'anxious crowd' turned inward upon the interior life of the president himself. Again though, Clinton sensed the popular mood was on his side. In his statement on 17 August 1998, when he talked about his affair with Monica Lewinsky, he observed that in appearing before the grand jury he had responded to questions about his private life which 'no American citizen would ever want to answer'. Seeking to restore the distinction between private morality and public conduct, he suggested that the affair was a personal matter, 'and I intend to reclaim my family life for my family. It's nobody's business but ours. Even Presidents have private lives'. And he went on to argue that 'it is time to stop the pursuit of personal destruction and the prying into public lives, and get on with our national life'.[45] Throughout the impeachment process, and emphatically during the 1998 mid-term elections, he retained popular support for that position, even though it failed to appease his political critics and opponents.

Clinton, however, made another attempt to reach out to the constituency most alienated by his conduct. In the manner if not the style of the Southern revivalist preacher Jimmy Swaggart, whose sexual conduct had also been the subject of scandal, he asked to find redemption through Christian forgiveness. In his remarks at a religious leaders' breakfast in September 1998, he confessed 'I don't think there is a fancy way to say that I have sinned'. But 'to be forgiven, more than sorrow is required'. So repentance was necessary. But Clinton also needed what 'my bible calls a broken spirit'. This does not imply a fractured sense of self so much as a realisation that through the acknowledgement of sin it was possible to achieve 'an understanding that I must have God's help to be the person that I want to be'.[46]

Then, in language reminiscent of that used in the immediate aftermath of Vietnam, the president asked 'for your help in healing our nation. And though I cannot move beyond or forget this – indeed I must always keep it as a caution light in my life – it is very important that our nation move forward'.[47] It as if he is offering himself as a sacrifice: if he continues to accept responsibility for what has occurred, the nation can do what he will never be able to do, forget and move on. It might be, by analogy, a metaphor for Vietnam: accepting the need to make a similar heroic gesture would indeed be the ultimate test of presidential character.

Clinton, as he had done before, survived. And as the trauma of his impeachment came to its end, he summed up his experience: 'I believe any person who asks for forgiveness has to be prepared to give it'.[48] It was another symbolic moment. The president's pyrrhic victory, just like the nation's defeat in Southeast Asia had become framed in the rhetoric of reconciliation. But the political and cultural divisions, along the fault-line of Vietnam, remained.

NOTES

1. The letter is reproduced in Maraniss, *First in His Class*, pp. 199–204. See p. 202.
2. Ibid. p. 201.
3. Ibid. p. 173.
4. Ibid. p. 194.
5. Ibid. p. 200.
6. Bush, 'Remarks at a Victory '92 Dinner', 8 October 1992, Houston, Texas (see Website: George Bush Digital Library).
7. Bush, Clinton and Perot, 'First Presidential Debate' 11 October 1992, St. Louis, Missouri (see Website: George Bush Digital Library).
8. Ibid.
9. Bush, Clinton and Perot, 'Third Presidential Debate' 19 October 1992 in East Lansing, Michigan (see Website: George Bush Digital Library).
10. Ibid.
11. Liebovich, *The Press and the Modern Presidency*, p. 187.
12. Whitman, 'Democratic Vistas', p. 324.
13. Williams, 'Vietnam and the Revival of an Anti-Imperial Mood?', p. 226.
14. Ibid. p. 228.
15. Ibid. p. 234.
16. Ibid. p. 236.
17. Hartz, *The Liberal Tradition in America*, p. 287.
18. Greenstein, 'Political Style and Political Leadership', p. 140.
19. Clinton, 'First Inaugural Address', Thursday, 20 January 1993 (see Website: Presidential Inaugural Addresses).
20. Liebovich, *The Press and the Modern Presidency*, p. 190.
21. Clinton, 'Remarks by the President to the 1993 Annual Convention of the Newspaper Association of America', 25 April 1993' (see Website: White House Electronic Publications).

22. Ibid.
23. Clinton, 'Remarks by the President at National Defense University', 19 July 1993 (see Website: White House Electronic Publications).
24. Hart, 'The Presidency in the 1990s', p. 117.
25. Greenstein, 'Political Style and Political Leadership', p. 139.
26. Clinton, 'Remarks by the President at American University Centennial Celebration', 26 February 1993 (see Website: White House Electronic Publications).
27. Ibid.
28. Ibid.
29. Talbott, 'The New Geopolitics', pp. 3 and 4.
30. Ibid. p. 6.
31. Clinton, 'Remarks by the President in Freedom House Speech' 6 October 1995 (see Website: White House Electronic Publications).
32. Clinton, 'Remarks by the President at American University'.
33. Mandelbaum, 'Foreign Policy as Social Work', p. 16.
34. Ibid. p. 17.
35. Ibid. p. 19.
36. Ibid. p. 32.
37. Clinton, 'Remarks by the President in Address to the Nation', 26 June 1993 (see Website: White House Electronic Publications).
38. Krauthammer, 'The End of Heroism', p. 68.
39. Ibid. p. 68.
40. Clinton, 'Remarks by the President in Reception to Mark the Dedication of the United States Holocaust Memorial Museum', 21 April 1993 (see Website: White House Electronic Publications).
41. *Forrest Gump* was directed by Robert Zemeckis, who also directed *Back to the Future*.
42. Clinton, 'Second Inaugural Address', Monday, 20 January 1997, (see Website: Presidential Inaugural Speeches).
43. Clinton, 'Remarks by the President at the After-School Event', 26 January 1998 (see Website: White House Electronic Publications).
44. Clinton, 'Statement by the President', 17 August 1998 (see Website: White House Electronic Publications).
45. Ibid.
46. Clinton, 'Remarks by the President at Religious Leaders Breakfast', 11 September 1998 (see Website: White House Electronic Publications).
47. Ibid.
48. Clinton, 'Statement by the President', 12 February 1999 (see Website: White House Electronic Publications).

CHAPTER TEN

All-American Heroes?

INTRODUCTION: SEARCHING FOR 'STAR QUALITY'

'I'm an authentic American hero. Really. That's what I am'.[1] Joe Broz, the central character in Larry Beinhart's novel *American Hero* (1993) is an ex-marine, a Vietnam veteran who uncovers a conspiracy. Acting on a deathbed memo from his 1988 campaign strategist Lee Atwater, President George Bush colludes with a top Hollywood producer and director to stage-manage the Gulf War as if it were a studio production. A successful conflict, scripted by professional movie-makers, and designed as a media event, will boost the president's flagging poll ratings and ensure his re-election. Broz, having learnt this sinister truth, is pursued by former colleagues who, like him, had been involved with Operation Phoenix – a CIA-sponsored assassination programme – in Vietnam. At the end of the novel he is revealed as the source of the story which Beinhart has been relating and 'authenticating' through detailed footnotes and references.

In this novel Vietnam veterans apply their 'warrior knowledge' of guerilla warfare in working for a large security corporation in the United States, using techniques of surveillance, and if necessary violence, in the service of American capitalist enterprise. Presidents, focused upon re-election, use any kind of 'dirty trick', even creating a war, in order to achieve their ambition. Hollywood supplies the plot, the script and even the systems of financial management, that guarantee that the conflict will be a 'success'. When a movie director has to develop the scenario for such a war, he finds that his model cannot be Vietnam, the 'mission-impossible'. For

> that was the final insight. The real fundamental problem was that Vietnam wasn't Vietnam. It was never intended to be its own thing. To go back to

Vietnam was to miss the point. The point was to be what Vietnam was supposed to be in the first place – a remake – not for the theaters, for television – of 1942–45: *World War II Two – The Video*.[2]

This, then, becomes the premise of the Gulf War. As Beinhart observes, a story in the *Nation* in May 1992 – 'Pentagon-Media Presents – The Gulf War as Total Television' neatly captured the argument: 'with its million or more uniformed extras, its vast sets . . . its own built-in coming attractions . . . dazzling Star Wars-style graphics, theme music and logos, as well as stunningly prime-timed first moments (Disney-esque fireworks over Baghdad) . . .' the Gulf War was the perfect made-for-television war.[3]

Beinhart's novel would become the basis for a Hollywood movie: *Wag the Dog* (1998), its plot transposed to the Clinton era, so that instead of merely facing low ratings in the public opinon polls, now a president is threatened by the revelation of a sexual scandal in the Oval Office. Both novel and film point to the distance that has been travelled from the time when John F. Kennedy could project himself in the role of heroic president and be believed in it. Following Vietnam and Watergate, a more cynical view of leadership developed, and popular culture reflects the far less heightened climate of expectations surrounding the presidency. And yet, at the same time, the president is still the central character in the drama of national politics.

When JFK came to the office, therefore, Norman Mailer had sensed that as well as the existential hero, he might also be the star of a presidential soap opera. So

> no one had too much doubt that Kennedy would be nominated, but if elected he would be not only the youngest President ever to be chosen by voters, he would be the most conventionally attractive young man ever to sit in the White House, and his wife – some would claim it – might be the most beautiful first lady in our history . . . America's politics would now be also America's favorite movie, America's first soap opera, America's best-seller.[4]

This image of the president as a soap-opera star is one that Mailer himself has reworked during the subsequent forty years. In his estimation there have been only three presidents during this time who qualify, in separate ways, for such an accolade: Kennedy, Reagan and Clinton. Through a combination of personality and personal drama surrounding their time in office, this trio may be seen as one which illustrates the overwhelming significance now attached to the visual image in presidential politics, and the search for elusive 'star quality'.

Kennedy had it. Nixon, his opponent in 1960, did not.[5] Critically, in the mythology of that campaign, the first ever televised debate was lost and won not because of anything the candidates said, but because of how they looked and how they managed the medium. Those who saw Kennedy on television judged him the winner: those who listened on radio thought that Nixon had the better of it. Thereafter, JFK's short tenure as president would be punctuated by lasting images that became part of contemporary television news: speeches such as that which announced America's mission to place a man on the moon, or that claiming 'Ich bin ein Berliner' on a visit to that city. Kennedy on television, talking the nation through the Cuban missile crisis, or seen listening to Marilyn Monroe sing 'Happy Birthday, Mr. President'. But he was not being watched by television cameras, ironically, at the time of the biggest story of them all: the assassination. The film that captured the tragic moment, the Zapruder 8mm home movie of the event, became familiar to most only some twenty-eight years afterwards, as it was incorporated into Oliver Stone's fictionalised account, *JFK*. Kennedy, then, lived in an unprecedented spotlight of media attention. At the moment of his death, its focus was elsewhere.

The four presidents who followed him – Johnson, Nixon, Ford and Carter – could not invest the office with a similar Hollywood-inspired style and glamour. And then a movie star became president. Even so, he was no Kennedy. For as Norman Mailer had observed in 1968, 'Jack Kennedy had looked like the sort of vital leading man who would steal the girl from Ronald Reagan every time'.[6] But by the time he became president, expectations had changed and if Reagan could not lead in an imitation of Kennedy's existential heroic style, like him he could be a soap-opera star. Reflecting on his presidency in 1991, Mailer returned to this theme.

> Reagan established the principle: You cannot be a good President unless you keep the populace entertained. Reagan understood what hard workers like Lyndon Johnson, Richard Nixon, and Jimmy Carter did not – he saw that the President of the United States was the leading soap-opera figure in the great American drama, and one had better possess star value. The President did not have to have executive ability nearly as much as an interesting personality.[7]

Reagan's presidency was kept alive not simply by the fact that he survived an assassination attempt and recovered to become the first president since Eisenhower to complete two terms in the White House.

It was his ability to recognise the power of the image as a tool of political communication, and to be able to connect it with a revisionist rhetoric that many of his audience wished to hear, which made him the popular choice for the role of presidential hero for almost a decade.

If American presidential politics had indeed become a soap opera, then in Bill Clinton it found its perfect lead. He too had star quality, and, like Larry Hagman's character in *Dallas*, his public image would be based upon his uncanny ability to come back from personal and political disasters which would have defeated most other people. So, when he was re-elected in 1996, his legislative agenda having been all but swept away in Newt Gingrich's Republican revolution of the mid-term elections, again in Mailer's view,

> it was likely that Clinton was by now the most fascinating character to come along since J.R. That large share of America's viewers would not wish the Clintons to go off the air. For this is a TV entertainment with the potential to rise above all the video heights of the past, and even the Simpson case could pale before the future adventures of Bill and Hillary.[8]

It was a prescient comment. For the plot and the script of Clinton's presidency during its second term seemed at times to owe more to Hollywood than anything that had come before.

At the same time that the White House became the location of a national political soap opera, and particularly during the 1990s, the presidency also has provided stories for major Hollywood productions. Some, such as Oliver Stone's *JFK* (1991) and *Nixon* (1995) have dramatised events – the assassination, Watergate – to create new and powerful mythologies around the protagonists of the 1960 election. Building upon such fascination with the politics of conspiracy, some films – such as *Absolute Power* (1997) – portray a corrupt president abusing his position to cover up personal indiscretions. On the other hand, others – *Independence Day* (1996) and *Air Force One* (1997) – have tried to reinvent the president as an action hero. Hollywood's contemporary fascination with the presidency appears undiminished.

Again, a little over seven months after *Wag the Dog* opened at cinemas in America, it seemed that the president had taken heed of the plot. In August 1998, four days after he had confessed on nationwide television to an affair with Monica Lewinsky, Bill Clinton ordered the bombing of terrorist bases abroad. His press secretary, Mike McCurry, was asked an obvious question about what the media styled, immediately and inevitably, the 'Wag the Dog theory'. 'Could you at least say that it is life imitating art, possibly, in some ways.' McCurry's reply, 'I'm not a movie critic', stonewalled the enquiry.[9] Nevertheless, the broader question is raised as to the extent to which images of the president and the presidency in popular culture have come to define both the style of the incumbent and the climate of expectations surrounding the office. So Hollywood has cast its contemporary presidents either as personally corrupt and using government as a conspiracy intent on deception, or as straightforward action heroes whose exploits on celluloid may redress the inadequacies of their real counterparts in office.

THE PRESIDENT AT THE MOVIES

Oliver Stone's movie *JFK* takes the idea that had Kennedy lived, Vietnam would have been neither so traumatic nor so disastrous, and seeks to confirm it as a popular cultural myth. As Marcus Raskin suggests, after the assassination, 'some came to believe that if John Kennedy had lived and won a second term, the politics of America would have been much different and the nation would not have passed through the Indochina agony'. *JFK* promotes that belief. So 'in Freudian terms, for Stone President Kennedy is transformed into an imago who would have warded off the evil and difficulties his generation and others passed through'.[10] In the movie version of the event, the mythology of the assassination contributes to the myth of Kennedy himself, and is moulded to generic conventions reminiscent, ironically, of Hollywood's portrayal of the Watergate conspiracy in *All the President's Men* (1976).

Stone's imagination of a vast conspiracy, of which Johnson too was a part, to kill Kennedy because he intended to withdraw American forces from Vietnam, is suggestive of a paranoid style run wild. As John Hellmann puts it, 'viewed in terms of historical fact, the revelation of Vietnam as the motivation for Kennedy's assassination is the most ludicrous aspect of Stone's film'. But 'Stone chooses this explanation because it mythically constructs a powerfully simple version of the more complicated, ambiguous conclusion that things would have been better if Kennedy had lived'.[11] It is in such simplification and exaggeration of the earlier suggestions of Bernard Brodie and others that the popular appeal of the movie lies. When Stone turned his attention to a film biography of Richard Nixon, moreover, it was unsurprising that he embarked on a similar treatment of the historical record based upon the selective interpretation of certain myths.

It was *All the President's Men*, the film based upon the account by the two *Washington Post* reporters Bob Woodward and Carl Bernstein of how they broke the story of Watergate, which established an image of the presidency in the popular imagination. Here government exists not for the benefit of the people, but for those in power. If they are corrupt, they have vast resources at their disposal to maintain a conspiracy of silence that the two journalists can expose only through hard work, bravery and luck. Critical to the movie's plot are the revelations of 'Deep Throat', the informer inside the government who provides vital direction in his meetings with Woodward that allows the journalists to unravel the web of the Watergate scandal. As the investigation proceeds, the president at its centre, Nixon, is seen in documentary, black and white television footage, adding a sense of realism and immediacy to the story.

Similar techniques characterise Oliver Stone's portrayal of the conspiracy surrounding the assassination of *JFK*. The director intercuts documentary and fictional material, and rapid montages of presidential speeches and contemporary images seek to establish a sense of authenticity for the plot. Again, revelations come from an informant, 'X' (Donald Sutherland), who provides the hero of the movie, Jim Garrison (Kevin Costner), with vital information, presumably credible because it comes from a renegade government 'source'. Both 'Deep Throat' and 'X', former members of the conspiracy, by revealing their privileged knowledge, allow other characters and the audience a glimpse of an alternative reality, which, for the sake of the story, is accepted as true. In *All the President's Men*, the denouement is known: by the time the film was released, Nixon had resigned. In the case of *JFK* however, the fictional conspiracy exposed in the movie masquerades as truth and for audiences who now accept the possibility of corruption in government, no theory is too far-fetched.

When the conspiracy genre established in *All the President's Men* and *JFK* is moulded with the biographical portrait of Stone's *Nixon*, the image of a president using the power of the office for corrupt purposes is reinforced. Such a stereotype then reappears in purely fictional accounts of high crimes and misdemeanours at the White House. Even when the corruption involves the cover-up of sexual indiscretion – *Absolute Power* for example – the president (in this case played by Gene Hackman) appears as a Nixon-like character, despite the fact that throughout his political career there was never any question of Nixon's fidelity to his wife. What is equally apparent, however, is the way in which the president as heroic leader has also been re-created on celluloid – an action hero who appears as an idealised image of the times: an integrated portrait of John F. Kennedy and Bill Clinton.

In both *Independence Day* and *Air Force One* the president is young, activist, independent minded and capable of inspirational rhetoric: all stereotypical qualities associated with JFK. His family circumstance – married with a daughter – is, however, an image of the Clintons. But unlike him, both these movie presidents are authentic war heroes, one of the Gulf War, the other of Vietnam. And in the face of crisis, they too can use their 'warrior knowledge' to survive the threat, whether it is alien invasion or terrorist kidnap. These, then, are presidents with courage, moral integrity, and charismatic style, who are ennobled by the office they hold. Such films appear as nostalgic attempts to reinvent the president as heroic leader in a world where such leadership has failed. Yet in this confusion of popular culture and political life, if Bill Pullman is no Jack Kennedy, so Bill Clinton, indeed, is no Harrison Ford.

There is, then, a symbiotic relationship between Hollywood and the presidency. Those presidents – notably Kennedy and Reagan – who have had what George Bush famously called 'the vision thing' have been able to articulate their political ideals in a rhetoric which connects their contemporary view of the nation with the mythologies of its past. That too has been the business of Hollywood. It has created images of America – notably the American west – that have become 'real' in the minds of its audience. And just as movie-makers can look to the White House for scenarios, narratives and plots, so presidents may co-opt the myths made in Hollywood as a way of similarly appealing to a mass audience. It was Kennedy's particular genius, then, to recast the rhetoric of the cold war in an accessible Hollywood idiom. For many – including intellectuals and historians – brought up in movie-made America would understand immediately the attractive appeal of the enduring metaphor of the frontier.

THE ENDURING METAPHOR OF THE FRONTIER

Kennedy was not alone in exploiting the mythological cachet of the frontier. It had been explored in the work of the consensus historians of the 1950s, and again, in 1992, Francis Fukuyama's book *The End of History and the Last Man* ended with a reference to the familiar historical myth, encapsulated in an extended metaphor. So mankind will come to seem like a long wagon train strung out along a road. Some wagons will be pulling into town sharply and crisply, while others will be bivouacked back in the desert, or else stuck in ruts in the final pass over the mountains. Several wagons, attacked by Indians, will have been set aflame and abandoned along the way. There will be a few wagoneers who, stunned by the battle, will have lost their sense of direction and are temporarily heading in the wrong direction, while one or two wagons will get tired of the journey and decide to set up permanent camps at particular points back along the road. Others will have found alternative routes to the main road, though they will discover that to get through the final mountain range they must all use the same pass. But the great majority of wagons will be making the slow journey into town, and most will eventually arrive there.[12]

Here, then, the advance of democracy in the post-cold war era is connected once again with images of America's pioneer experience and the expansion of the democratic frontier. If the consensus historians of the 1950s had circled their wagons in defence of the 'vital center' against the extremes of the totalitarian left, now, with the resolution of the cold war, the intellectual wagon train may resume its journey, re-creating the triumphant mythology of the nation's providential mission. Then, as now, the enduring metaphor of the frontier endorses and justifies America's distinctive liberal democratic and capitalist world-view.

During the 1950s, American historiography reflected the contemporary concerns of the 'culture of contingency'. Events such as the slump of the 1930s, the second world war and the revelations of the holocaust reflected a reality that differed from the relentless optimism of the American dream. Moreover, the invention and use of the atomic bomb now defined the terms of what might be possible should international tensions – the cold war – escalate to superpower confrontation. In such an atmosphere, consensus history offered both reassurance and hope. By recasting their past as a pageant, and imbuing their progress across both space and time with a sense of providential mission and purpose, Americans might escape from Marx's historical determinism into a narrative of exceptionalism and an alternative rendezvous with destiny. And it was the mythology of the frontier which gave both intellectual and populist appeal to such an argument. The frontier experience, Turner had argued, made not simply America but also Americans exceptional. In the 1950s, as Richard Hofstadter outlined the American political tradition, he focused on those who, like the pioneers, appeared to transcend the mundane flow of history, who

through their ideas or their actions had been able to shape the pattern of America's past into a heritage that defined both the present and the future. Similarly, Daniel Boorstin isolated the genius of American politics through recasting the relevance of Turner's frontier thesis for the cold war generation. And yet, if consensus atrophied into 1950s' conformity, then Louis Hartz also recognised the potential limitations of cold war historiography. Exceptionalism was built upon philosophical myopia and an inability to appreciate cultural diversity. Hartz, who would eventually leave America for an itinerant life overseas, could not resolve the intellectual dilemma at the heart of consensus history: can a people 'born equal' understand those struggling to become so? For many of his contemporaries, however, it was an irrelevant question.

The principal task of consensus history was instead to focus upon the maintenance of the 'vital center' which might be under attack from everywhere: from the totalitarianisms of the right and the left, from un-American activities at home and a communist conspiracy abroad. And yet, the 'great fear' of ideological subversion impacted upon American culture in a variety of ways. On the one hand, it encouraged conformity: the alien was mistrusted, the aberrant abhorred. On the other it created complacency. The comforting stereotype of the 1950s was one of affluence, peace and harmony: the reality was a society increasingly under pressure as the 'vital center' appeared robbed of vitality. As the decade wore on, the veneer cracked. Events as apparently disconnected as the attempt to desegregate the school system in Little Rock, Arkansas in 1957 – a seminal event in the story of the struggle for civil rights – and the Soviet Union's launch of sputnik in the same year served to show that America had problems at home and abroad which required new leadership, if not fresh vision.

'Probably, we will never be able to determine the psychic havoc of the concentration camps and the atom bomb upon the unconscious mind of almost everyone alive in these years.' The opening sentence of Norman Mailer's 1959 essay, 'The White Negro: Superficial Reflections on the Hipster' contextualises not only the continuing horrors of the holocaust but also the fear which characterised the postwar world: when the prospect of nuclear conflict between two ideologically opposed superpowers rendered individuals powerless in the face of such an apocalyptic prospect. Indeed, for Mailer,

no wonder, then, that these have been the years of conformity and depression. A stench of fear has come out of every pore of American life, and we suffer from a collective failure of nerve. The only courage, with rare exceptions, that we have been witness to has been the isolated courage of isolated people.[13]

The choice, then, is clear: to become the existential 'hipster' or to remain the conformist 'square'.

> One is Hip or one is Square (the alternative that each new generation coming into American life is beginning to feel), one is a rebel or one conforms, one is a frontiersman in the Wild West of American night life or else a Square cell, trapped in the totalitarian tissues of American society, doomed willy-nilly to conform if one is to succeed.[14]

The prospect of action, excitement and adventure is contained in another image of the frontier. It exists as a metaphorical space, co-opted by successive generations of Americans as an enduring motif: symbol of the nation's political culture and indeed, for Mailer, of its counter-culture.

Then came Kennedy. Whereas Eisenhower had been a hero rewarded in his election as leader, here was a new president who would define himself in office through acts of heroic leadership. In his inaugural address, he emphasised the fact that his election represented a generational shift in American political leadership:

> Let the word go forth from this time and place, to friend and foe alike, that the torch has been passed to a new generation of Americans – born in this century, tempered by war, disciplined by a hard and bitter peace, proud of our ancient heritage – and unwilling to witness or permit the slow undoing of those human rights to which this Nation has always been committed, and to which we are committed today at home and around the world.[15]

At the same time, the new frontier was like the old frontier: a place of challenge, of achievement, shaping national character and defining national purpose. President Kennedy – indeed the 'focus of the anxious crowd' – created and projected the image of the heroic leader, facing and meeting the crises of cold war confrontations.

THE 'TRUE HERO' AND THE 'SHAM HERO'

Kennedy's legacy was not simply his heroic style. His administration had set an agenda for international activism that included a continuing commitment to 'nation building' in South Vietnam. This would persist even though increasing disillusionment in the choice of domestic

architect – Ngo Dinh Diem – led to at the least a moral complicity in the
coup that ousted him. Kennedy's assassination then came as South
Vietnam was entering a time of extreme political instability, presenting
the United States with choices that JFK – the fallen hero – did not have
to make. As Brian VanDeMark observes,

> Diem's overthrow – however predictable given his peremptory rule – un-
> leashed powerful and unpredictable forces of fateful significance to U.S.-
> Vietnamese relations. The responsibility for this development rested with
> John Kennedy; its consequences confronted his successor, Lyndon John-
> son.[16]

And from LBJ through to Bill Clinton, presidential leadership would be
projected not simply in the shadow of JFK but also of the war for which
he wrote the score but never had the opportunity to orchestrate.

America's war in Vietnam destroyed Johnson's presidency. It defined
Richard Nixon's term in the White House, and its aftershocks continue.
In Gerald Ford's administration, North Vietnam invaded the South
and unified the nation. Jimmy Carter then exploited the popular feeling
of disillusionment caused by war and Watergate to be elected president,
only to find that the national 'malaise' – of which the 'Vietnam
syndrome' was a part – effectively undermined faith in his ability to
lead. Ronald Reagan, redefining Vietnam as a 'noble cause', embarked
on a process of historical revisionism aimed at absorbing popular
memories of the war into the mythologies of American history; a
process continued by his successor George Bush, who fought a war
in the Gulf in part to try finally to 'overcome the Vietnam syndrome'.
And Bill Clinton, the first commander-in-chief to have personal experience of the political dilemmas forced upon his generation as a result
of the nation's involvement in the Vietnam war encapsulates the
ambiguities of its legacy. So presidential leadership after Kennedy
must be contextualised in relation to America's war in Southeast Asia:
the most significant event in the nation's late twentieth-century history.
Vietnam, and its impact upon American politics, society and culture,
has been the challenge which, in separate and distinctive ways, has
faced each American president from Kennedy through to Clinton. In
the beginning, it was a cold war crisis which might help define the
president's heroic style of leadership. In the end, it has become a
continuing reminder of the fault-lines in American political culture
which make the task of heroic leadership Kennedy-style that much
more difficult.

At the Republican convention in 1992 a five-minute film was shown, the star of which was George Bush. This home movie as political advertisement reached 'back into the past in an attempt to carry over the ethos of past presidents to the current one'. There were brief references to the administrations of George Washington, Thomas Jefferson and Abraham Lincoln, and to twentieth-century presidents: the Roosevelts, Eisenhower, Kennedy, Nixon – a measure of Republican self-confidence and the success of his post-Watergate political rehabilitation – and Ronald Reagan. As David Timmerman suggests,

> the portrayal of the nine presidents places them in the role of epic figures. These were men who changed the course of history and fought battles for American sovereignty, individual freedom, democracy and world peace. They stood fast in the face of superior odds and tremendous obstacles. They led the nation at critical moments and their actions always led to victory. Bush is not only shown to be their equal, he is shown to possess all the qualities they demonstrated . . . The film presents George Bush as the present day embodiment of these great presidents from the past. He too is a heroic leader.[17]

But Bush existed only as a celluloid hero. By 1992, the idea of presidential heroic leadership – a manifestation of America's cold war culture and symbolised in the Kennedy myth – had become tainted by the legacy of Vietnam. The campaign drama of that year reflected an idiom which, when combined with Bush's own popular image – the 'wimp factor' – once more demonstrated the credibility gap that had emerged between leader and led. Twenty years earlier, writing his history of the Kennedy administration, David Halberstam had recollected a different mood.

> It seems so long ago now, that excitement which swept through the country, or at least the intellectual reaches of it, that feeling that America was going to change, that the government had been handed down from the tired, flabby, chamber-of-commerce mentality of the Eisenhower years to the best and brightest of a generation.[18]

The Kennedy and the Bush presidencies had been separated by wars of different kinds and fought for different purposes: Vietnam and its legacy, the cold war and its denouement and the Gulf War and its aftermath. The president's capacity to lead – and lead in the heroic style of a JFK – had been tried and tested, and had been found wanting.

Vietnam, compounded by Watergate, destroyed collective faith in the ideal of the hero as president. The revisionism of the 1980s attempted to change popular attitudes to such events. For Paul Brace and Barbara Hinckley, indeed, 'they have been redefined from problems of decision making to problems of public support'. Reagan's success in defusing the Iran-Contra scandal – potentially more serious than Watergate in that it amounted to the partial privatisation of American foreign policy itself – showed that 'illegal and unconstitutional acts might continue, but they would not result in impeachment or resignation, given proper management at the White House'. The shadow of defeat in Vietnam might be similarly air-brushed from history by the clarity of victory in the Gulf. So 'the nation would continue to go to war, but the wars would not be unpopular, nor would they show the casualties and civilian damage that might make them so'. Irangate and the Gulf become derivatives of Watergate and Vietnam: each 'in its own way was a public-relations victory'.[19] But both gave no hint of what was to come: the impeachment crisis that threatened Bill Clinton's presidency.

Consider, then, Thomas Carlyle. His nineteenth-century theory of hero worship was, for Ernst Cassirer, perhaps the most important philosophical basis for the establishment of 'the modern ideals of political leadership'. And so,

> according to Carlyle there are two criteria by which we can easily distinguish the true hero from the sham hero: his 'insight' and his 'sincerity'. Carlyle could never think or speak of lies as necessary or legitimate weapons in great political struggles.[20]

What Irangate, the Gulf War and then Clinton's behaviour in office demonstrated is the continuing tendency of presidents to act as Carlyle's sham hero for reasons of political expediency and when faced with the complicated legacy of the Vietnam war.

If Clinton's election, like Kennedy's, represented a generational transformation of American politics, he could not escape his history. In Norman Mailer's words, 'after two years in the White House, it was clear that Clinton's past was a puddle and he was sitting in it'.[21] His inability to project himself as an authentic heroic leader depended as much on the persistence of a credibility gap between president and public – demonstrated in the way in which personal and political scandals had become both accepted and dismissed as only to be expected in the public sphere – as it does on force of circumstance. Clinton survived in part because since Vietnam, and particularly in the 1990s, the president had been exposed as a sham hero: in an era of diminished expectations, standards of political and personal morality were of less concern than the continuing drama of the soap-opera presidency.

CONCLUSION: HEROIC LEADERSHIP FROM KENNEDY TO CLINTON

The presidency is a historic theatre in which the hero seeks the centre stage. In the history of the republic, the men who have thus far held the office number no more than might play in a season for an average size American football team. The focus of this book has been on those who became chief executive over a span of forty years, from the thirty-fifth president, John Fitzgerald Kennedy, to the forty-second, William Jefferson Clinton. For each of them, on coming to the office, there is the reminder that whatever they achieve as president, it will be measured against the legacy of their predecessors in the office. Where will they rank in terms of greatness? Will they be members of the presidential hall of fame alongside George Washington, Abraham Lincoln and Franklin Roosevelt? Or will their administrations be as immemorable as those of Millard Fillmore, Franklin Pierce and Chester Arthur? And after Kennedy's assassination, in contemporary terms too, how might his successors deal with the shadow of JFK?

For Kennedy took office at the height of the cold war. His aim was to win it. Using the rhetoric of the new frontier and by facing and overcoming crises, he created an image and a style of heroic leadership which his assassination crystallised in the popular mind. Moreover, the mythic intuition of his admirers, that if he had lived things would not only have been different but better, implied that those who immediately followed him in office had 'usurped' his legacy, a view reinforced when his brother Bobby, the 'rightful heir', was murdered too. But Kennedy also left behind both a commitment and a problem: Vietnam.

Lyndon Johnson's involvement in the Vietnam war was the product both of the rhetoric of mission and exceptionalism which fuelled the cold war, and his interpretation of his predecessor's policy in Southeast Asia. As the war unravelled, Johnson was left with a rhetoric that no longer made sense in the face of a reality that contradicted it at every turn. His critics, particularly those for whom the myth of Kennedy held a transcendent appeal, looked to the messenger – Johnson – rather than the message. The president was neurotic, dsyfunctional. An impulse to use the language of psychoanalysis as a means of expressing personal and political opposition to a president and his policies became part of a consistent critique. It would create a presidential stereotype and be applied to others, not least to Richard Nixon, but also to Bill Clinton.[22]

If Lyndon Johnson was a casualty of war, Richard Nixon was a heroic failure. Defining himself in the shadow of JFK, his political motivation was to outdo Kennedy: one part of that objective was to win the war in Vietnam. As president, however, Nixon, like Johnson, had to face the credibility gap that had emerged between political rhetoric and popular belief in the capacity of the chief executive to act in the role of heroic leader. Instead of solving this problem, Nixon exacerbated it. His covert policies in Southeast Asia had the effect of widening the war and of giving his administration something to hide. As Watergate eventually forced him to resign, and brought about the collapse of the 'imperial presidency', he too would be portrayed by his critics as psychologically flawed and disturbed.

After over a decade of war and Watergate, Gerald Ford correctly diagnosed a sickness in the body politic. He co-opted the rhetoric of his hero, Abraham Lincoln, in an attempt to 'heal' the nation after the symbolic civil war that had been waged within America over such divisive issues. His temporary and unelected tenure of office then was broken by the born-again 'outsider', Jimmy Carter. Yet Carter's transient populist appeal rapidly ruptured when his administration was metaphorically taken hostage along with the Americans in the embassy in Tehran, and all he could offer in his defence was a diagnosis of America's 'malaise'.

Ronald Reagan was a more successful therapist than either of his two immediate predecessors. His successful use of rhetoric, like that of JFK, was based upon his ability to connect his ideas with images from America's past: a nostalgic vision that, because of his age, he seemed to embody within his own experience and lifetime. In surviving the attempt to assassinate him he endorsed the mythology that if Kennedy had lived things would have been different: Reagan lived, and throughout the 1980s, his supporters would argue, things *did* become better. Vietnam was reinvented as a 'noble cause': revisionist sentiments played well to a receptive audience. The president was able to survive the Irangate scandal – again proving himself more than Nixon's equal – because many still wanted to believe in Reagan's world.

Although he identified the 'Vietnam syndrome' as a constraint upon the projection of American power abroad, Reagan could not overcome it. In this respect, George Bush tried to outdo his predecessor. The Gulf War became a symbolic event which aimed to eviscerate the effects of Vietnam upon American political life. It was fought with such a revisionist agenda in mind. But as long as Saddam Hussein, Bush's demonised opponent, remained in power, the impact of the president's 'victory' was diluted. Nor did his attempt to undermine the challenge of Bill Clinton in 1992 through references to his conduct during the Vietnam war ultimately improve Bush's political credibility. When he lost that election, the second generational shift in post-war American politics occurred.

Bill Clinton was not Jack Kennedy. His problem, if he was to reinvent himself as a potentially heroic president, was that he came to the White House in a complex and fragmented multi-cultural age: one disillusioned by its heroes, and – influenced by Hollywood – more cynical in its view of the president as leader in the post-cold war era. Clinton thus was not able to offer the nation a fresh vision, a rhetoric connected with historical myth, when such myths themselves were challenged by those who sought to construct a more heterogeneous sense of America's past. Instead there seemed only his belief in 'a place called Hope'. His fortunately named home-town proved at times to be a metaphor for his presidency. At times it seemed that it was all he could do. Clinton's image became defined in terms of his conduct in a series of personal crises, culminating in what turned out to be the *ersatz* drama of impeachment: a challenge that in political terms he was able to survive – his opponents in Congress never had the votes to convict him – but which had still to be played out to dramatic effect on the world's television screens. Yet for some, the president did become a hero of sorts.

In October 1998 in *The New Yorker* the novelist Toni Morrison thus wrote:

> African-American men seemed to understand it right away. Years ago, in the middle of the Whitewater investigation, one heard the first murmurs: white skin notwithstanding, this is our first black President. Blacker than any actual black person who could ever be elected in our children's lifetime. After all, Clinton displays almost every trope of blackness: single-parent household, born poor, working-class, saxophone-playing, McDonald's-and-junk-food-loving boy from Arkansas. And when virtually all the African-American Clinton appointees began, one by one, to disappear, when the President's body, his privacy, his unpoliced sexuality became the focus of the persecution, when he was metaphorically seized and body-searched, who could gainsay these black men who knew whereof they spoke?[23]

Such a characterisation then begs further questions. Could the 'black president' be the 'white negro'? Is Clinton to be seen as a version of

Mailer's infamous character, who adopts an existential perspective on life, gambling 'with all his energies through all those small or large crises of courage and unforeseen situations that beset his day'?[24] Like Kennedy, then, Clinton might be the 'hipster' as president: perhaps, indeed, more comfortable in that role than was JFK. He becomes the product of what, for Mailer was a cultural 'menage-à-trois'. When 'the bohemian and the juvenile delinquent came face-to-face with the Negro, . . . the hipster was a fact in American life'. Moreover, 'if marijuana was the wedding ring' (although Clinton never inhaled), 'the child was the language of Hip' (which became the slang of the baby-boomers), and the music was jazz (as the aspiring president reminded an audience on the Arsenio Hall show with an improvised saxophone solo).[25] Clinton, then, is representative of his generation. Like Kennedy, he helps to define the 'spirit of the age'. He is a president in whom the cultural and counter-cultural values of contemporary America may collide and coexist in uneasy tension.

From Theodore White's account of the 1960 election campaign, the first in his *The Making of the President* series, in which the hero of his story was undoubtedly JFK, to the best-selling satire of Clinton's first campaign, *Primary Colors* (which in turn became a Hollywood movie), the contemporary presidency has continued to fascinate the 'anxious crowd of the age'. The inspirational rhetoric of Kennedy's inaugural address and the bathos of Clinton's impeachment become scenes in the continuing drama of American political life. They are connected. For in the last forty years of the twentieth century – the American century – the nation's political culture may be seen as a product of that rare combination of politics, personalities and events which focuses attention upon the abilities and the actions of its leader. Each president has had to build upon or battle against the achievements and the mistakes of those who have gone before. When he recalls his meeting with John F. Kennedy in that summer of 1963, therefore, with America's war in Vietnam yet to be fought, and its cultural aftershocks unimagined, Bill Clinton might reflect that history is moulded by more than just a handshake.

NOTES

1. Beinhart, *American Hero*, p. 7.
2. Ibid. p. 214.
3. Ibid. p. 395.
4. Mailer, 'Superman Comes to the Supermarket', p. 21.

5. Eisenhower once observed of Nixon that he 'lacked star quality'. Quoted in Evans, *The American Century*, p. 483.
6. Mailer, 'Miami and the Siege of Chicago', p. 632.
7. Mailer, 'How the Wimp Won the War', p. 1084.
8. Mailer, 'Clinton and Dole', p. 1150.
9. Berger and McCurry, Press Briefing, 21 August 1998 (see Website: White House Electronic Publications).
10. Raskin, '*JFK* and the Culture of Violence', p. 490.
11. Hellmann, *The Kennedy Obsession*, pp. 160 and 161.
12. Fukuyama, *The End of History and the Last Man*, pp. 338–9.
13. Mailer, 'The White Negro: Superficial Reflections on the Hipster', pp. 211 and 212.
14. Ibid. p. 212.
15. Kennedy, 'Inaugural Address', Friday 20 January 1961, (see Website: Presidential Inaugural Addresses).
16. VanDeMark, *Into the Quagmire*, p. 8.
17. Timmerman, '1992 Presidential Candidate Films', p. 370.
18. Halberstam, *The Best and the Brightest*, pp. 50–1.
19. Brace and Hinckley, *Follow the Leader*, pp. 162–3.
20. Cassirer, *The Myth of the State*, p. 216.
21. Mailer, 'Clinton and Dole', p. 1148.
22. See Fick, *The Dysfunctional President*, as an example of speculative psychoanalysis.
23. Morrison in 'The Talk of the Town' p. 32. Her characterisation of Clinton was widely quoted. See, for example, Powell, 'For Democrats a Defining Moment'; and Morrow, 'Why I'm Still Angry'.
24. Mailer, 'The White Negro', p. 212.
25. Ibid. p. 213.

Bibliography

Presidential Speeches and Documents

A number of relevant speeches and documents are available on the Internet. The following have been used for citations in the text.

Presidential Inaugural Addresses
  http://www.ideasign.com/chilast/pdocs/inaugural/inaug.html
Annual Messages to Congress on the State of the Union
  http.//www.castle.net/~rfrone/history/
Gerald Ford Library and Museum
  http://www.lbjlib.utexas.edu/ford/
Ronald Reagan Speeches
  http://www.Reagan.webteamone.com/speeches/
George Bush Digital Library
  http://www.csdl.tamu.edu/bushlib/papers
  (also includes transcripts of Bush-Clinton-Perot presidential debates, 1992)
White House Electronic Publications
  http://www1.ai.mit.edu/publications.html
  (for transcripts of Clinton's speeches, statements and remarks, and press conferences)
Bentsen-Quayle Vice-Presidential Debate, 1988
  http://www.debates.org/Debates/bq-88.htm

Other Sources

Aitken, J. (1993) *Nixon: A Life*, London: Weidenfeld & Nicolson.
Aldridge, J. (1971) 'From Vietnam to Obscenity', in R. Lucid (ed.), *Norman Mailer: The Man and His Work*, Boston: Little, Brown & Co., 1971.
Ambrose, S. (1987) *Nixon: The Education of a Politician*, 1913–1962, New York: Simon & Schuster.

Ambrose, S. (1989) *Nixon: The Triumph of a Politician, 1962–1972*, New York: Simon & Schuster.

Anonymous (1996) *Primary Colors*, London: Vintage.

Bagehot, W. (1900) *Physics and Politics*, London: Kegan Paul, Trench, Trubner & Co.

Bailey, T. and Kennedy, D. (1991) *The American Spirit*, Lexington, Mass.: D.C. Heath & Co.

Baker, J. (1989) 'A New Europe, a New Atlanticism: Architecture for a New Era', Washington DC: US Department of State.

Ball, G. (1982) *The Past Has Another Pattern*, New York: W. W. Norton & Co.

Bass, J. (1992) 'The Paranoid Style in Foreign Policy', in M. Weiler & W. B. Pearce (eds.), *Reagan and Public Discourse in America*, Tuscaloosa: University of Alabama Press.

Bassett, L. and Petz, S. (1989) 'The Failed Search for Victory: Vietnam and the Politics of War', in T. Paterson (ed.), *Kennedy's Quest for Victory*, New York: Oxford University Press.

Beinhart, L. (1995) *American Hero*, London: Arrow Books.

Benson, L. (1969) 'The Historian as Mythmaker: Turner and the Closed Frontier', in D. Ellis (ed.), *The Frontier in American Development*, Ithaca: Cornell University Press.

Beschloss, M. (1997) *Taking Charge*, New York: Simon & Schuster.

Billington, R. (1973) *Frederick Jackson Turner*, New York: Oxford University Press.

Blankenship, J. and Muir, J. (1992) 'The Transformation of Actor to Scene: Some Strategic Grounds of the Reagan Legacy', in M. Weiler & W. B. Pearce (eds), *Reagan and Public Discourse in America*, Tuscaloosa: University of Alabama Press.

Bonazzi, T. (1993) 'Frederick Jackson Turner's Frontier Thesis and the Self-Consciousness of America', *Journal of American Studies*, vol. 27, no. 2, pp. 149–71.

Boorstin, D. (1953) *The Genius of American Politics*, Chicago: University of Chicago Press.

Boyer, P. (ed.) (1990) *Reagan as President*, Chicago: Ivan R. Dee.

Brace, P. and Hinckley, B. (1992) *Follow the Leader*, New York: Basic Books.

Bradlee, B. (1975) *Conversations with Kennedy*, New York: W. W. Norton & Co.

Brammer, B. L. (1983) *The Gay Place*, London: Blond & Briggs.

Brodie, B. (1973) *War and Politics*, New York: Macmillan.

Brodie, F. (1983) *Richard Nixon: The Shaping of His Character*, Cambridge, Mass.: Harvard University Press.

Brown, T. (1988) *JFK: History of an Image*, London: I. B. Taurus & Co.

Brzezinski, Z. (1966) 'Tomorrow's Agenda', *Foreign Affairs*, vol. 44, pp. 662–70.

Burdick, E. and Wheeler, H. (1962) *Fail Safe*, New York: McGraw-Hill.

Bussey, C. (1996) 'Jimmy Carter: Hope and Memory versus Optimism and Nostalgia', in E. Hurup (ed.), *The Lost Decade: America in the Seventies*, Aarhus: Aarhus University Press.

Campbell, J. (1968) *The Hero with a Thousand Faces*, Princeton: Princeton University Press.

Campbell, K. and Jamieson, K. (1990) *Deeds Done in Words: Presidential Rhetoric and Genres of Governance*, Chicago: University of Chicago Press.

Carter, J. (1982) *Keeping Faith*, New York: Bantam Books.

Cassirer, E. (1975) *The Myth of the State*, New Haven: Yale University Press.

Caute, D. (1978) *The Great Fear*, New York: Simon & Schuster.

Chomsky, N. (1973) *The Backroom Boys*, London: Fontana/Collins.

Combs, J. (1993) *The Reagan Range: The Nostalgic Myth in American Politics*, Bowling Green: Bowling Green State University Popular Press.

Commager, H. (1951) *Living Ideas in America*, New York: Harper & Brothers.

Congressional Quarterly Weekly Report.

Crèvecœur, H. St. John de (1951) *Letters from an American Farmer*, New York: E. P. Dutton & Co.

Crowley, M. (1998) *Nixon in Winter*, New York: Random House.

Cunliffe, M. (1974) 'New World, Old World: The Historical Antithesis', in Richard Rose (ed.), *Lessons from America: an Exploration*, London: Macmillan.

Dallek, R. (1991) *Lone Star Rising: Lyndon Johnson and His Times, 1908–1960*, Oxford: Oxford University Press.

Degler, C. 'Remaking American History', *Journal of American History*, vol. 67, no. 1. pp. 7–25.

Diggins, J. (1988) 'Knowledge and Sorrow: Louis Hartz's Quarrel with American History', *Political Theory*, vol. 16, no. 3, pp. 355-76.

Doctorow, E. L. (1992) 'The Character of Presidents', *Nation*, 9 November

Dugger, R. (1982) *The Politician: The Life and Times of Lyndon Johnson*, New York: W. W. Norton & Co.

Dumbrell, J. (1995) *The Carter Presidency: A Re-Evaluation*, Manchester: Manchester University Press.

Efaw, F. (1976) 'Amnesty: Carter's First Issue', *Nation*, 4 December.

Ehrhart, W. D. (1999) *Ordinary Lives: Platoon 1005 and the Vietnam War*, Philadelphia: Temple University Press.

Emerson, R. (1903) 'Heroism', in J. Cabot (ed.), *Complete Works*, vol. I, London: Routledge.

Emerson, R. (1960–1) 'The Erosion of Democracy', *Journal of Asian Studies*, vol. 20, no. 1, pp. 1–8.

Emery, F. (1994) *Watergate: The Corruption and Fall of Richard Nixon*, London: Pimlico.

Engelhardt, T. (1995) *The End of Victory Culture*, New York: Basic Books.

Evans, H. (1998) *The American Century*, London: Jonathan Cape/Pimlico.

Fick, P. (1995) *The Dysfunctional President: Inside the Mind of Bill Clinton*, New York: Citadel Press.

FitzGerald, F. (1972) *Fire in the Lake*, Boston: Little, Brown & Co.

Ford, G. (1979) *A Time to Heal*, London: W. H. Allen & Co.

Foster, R. (1971) 'Norman Mailer', in R. Lucid (ed.), *Norman Mailer: The Man and His Work*, Boston: Little, Brown & Co.

Freud, S. (1930) *Civilization and Its Discontents*, London: The Hogarth Press.

Freud, S. (1955) 'Totem and Taboo', in J. Stachey (ed.) *Complete Psychological Works*, vol. XIII, London: The Hogarth Press.

Freud, S. and Bullitt, W. (1967) *Thomas Woodrow Wilson*, London: Weidenfeld & Nicolson.

Friedman, R. and Moore, J. (1990) 'Introduction', in J. Moore (ed.), *The Vietnam Debate: A Fresh Look at the Arguments*, Maryland: University Press of America.

Frielander, S. (1978) *History and Psychoanalysis*, New York: Holmes & Meier Publishers.

Fuchs, L. W. (1967) *Those Peculiar Americans*, New York: Meredith Press.

Fukuyama, F. (1989) 'The End of History?', *Public Interest*, Summer, pp. 3–18.

Fukuyama, F. (1992) *The End of History and the Last Man*, New York: The Free Press.

Gaffney, F. (1991) 'Return of the Syndrome', *The Washington Times*, 18 April.

Gay, P. (1988) *Freud: A Life for Our Times*, New York: W. W. Norton & Co.

Germond, J. and Witcover, J. (1981) *Blue Smoke and Mirrors: How Reagan Won and Why Carter Lost the Election of 1980*, New York: The Viking Press.

Gibbons, W. (1986) *The US Government and the Vietnam War*, Princeton: Princeton University Press.

Gibson, J. W. (1988) *The Perfect War*, New York: Vintage Books.

Gibson, J. W. (1991) 'The Return of Rambo: War and Culture in the Post-Vietnam Era', in A. Wolfe (ed.), *America at Century's End*, Berkeley: University of California Press.

Gordon, M. and Trainor, B. (1995) *The Generals' War: The Inside Story of the Conflict in the Gulf,* Boston: Little, Brown & Co.

Godden, R. (1990) *Fictions of Capital*, Cambridge: Cambridge University Press.

Graebner, W. (1990) *The Age of Doubt: American Thought and Culture in the 1940s*, Boston: Twayne.

Graham, K. (1997) *Personal History*, London: Weidenfeld & Nicolson.

Grazia, A. de (1969) 'The Myth of the President', in A. Wildavsky (ed.), *The Presidency*, Boston: Little, Brown & Co.

Gelb, L. and Betts, R. (1979), *The Irony of Vietnam: The System Worked*, Washington, DC: The Brookings Institution.

Greene, J. (1995) *The Presidency of Gerald R. Ford*, Kansas: University of Kansas Press.

Greenstein, F. (1995) 'Political Style and Political Leadership: The Case of Bill Clinton' in S. Renshon (ed.), *The Clinton Presidency*, Boulder: Westview Press.

Halberstam, D. (1973) *The Best and the Brightest*, London: Pan Books.

Haldeman, H. R. (1978) *The Ends of Power*, London: Sidgwick & Jackson.

Hamburg, E. (ed.) (1996) *Nixon: An Oliver Stone Film*, London: Bloomsbury.

Hart, J. (1994) 'The Presidency in the 1990s', in G. Peele, C. Bailey, B. Cain and B Peters, (eds), *Developments in American Politics 2*, London: Macmillan.

Hartz, L. (1955) *The Liberal Tradition in America*, New York: Harcourt Brace Jovanovich.

Hartz, L. (1968) 'The Nature of Revolution', *Senate Committee on Foreign Relations, 90th Congress 2nd Session*, Washington DC: US Government Printing Office.

Heinrichs, W. (1994) 'Lyndon Johnson: Change and Continuity', in W. Cohen and N. Tucker (eds), *Lyndon Johnson Confronts the World*, New York: Cambridge University Press.

Hellmann, J. (1986) *American Myth and the Legacy of Vietnam*, New York: Columbia University Press.

Hellmann, J. (1997) *The Kennedy Obsession: The American Myth of JFK*, New York: Columbia University Press.

Henderson, W. (1957) 'South Viet Nam Finds Itself', *Foreign Affairs*, vol. 35, no. 2, pp. 283–94.

Herr, M. (1987) *Dispatches*, London: Picador.

Herring, G. (1991) 'America and Vietnam: The Unending War', *Foreign Affairs*, vol. 70, no. 5, pp. 104–19.

Hinckley, B. (1990) *The Symbolic Presidency*, New York: Routledge.

Hofstadter, R. (1957) *The American Political Tradition*, New York: Alfred A. Knopf.

Hopkins, T. (ed.) (1964) *Rights for Americans: The Speeches of Robert F. Kennedy*, New York: The Bobbs-Merrill Co.

Hosenball, M. (1992) 'The Odd Couple', *New Republic*, 1 June.

Huizinga, J. (1955) *Homo Ludens: A Study of the Play Element in Culture*, Boston: Beacon Press.

Johnson, H. (1991) *Sleepwalking through History*, New York: W. W. Norton & Co.

Johnson, L. (1971) *The Vantage Point: Perspectives of the Presidency 1963–1969*, New York: Holt, Reinhart & Winston.

Johnston, W. (1990) 'Containment and Vietnam', in J. Moore (ed.), *The Vietnam Debate: A Fresh Look at the Arguments*, Maryland: University Press of America.

Jung, C. G. (1964) 'The Fight with the Shadow', in H. Read, M. Fordhamd and G. Adler (eds.), *Civilisation in Transition: Collected Works*, vol. 10, London: Routledge & Kegan Paul.

Jungk, R. (1959) *Brighter than a Thousand Suns: The Moral and Political History of the Atomic Scientists*, London: Gollancz.

Kaldor, M. (1986) 'Introduction', in E. P. Thompson and M. Kaldor, *Mad Dogs: The US Raids on Libya*, London: Pluto Press.

Karnow, S. (1991) *Vietnam: A History*, Harmondsworth: Penguin.

Kearns, D. (1976) *Lyndon Johnson and the American Dream*, New York: Harper & Row.

Kellerman, B. and Barrilleaux, R. (1991) *The President as World Leader*, New York: St Martin's Press.

Kennan, G. (1987) 'The Sources of Soviet Conduct', reprinted in *Foreign Affairs*, vol. 65, no. 4: Containment 40 Years Later, pp. 852–68.

Kennedy, J. F. (1961) *Profiles in Courage*, New York: Harper & Brothers.

Kimball, W. (1990) *To Reason Why: The Debate about US Involvement in the Vietnam War*, New York: McGraw-Hill.

Kirk, R. (1992) *The Roots of American Order*, Washington DC: Regnery Gateway.

Kissinger, H. (1979) *White House Years*, Boston: Little, Brown & Co.

Klare, M. (1981) *Beyond the Vietnam Syndrome*, Washington DC: Institute for Policy Studies.

Knockton, J. (1991) 'Vietnamese Social Conflict and the Vietnam War', in P. Melling, and J. Roper, (eds) *America, France and Vietnam: Cultural History and Ideas of Conflict*, Aldershot: Avebury.

Kraus, S. (ed.), (1977) *The Great Debates: Kennedy vs. Nixon, 1960*, Bloomington: Indiana University Press.

Krauthammer, C. (1991) 'Good Morning Vietnam: The Syndrome Returns, Courtesy of George Bush', *The Washington Post*, 19 April.

Krauthammer, C. (1997) 'The End of Heroism', *Time* (European edition), 10 February.

Lam, A. (1990) 'My Vietnam, My America', *Nation*, 10 December.

Lasch, C. (1978) *The Culture of Narcissism*, New York: W. W. Norton & Co.

Lea, F. (1972) *The Tragic Philosopher: A Study of Friedrich Nietzsche*, London: Methuen & Co.

Lederer, W. and Burdick, E. (1958) *The Ugly American*, New York: Norton.

Lee, E. (1968) 'The Turner Thesis Re-examined', in R. Hofstadter and S. Lipset (eds), *Turner and the Sociology of the Frontier*, New York: Basic Books.

Levy, D. (1991) *The Debate over Vietnam*, Baltimore: The Johns Hopkins University Press.

Levy, M. (1982) *Political Thought in America: An Anthology*, Illinois: The Dorsey Press.

Liebovich, L. (1998), *The Press and the Modern Presidency*, Westport: Praeger.

McCarthy, M. (1973) *The Mask of State: Watergate Portraits*, New York: Harcourt Brace Jovanovich.

McKeever, R. (1989) 'American Myths and the Impact of the Vietnam War: Revisionism in Foreign Policy and Popular Cinema in the 1980s', in J. Walsh and J. Aulich (eds), *Vietnam Images*, Basingstoke: Macmillan.

Maclear, M. (1981) *Vietnam: The 10,000 Day War*, London: Eyre Methuen.

MacPherson, M. (1985) *Long Time Passing: Vietnam and the Haunted Generation*, New York: Signet.

McMahon, R. (ed.), (1990) *Major Problems in the History of the Vietnam War*, Lexington, Mass.: D. C. Heath & Co.

McNamara, R. (1995) *In Retrospect: The Tragedy and Lessons of Vietnam*, New York: Random House.

McNeill, W. (1982) 'The Care and Repair of Public Myth', *Foreign Affairs*, vol. 61, pp. 1–13.

McQuaid, K. (1989) *The Anxious Years,* New York: Basic Books.

Mailer, N. (1948) *The Naked and the Dead*, New York: Holt, Reinhart & Wilson.

Mailer, N. (1969) *Why Are We in Vietnam?*, London: Weidenfeld & Nicolson.

Mailer, N. (1971) '*Playboy* Interview', in R. Lucid (ed.), *Norman Mailer: The Man and His Work*, Boston: Little, Brown & Co.

Mailer, N. (1976) 'Superman Comes to the Supermarket', in his *Some Honorable Men*, Boston: Little, Brown & Co.

Mailer, N. (1995) *Oswald's Tale: An American Mystery*, Boston: Little, Brown & Co.

Mailer, N. (1998) 'Clinton and Dole', in his *The Time of Our Time*, London: Little, Brown & Co.

Mailer, N. (1998) 'How the Wimp Won the War', in his *The Time of Our Time*, London: Little, Brown & Co.

Mailer, N. (1998) 'Miami and the Siege of Chicago', in his *The Time of Our Time*, London: Little, Brown & Co.

Mailer, N. (1998) 'The White Negro: Superficial Reflections on the Hipster', in his *The Time of Our Time*, London: Little Brown & Co.

Manchester, W. (1983) *One Brief Shining Moment: Remembering Kennedy*, Boston: Little, Brown & Co.

Mandelbaum, M. (1996), 'Foreign Policy as Social Work', *Foreign Affairs*, vol. 75, no. 1, pp. 16–32.

Manso, P. (1985) *Mailer: His Life and Times*, New York: Simon & Schuster.

Maraniss, D. (1995) *First in His Class: A Biography of Bill Clinton*, New York: Simon & Schuster.

Mause, L. de (1991) 'The Gulf War as Mental Disorder', *Nation*, 11 March.

Mazlish, B. (1990) *The Leader and the Led and the Psyche: Essays in Psychohistory*, Middleton, Conn.: Wesleyan University Press.

Messenger, C. (1981) *Sport and the Spirit of Play in American Fiction*, New York: Columbia University Press.

Meyer, P. (1978) *James Earl Carter: The Man and The Myth*, Kansas City: Sheed Andrews & McMeel.

Molina, F. (1962) *Existentialism as Philosophy*, Englewood Cliffs, NJ: Prentice-Hall.

Moore, J. (ed.) (1990) *The Vietnam Debate: A Fresh Look at the Arguments*, Lanham, MD: University Press of America.

Morris, C. (1984) *A Time of Passion: America 1960–1980*, New York: Harper & Row.

Morrison, T. (1998) 'The Talk of the Town', *The New Yorker*, 5 October.

Morrow, L. (1999) 'Why I'm Still Angry', *Time*, 22 February.

Niebuhr, R. and Heimert, J. (1963) *A Nation So Conceived*, New York: Scribner's Sons.

Nevins, A. (1961) Introduction to J. F. Kennedy, *Profiles in Courage*, New York: Harper & Brothers.

Nietzsche, F. (1993) 'On the Uses and Disadvantages of History for Life', in R. Schacht (ed.), *Nietzsche: Selections*, New York: Macmillan.

Nixon, R. (1968) *Six Crises*, New York: Pyramid Books.

Nixon, R. (1978) *RN: The Memoirs of Richard Nixon*, New York: Grossat & Dunlap.

Novick, P. (1988) *That Noble Dream: The 'Objectivity Question' and the American Historical Profession*, Cambridge: Cambridge University Press.

O'Donnell, K. and Power, D. (1970) *Johnny We Hardly Knew Ye*, Boston: Little, Brown & Co.

Omestad, T. (1992–3) 'Why Bush Lost', *Foreign Policy*, vol. 89, pp. 70–81.

Osgood, R. (1981) 'The Revitalization of Containment', *Foreign Affairs*, vol. 60, no. 3, pp. 465–502.

Pilger, J. (1986) 'Bobby'; 'A Noble Cause', in his *Heroes*, London: Pan Books.

Pilger, J. (1992) 'Sins of Omission'; 'Turkey Shoots'; 'New Age Imperialism', in his *Distant Voices*, London: Vintage.

Pocock, J. (1975) *The Machiavellian Moment*, Princeton: Princeton University Press.

Podhoretz, N. (1971) 'Norman Mailer: The Embattled Vision', in R. Lucid (ed.), *Norman Mailer: The Man and His Work*, Boston: Little, Brown & Co.

Podhoretz, N. (1982) *Why We Were in Vietnam*, New York: Simon & Schuster.

Polenberg, R. (1980) *One Nation Divisible*, Harmondsworth: Penguin.

Powell, M. (1999) 'For Democrats a Defining Moment', *Washington Post*, 8 February.

Price, R. (1977) *With Nixon*, New York: The Viking Press.

Public Papers of the Presidents of the United States: John F. Kennedy (1961–4), Washington DC: US Government Printing Office.

Public Papers of the Presidents: Lyndon B. Johnson (1965–70), Washington DC: United States Government Printing Office.

Public Papers of the Presidents, Richard Nixon (1971–5), Washington DC: United States Government Printing Office.

Raskin, M. (1992) '*JFK* and the Culture of Violence', *American Historical Review*, vol. 97, no. 2, pp. 487–99.

Reedy, G. (1970) *The Twilight of the Presidency*, New York: The New American Library.

Roazen, P. (1986) *Freud: Political and Social Thought*, New York: Da Capo Press.

Roelofs, H. M. (1976) *Ideology and Myth in American Politics*, Boston: Little, Brown & Co.

Roth, P. (1971) *Our Gang*, London: Jonathan Cape.

Schacht, R. (1983) *Nietzsche*, London: Routledge & Kegan Paul.

Schlesinger jr., A. (1948–9) 'Review of Richard Hofstadter, The American Political Tradition', *American Historical Review*, vol. 54, no. 3, pp. 612–13.

Schlesinger jr., A. (1949) *The Vital Center*, Boston: Houghton Mifflin.

Schlesinger jr., A. (1960) 'On Heroic Leadership and the Dilemma of Strong Men and Weak Peoples', *Encounter*, vol. 15, no. 6, pp. 3–11.

Schlesinger jr., A. (1965) *A Thousand Days: John F. Kennedy in the White House*, London: André Deutsch.

Schlesinger jr., A. (1968) *The Bitter Heritage: Vietnam and American Democracy, 1941–1966*, Greenwich: Fawcett.

Schlesinger jr., A. (1978) *Robert Kennedy and His Times*, Boston: Houghton Mifflin.

Schlesinger jr., A. (1989) *The Imperial Presidency*, Boston: Houghton Mifflin.

Schlesinger jr., A. (1991) *The Disuniting of America*, New York: W. W. Norton & Co.

Schlesinger jr. A. (1998) 'On JFK: An Interview with Isaiah Berlin', *The New York Review of Books*, 22 October.

Schneider, W. (1987) ' "Rambo" and Reality: Having It Both Ways', in K. Oye, R. Lieber and D. Rothchild, (Eds.), *Eagle Resurgent?: The Reagan Era in American Foreign Policy*, Boston: Little, Brown & Co.

Sheehan, N. (1989) *A Bright Shining Lie: John Paul Vann and America in Vietnam*, London: Jonathan Cape.

Sidey, H. (1968) *A Very Personal Presidency*, London: André Deustch.

Slotkin, R. (1993) *Gunfighter Nation*, New York: HarperCollins.

Smith, H. Nash (1950) *Virgin Land*, New York: Random House.

Smith, H.Nash (1986) 'Symbol and Idea in Virgin Land', in S. Bercovitch and M. Jehlen, (eds.), *Ideology and Classic American Literature*, Cambridge: Cambridge University Press.

Solotaroff, R. (1974) *Down Mailer's Way*, Urbana: University of Illinois Press.

Sorensen, T. (1965) *Kennedy*, New York: Harper & Row.

Sorensen, T. (1975) *Watchmen in the Night: Presidential Accountability after Watergate*, Cambridge, Mass.: The MIT Press.

Spencer, D. (1988) *The Carter Implosion*, New York: Praeger.

Stack, G. (1992) *Nietzsche and Emerson: An Elective Affinity*, Athens: Ohio University Press.

Stourzh, G. and Lerner, R. (1959) *Readings in American Democracy*, New York: Oxford University Press.

Summers, H. (1981) *On Strategy: The Vietnam War in Context*, Pennsylvania: US Army War College.

Summers, H. (1987) 'Palmer, Karnow and Herrington: A Review of Recent Vietnam War Histories', in L. Matthews and D. Brown, (eds), *Assessing the Vietnam War*, Washington: Pergamon Group.

Talbott, S. (1992) 'Post-Victory Blues', *Foreign Affairs*, vol. 71, no.1 pp. 53–69.

Talbott, S. (1994) 'The New Geopolitics: Defending Democracy in the Post Cold-War Era', London: US Information Service.

Tanenhaus, S. (1997) *Whittaker Chambers: A Biography*, New York: Random House.

Timmerman, D. (1996) '1992 Presidential Candidate Films: The Contrasting Narratives of George Bush and Bill Clinton', *Presidential Studies Quarterly*, vol. 26, no. 2, pp. 364–73.

Tocqueville, A. de (1945) *Democracy in America*, 2 vols New York: Vintage Books edition, vol. 1.

Tuchman, B. (1990) *The March of Folly*, London: Sphere.

Tucker, R. (1989) 'Reagan's Foreign Policy', *Foreign Affairs*, vol. 68, no. 1, pp. 1–17.

Turner, B. (1992) *Max Weber: From History to Modernity*, London: Routledge.

Turner, F. J. (1920) *The Frontier in American History*, New York: Henry Holt & Co.

Turner, F. J. (1920) 'Significance of the Frontier in American History' in *F. J. Turner, The Frontier in American History*, New York: Henry Holt & Co., pp. 1–38.

Turner, F. J. (1942) 'International Political Parties in a Durable League of Nations', reprinted in the *American Historical Review*, vol. 47, no. 3, pp. 545–51.

Updike, J. (1979) *The Coup*, London: André Deustch.

VanDeMark, B. (1991) *Into the Quagmire: Lyndon Johnson and the Escalation of the Vietnam War*, New York: Oxford University Press.

Vlastos, S. (1991) 'America's "enemy": the Absent Presence in Revisionist Vietnam War History', in J. Rowe and R. Berg (eds.), *The Vietnam War and American Culture*, New York: Columbia University Press.

Wallerstein, I. (1987) 'The Reagan Non-Revolution, or the Limited Choices of the US', *Millennium: Journal of International Studies*, vol. 16, no. 3, pp. 467–72.

Warner, D. (1963) *The Last Confucian*, Harmondsworth: Penguin.

Warner, M. (1987) 'Bush Battles the "Wimp Factor"', *Newsweek*, vol. 110, 19 October, pp. 28–36.

Weiler, M. and Pearce, W. B. (1992) 'Ceremonial Discourse: The Rhetorical Ecology of the Reagan Administration', in M. Weiler and W. B. Pearce (eds), *Reagan and Public Discourse in America*, Tuscaloosa: University of Alabama Press.

Westmoreland, W. (1990) 'Vietnam in Perspective', in P. J. Hearden, (ed.), *Vietnam: Four American Perspectives*, Indiana: Purdue University Press.

White, T. (1968) *The Making of the President, 1964*, London: Jonathan Cape.

White, T. (1975) *Breach of Faith*, New York: Atheneum Publishers.

White, T. (1983) *America in Search of Itself*, New York: Warner Books.

Whitman, W. (1964) 'The Eighteenth Presidency', in C. Furness (ed.), *Walt Whitman's Workshop*, New York: Russell & Russell.

Whitman, W. (1982) 'Democratic Vistas', in M. van Doren (ed.), *The Portable Walt Whitman*, Harmondsworth: Penguin.

Wicker, T. (1995) *One of Us: Richard Nixon and the American Dream*, New York: Random House.

Wilkinson, R. (ed.), (1992) *American Social Character: Modern Interpretations*, New York: HarperCollins.

Williams, W. A. (1980) *Empire as a Way of Life*, Oxford: Oxford University Press.

Williams, W. A. (1991) 'Vietnam and the Revival of an Anti-Imperial Mood?' in P. Melling and J. Roper (eds), *America, France and Vietnam: Cultural History and Ideas of Conflict*, Aldershot: Avebury.

Wills, G. (1987) *Reagan's America: Innocents at Home*, New York: Doubleday & Co.

Wills, G. (1990) *Nixon Agonistes*, Atlanta: Cherokee Publishing Co.

Winkler, A. (1993) *Life under a Cloud*, New York: Oxford University Press.

Wolfe, T. (1979) *The Right Stuff*, London: Jonathan Cape.

Woodward, B. and Bernstein, C. (1976) *The Final Days*, New York: Simon & Schuster.

Index

Abrahamson, David, 107
Absolute Power (film), 210, 212
Adams, John Quincy, 45
Agnew, Spiro, 116
  Air Force One (film), 213
Aitken, Jonathan, 108
Aldridge, John, 80, 81, 82, 83, 170
All the President's Men (film),
  211, 212
Altman, Robert, 129
Ambrose, Stephen, 92, 98, 110
American Dream, An (Mailer), 13
American Hero (Beinhart), 207–8
American Political Tradition, The
  (Hofstadter), 16, 17–20, 41
'Apocalypse Now'
  (memorandum), 129
Arthur, Chester, 220
Atwater, Lee, 207

Back to the Future (film), 138, 155
Backroom Boys, The (Chomsky), 54
Bagehot, Walter, 34
Baker, James, 162
Ball, George, 50, 54, 55
Barnet, Richard, 128
Bass, Jeff, 143, 149
Beinhart, Larry, 207, 208
Benton, Thomas Hart, 45
Bentsen, Lloyd, 161
Berlin, Isaiah, 4, 5
Bernstein, Carl, 108, 212

Beschloss, Michael, 69
Betts, Richard, 147
Billington, Ray, 33, 34
Billy the Kid, 1
Bitter Heritage, The (Schlesinger),
  72
Bonazzi, Tiziano, 33, 35
Boorstin, Daniel, 10, 16, 17, 20,
  21, 23, 215
Bosnia, 197
Brace, Paul, 219
Brammer, Billy Lee, 80
Brodie, Bernard, 72, 73, 105, 211
Brodie, Fawn, 105, 106, 107, 108
Brown, Thomas, 51
Brownson, Orestes, 133
Bryan, William Jennings, 19
Brzezinski, Zbigniewi, 83
Bullitt, William, 75
Burdick, Eugene, 54, 68, 69
Burns, James McGregor, 63
Bush, George, 159, 162, 170, 196,
  197, 198, 213
  Clinton, Bill and, 175–7, 179,
    182, 185–6, 190, 191, 222
  confronts 'Vietnam Syndrome',
    161, 166, 169, 172–3, 174–5,
    177–80, 217, 221
  Gulf War and, 165–9, 207, 217,
    221
  as heroic leader, 12, 165, 179,
    218

Inaugural Address (1989), 161
Saddam Hussein and, 12, 165–7, 173–4, 178–9, 222
State of the Union Address (1990), 165
Vietnam and, 161, 164–9, 171–9, 190, 218
'wimp factor', 159–60, 161, 171

Caddell, Pat, 129
Calhoun, John, 18
Cambodia, 97, 148, 176
Campbell, Joseph, 83, 154
Carlyle, Thomas, 2, 219
Carter, Jimmy, 11, 115, 124, 133, 139, 141, 160, 209
diagnoses contemporary 'malaise', 116, 129–31, 221
human rights, 127, 197
Inaugural Address (1976), 127, 142
as moral leader, 125–7, 140
Vietnam and, 125–34, 148, 189, 217
'Vietnam Syndrome' and, 116, 131
Watergate and, 124–7, 130, 132, 217
Cassirer, Ernst, 48, 219
Castro, Fidel, 198
Caute, David, 8
Chambers, Whittaker, 94, 95
China, 10, 59, 61, 69, 70, 71, 101, 103, 159
Chomsky, Noam, 54
Churchill, Winston, 2, 59
Civilization and its Discontents (Freud), 153
Clifford, Clark, 145
Clinton, Bill, 2, 173, 192, 199, 200, 201, 208, 210, 213, 220, 221
Bush, George and, 12, 175–7, 179, 185–6, 190, 191, 222
first term foreign policy, 194–8
impeachment, 119, 155, 202–5, 219

Inaugural Address (1993), 191
Inaugural Address (1997), 202
Kennedy, John F. and, 1, 12, 13–14, 182, 187, 194, 198, 208, 209, 219, 222, 223
Nixon, Richard and, 176–7, 183, 191, 202
Vietnam and, 101, 182–7, 202, 204–5, 217, 219
as 'white negro', 222–3
Clinton, Hillary, 202, 210
Combs, James, 138
Congressional Quarterly, 175
Corbett, Jim see Gentleman Jim
Costner, Kevin, 212
Coup, The, (Updike), 124
Crèvecœur, H. St John de, 10, 23, 28, 29, 30
Cronin, John, 95
Cuba, 4, 10, 68
Culture of Narcissism, The (Lasch), 132

Daily Telegraph, 119
Dallas (TV series), 138, 210
Dallek, Robert, 67
Day of the Locust, The (West), 140
de Crèvecoeur, H. St. John see Crèvecoeur
de Gaulle, Charles see Gaulle
de Grazia, Alfred see Grazia
de Mause, Lloyd see Mause
de Niro, Robert see Niro
de Tocqueville, Alexis see Tocqueville
Deer Park, The (Mailer), 43
Degler, Carl, 144
Dempsey, Jack, 1, 139
Diem, Ngo Dinh see Ngo Dinh Diem
Dien Bien Phu, 51, 52
Diggins, J. P., 27
Dispatches (Herr), 170
Dobrynin, Anatoly, 104
Doctorow, E. L., 176

Dole, Bob, 190
Dos Passos, John, 16
Dr. Strangelove (film), 68, 69
Drive for Power, The
    (Hutschnecker), 106
Dugger, Ronnie, 79
Dukakis, Michael, 160, 161
Dulles, John Foster, 57
Dumbrell, John, 127

Eagleton, Thomas, 107
Efaw, Fritz, 128
Eisenhower, Dwight D., 2, 5, 42,
    82, 84, 156, 209, 218
  as anti-imperial leader, 189
  as hero, 3, 4, 123, 216
  Inaugural Address (1953), 6
  Nixon, Richard and, 93, 101,
    160
  poker and, 110
  Vietnam and, 51, 56, 57
El Salvador, 153, 154
Eliot, T. S., 50
Ellsberg, Daniel, 103, 104, 105,
Emerson, Ralph Waldo, 13, 62, 63
Emerson, Rupert, 56
Emery, Fred, 108
Encounter, 61
End of History and the Last Man,
    The (Fukuyama), 213
Engelhardt, Tom, 8, 103, 104
English Patient, The (film), 199
'Erosion of Democracy, The'
    (Emerson), 56
Evans, Harold, 137
Evita (film), 199

Fail Safe (film), 68
Fairlie, Henry, 63
'Fight with the Shadow, The'
    (Jung), 82
Fillmore, Millard, 220
Final Days, The (Woodward and
    Bernstein), 108
Fire in the Lake (FitzGerald), 51
Fishel, Wesley, 58

Fisher, Walter, 4
Fiske, Robert, jr., 203
FitzGerald, Frances, 51, 57, 58
Fonda, Henry, 68
Ford, Gerald, 129, 132, 136, 159,
    209
  Lincoln, Abraham and, 11, 116,
    117, 118, 120, 121, 123, 221
  as moral leader, 124
  Nixon's pardon and, 115, 118–
    20, 121
  State of the Union Address
    (1976), 123
  Vietnam and, 115–24, 132, 189,
    217
  Watergate and, 112, 117, 119–
    21, 123–4, 221
Ford, Harrison, 213
Ford, Henry, 132
Foreign Affairs, 32, 55, 140, 141,
    173, 196
Forrest Gump (film), 199, 200–2
Foster, Jodie, 139
Foster, Richard, 47
Foster, Vince, 203
France, 50, 52
Frazer, J. G., 82
Freud, Sigmund, 83, 105, 107,
    109, 176, 211
  Civilisation and its Discontents,
    153
  'delusional transformation of
    reality', 153, 154, 173
  Oedipus complex, 75, 84
  Totem and Taboo, 82
Frielander, Saul, 80
Fukuyama, Frances, 162, 163,
    164, 195, 198, 213
Fulbright, William J., 184

Gaffney, Frank, 173
Gaulle, Charles de, 2, 50, 51, 67,
    78, 108
Galbraith, John Kenneth, 72
Garfield, James, 2
Gay Place, The (Brammer), 80

Gelb, Leslie, 147
Genius of American Politics
(Boorstin), 17, 20–2
Gentleman Jim (Corbett), 1
Germany, 14, 16, 162, 167
Germond, Jack, 159
Gibson, William, 54, 132, 149
Gingrich, Newt, 202, 210
Glaspie, April, 171
Godden, Richard, 81
Goldwater, Barry, 69, 70, 103,
136, 156, 160
Goodwin, Richard, 72, 73, 74
Graebner, William, 7
Graham, Katherine, 160
Grazia, Alfred de, 4
Greece, 59
Greene, John, 118, 122, 124
Greenstein, Fred, 191
Grenada, 152, 169
Grund, Francis, 31
Guevara, Che, 184
Gulf War, 12, 161, 179, 198, 208,
213, 218
Bush, George and, 165–9, 207,
217, 221
Vietnam and, 168–9 170, 174
'Vietnam Syndrome' and, 162,
166, 171, 172–3, 175, 177

Hackman, Gene, 212
Hagman, Larry, 210
Haiti, 197
Halberstam, David, 53, 55, 57, 58,
60, 68, 74, 218
Haldeman, Bob, 100, 104, 107
Hall, Arsenio, 223
Hamilton, Alexander, 24
Harlot's Ghost (Mailer), 13
Hart, John, 193
Hartz, Louis, 16, 27, 34, 36, 164,
189, 215
*The Liberal Tradition in
America*, 9, 17, 23–6
'The Nature of Revolution', 26
Heimert, Alan, 37

Hellmann, John, 37, 48, 49, 64, 211
Hemingway, Ernest, 1, 44
Henderson, William, 55, 56
Heroes (Pilger), 87
Herr, Michael, 170
Herring, George, 167, 174, 178
Hickel, Walter, 111
Hinckley, Barbara, 151, 219
Hinckley, John, 139, 140
Hiss, Alger, 93, 94, 95, 96
History and Psychology
(Frielander), 80
Hitler, Adolf, 2, 165, 167
Ho Chi Minh, 4, 55, 104, 147, 165
Hobbes, Thomas, 199
Hofstadter, Richard, 10, 16, 17,
18, 19, 36, 68, 214
Holmes, Eugene, 182, 183, 184
Hoover, Herbert, 19, 116
Hosenball, Mark, 171
House Committee on Un-
American Activities, 20, 21,
94, 95
House Judiciary Committee, 203
Houston, Sam, 45
Huizinga, Johan, 110, 111
Humphrey, Hubert, 88
Hussein, Saddam *see* Saddam
Hussein
Hutschnecker, Arnold, 106

Imperial Presidency, The
(Schlesinger), 100
Independence Day (film), 210, 213
Iran, 10, 125, 131, 152, 171
Irangate, 152, 154, 155, 162, 219,
221
Iraq, 168, 169, 172, 173, 174, 178
invasion of Kuwait, 161, 165,
167, 170, 171

Jackson, Andrew, 18, 19
Japan, 3
Jefferson, Thomas, 1, 18–19, 25,
26, 36, 45, 146, 218
JFK (film), 209, 210, 211–12

Johnson, Andrew, 45
Johnson, Haynes, 138, 139, 154, 160
Johnson, Lyndon, 11, 48, 83, 84, 98, 100, 108, 111, 115, 116, 159, 161
  election campaign (1964), 69–70, 160, 175
  as heroic leader, 10
  Kearns, Doris and, 74–7, 78, 82, 105
  Kennedy, John F. and, 2, 11, 51, 59–60, 67, 70, 73, 81, 191, 194, 198, 209, 221
  Kennedy, Robert and, 87–8
  mental health questioned, 68, 72–4, 77, 86, 109
  Nixon, Richard and, 101, 103, 112
  resignation, 71, 82, 85–6
  style of leadership, 79
  Vietnam and, 9, 59–61, 67–8, 71–7, 80–6, 102, 103, 109, 111–12, 117, 126, 156, 176, 217, 220
Jones, Paula, 203, 204
Jordan, Vernon, 119
Jung, Carl-Gustav, 82

Kaldor, Mary, 149
Karnow, Stanley, 51, 144, 145, 147
Kearns, Doris, 73, 74, 78, 82, 105
  Lyndon Johnson and the American Dream, 75–7
Kennan, George, 32
Kennedy, John F., 7, 13, 27, 68, 86, 93, 99, 110, 111, 116, 156, 161, 218
  assassination, 2, 64, 73, 79, 82, 84, 105, 117, 138–9, 170, 209, 210–12, 216, 217, 220
  Clinton, Bill and, 1, 13–14, 182, 187, 208, 219, 222, 223
  as heroic leader, 1, 2, 4, 5, 61–4, 98, 103, 115, 151, 208, 216, 220

Inaugural Address (1961), 49, 62–3, 216
JFK (film), 209, 210, 211–12
  Johnson, Lyndon and, 2, 11, 51, 59–60, 67, 70, 73, 81, 191, 194, 198, 209, 221
  Kennedy, Robert and, 87–8
  Mailer, Norman and, 1, 10, 13, 42–4, 47, 152, 208–9
  New Frontier, 10, 38, 47–50, 64, 140, 213
  Nixon, Richard and, 47, 91–2, 94, 97, 105, 108, 209, 221
  Profiles in Courage, 44–6, 48, 61, 92
  Reagan, Ronald and, 137, 138–9, 140, 141, 147, 151, 208, 209, 213
  State of the Union Address (1961), 63
  State of the Union Address (1963), 60
  Vietnam and, 5, 8, 10, 49, 50–4, 57–61, 63, 68, 72–3, 78, 81, 102, 111, 147, 211, 216–18, 220
Kennedy, Robert, 51, 73, 82, 87–8, 99, 105, 106, 108, 220
Kennedy (Sorensen), 59–60
Khrushchev, Nikita, 4, 5, 50, 61, 68, 93, 96, 110, 165
King, Martin Luther, 46, 82, 201, 202
Kirk, Russell, 133
Kissinger, Henry, 72, 103, 104, 149
Klare, Michael, 131
Korea, 59, 82
  Korean War, 71, 79, 101, 189
Kovic, Ron, 128
Krauthammer, Charles, 173, 198, 199
Kubrick, Stanley, 68
Kuwait, 19, 166, 168, 173, 174, 178
  Iraq's invasion of, 161, 165, 167, 170, 171

Lamar, Lucius, 45
Laos, 148
Lasch, Christopher, 132, 133
Lederer, William, 54
Lenin, Vladimir, 2
Letters from an American Farmer
(Crèvecœur), 28–30
Lewinsky, Monica, 202, 203, 204,
210
Liberal Tradition in America, The
(Hartz), 9, 17, 23–6
Libya, 149, 169
Liebovich, Louis, 187
Lincoln, Abraham, 2, 108, 129,
130, 142, 179, 180, 186
Ford, Gerald and, 11, 116, 117,
118, 120, 121, 123, 221
Gettysburg Address, 63, 81
as heroic leader, 1, 18, 218,
220
as 'Redeemer President'
(Whitman), 42
Locke, John, 24, 37, 62, 199
Lodge, Henry Cabot, 84
London, Jack, 1
Lone Star Rising (Dallek), 67
Louis, Joe, 1
*Lyndon Johnson and the American
Dream* (Kearns), 74, 75–7
Lyotard, Jean-François, 9

McCarthy, Eugene, 73
McCarthy, Joe, 44, 46, 57, 95,
154
McCarthy, Mary, 100
McCurry, Mike, 210, 211
McGovern, George, 107, 160
McKeever, Robert, 140
McKinley, William, 2
Maclear, Michael, 51, 78, 82
McNamara, Robert, 60, 67, 72,
81
McNeill, William, 140, 141
MacPherson, Myra, 119, 122
McQuaid, Kim, 100, 109
Madison, James, 49

Mailer, Barbara, 13
Mailer, Norman, 10, 13, 49, 50,
61, 152, 153–4, 170, 219
Deer Park, The, 43
Naked and the Dead, The, 41,
43
'Superman Comes to the
Supermarket', 1–2, 4, 43–4,
47
'White Negro, The', 215–16,
222–3
Why Are We in Vietnam?, 80,
83–5
Making of the President (White),
223
Manchester, William, 2
Mandelbaum, Michael, 196, 197
Mansfield, Mike, 56, 102
Mao Tse Tung, 4, 165
Maraniss, David, 183, 184
Marx, Karl, 6, 7, 18, 23, 25, 163,
214
Mause, Lloyd de, 170
Mayaguez, 122
Mayflower, 36
Mazlish, Bruce, 107
Melville, Herman, 9
Messenger, Christian, 109
Mexico, 153
Meyer, Peter, 126
Minh, Ho Chi *see* Ho Chi Minh
Mission Impossible (TV series),
15n
Mondale, Walter, 160
Monroe, Marilyn, 209
Morris, Charles, 61
Morrison, Toni, 222
Moyers, Bill, 72, 73, 74
Muller, Bobby, 146
Murrow, Edward, 7

Naked and the Dead, The (Mailer),
41, 43
Nashville (film), 129
Nation, The, 148, 170, 208
National Interest, The, 162

Nevins, Allan, 48
New Frontier, 2, 14, 44, 50, 52, 86, 87, 112, 140
  Kennedy, John F. and, 10, 38, 42, 47–50, 64, 220
New Republic, The, 170, 171
New World Order, 165, 179, 193
New York Times, The, 60, 104
New Yorker, The, 222
Newsweek, 159, 160
Ngo Dinh Diem, 55–60, 216
Nguyen Van Thieu, 121
Nicaragua, 152 , 153, 154
Niebuhr, Reinhold, 37, 125

Nietzsche, Friedrich, 83, 126, 143, 146, 148
  Kennedy, John F. as Nietzschean hero, 10, 41–3, 49, 61–4
Niro, Robert de, 139
Nixon (Aitken), 108
Nixon (film), 107–8, 210, 212
Nixon, Richard, 71, 84, 88, 136, 146, 155, 160, 211, 212, 218
  Clinton, Bill and, 176–7, 183, 191, 202
  Ford, Gerald and, 115, 118–20, 121
  Kennedy, John F. and, 47, 91–2, 94, 97, 105, 209, 221
  mental health questioned, 68, 103–4, 105–7, 108–9, 112
  poker and, 95, 96–7, 110
  'silent majority', 102, 201
  Six Crises, 91–7, 110, 112
  Vietnam and, 9, 51, 97–8, 100, 101–3, 109, 111–12, 124, 126, 132, 152, 176, 217
  Watergate and, 11, 97–8, 100, 104–5, 107–9, 111–12, 115–16, 119, 124, 126, 152, 161, 176, 217, 218
Nixon, Tricia, 97
Noriega, Manuel, 165, 171
Norris, George, 46

North, Oliver, 152
Novick, Peter, 16, 120

Oates, Stephen, 67
Oedipus complex, 75, 84
Omestad, Thomas, 174
On Heroes (Carlyle), 2
Osgood, Robert, 141
Oswald, Lee Harvey, 140
Our Gang (Roth), 111–12
O'Neill, Owen Roe, 87

Paine, Tom, 142, 169
Panama, 165, 169
Pentagon Papers, 104
People versus Larry Flint, The (film), 199
Perot, Ross, 171
Peru, 95
Phillips, Wendell, 18
Physics and Politics (Bagehot), 34
Pierce, Franklin, 220
Pilger, John, 87, 145, 146, 147, 169, 171
Platoon (film), 145
Playboy, 127
Pocock, J. G. A, 12, 37
Podhoretz, Norman, 43, 147, 148
Poland, 165, 167
Polenberg, Richard, 131
'Political Uses of Madness, The' (Ellsberg), 103
post traumatic stress disorder, 149, 170
'Post Victory Blues', Talbott, 173–4
Powell, Colin, 172
Price, Ray, 107, 109
Primary Colors (Anonymous), 223
Profiles in Courage (Kennedy), 44–6, 48, 61, 92
Pullman, Bill, 213

Quayle, Dan, 160, 161, 183

Rambo (film), 154, 155
Raskin, Marcus, 211
Reagan, Nancy, 139
Reagan, Ronald, 134, 136, 149,
    169, 170, 190, 196, 201, 218
  assassination, 138–40, 221
  Bush, George and, 159, 160,
    161, 165, 171
  Farewell Address (1989), 155–6
  Inaugural Address (1981), 142,
    151
  Inaugural Address (1985), 137
  Irangate, 152, 154, 155, 162,
    219, 221
  Kennedy, John F. and, 137,
    138–9, 140, 141, 147, 151,
    208, 209, 213
  State of the Union Address
    (1986), 155
  Vietnam and, 12, 126, 138, 140–
    8, 150–3, 172, 178, 217
Reedy, George, 74, 77, 78
Reeves, Richard, 126
*Richard Nixon: The Shaping of his
  Character* (Brodie), 105–7
Rights for Americans (Hopkins), 87
Roazen, Paul, 83
Robert Kennedy and His Times
  (Schlesinger), 72
Rockwell, Norman, 151
Roosevelt, Franklin, 3, 5, 19, 99,
    110, 129, 167, 220
  Clinton, Bill and, 187, 194, 202
  as hero, 2, 218
  Johnson, Lyndon and, 71, 88
Roosevelt, Theodore, 19, 98, 115,
    218
Roots of American Order, The
  (Kirk), 133
Ross, Edmund, 45
Roth, Philip, 111, 112
Rusk, Dean, 60

Saddam Hussein, 168, 170, 171, 198
  Bush, George and, 12, 165–7,
    173–4, 178–9, 222

Saudi Arabia, 166
Schindler's List (film), 199, 200
Schlesinger, Arthur M. jr., 4, 16,
    17, 19, 28
  on Johnson, Lyndon, 72, 73–4,
    76–8, 87
  on Kennedy, John F., 43, 47,
    50, 51, 57, 60, 61–2
  on Nixon, Richard, 92, 98–9
Schlesinger, James, 117
Senate Committee on Foreign
  Relations, 26, 184
Severaid, Eric, 127
Sheehan, Neil, 52
Sidey, Hugh, 79, 80
'Significance of Frontier in
  American History, The'
  (Turner), 28, 31–3, 36
Sirhan, Sirhan, 106
Six Crises (Nixon), 91–7, 110,
    112
Slotkin, Richard, 36, 122, 128,
    141, 155
  on Kennedy, John F., 61, 62,
    63
Smith, Al, 46
Smith, Henry Nash, 30
Solotaroff, Robert, 13, 44
Somalia, 197
Sorensen, Theodore, 2, 46, 48, 51,
    59, 60, 73
'South Viet Nam Finds Itself'
  (Henderson), 55–6
Soviet Union, 3, 16, 21, 42, 67,
    137, 163, 164, 188, 215
Spencer, Donald, 129, 165
Spielberg, Steven, 146, 199, 200
Stalin, Joseph, 4
Star Wars (film), 155
Starr, Kenneth, 203, 204
Stone, Oliver, 145
  JFK (film), 209, 210, 211–12
  Nixon (film), 107–9, 210, 212
Stripling, Robert, 94
Sullivan, William, 147
Summers, Harry, 143, 147

'Superman Comes to the
      Supermarket' (Mailer), 1–2,
      4, 43–4, 47
Sutherland, Donald, 212
Swaggart, Jimmy, 204

Taft, Robert, 46
Taking Charge (Beschloss), 69
Talbott, Strobe, 173, 174, 195, 197
Taxi Driver (film), 139
terHorst, Jerry, 120
Tet offensive, 76, 79, 81
Thieu, Nguyen Van *see* Nguyen
      Van Thieu
Thomas Woodrow Wilson (Freud
      and Bullitt), 75
Thoreau, Henry David, 13
Thousand Days, A (Schlesinger),
      57
Time, 131, 198
Time to Heal, A, (Ford), 116
Timmerman, David, 218
Tocqueville, Alexis de, 4, 35
Totem and Taboo (Freud), 82
Tripp, Linda, 203
Truman, Harry, 3, 5, 6, 110
      Truman Doctrine, 3, 188
Tuchman, Barbara, 80, 97
Tucker, Robert, 143
Tunney, Gene, 139
Turner, Frederick Jackson, 10,
      21, 30, 34, 38, 67, 141, 214,
      215
   'The Significance of the
      Frontier in American
      History', 28, 31–3, 36
Twain, Mark, 1
Twilight of the Presidency, The
      (Reedy), 77

Ugly American, The (Lederer and
      Burdick), 54
Updike, John, 124, 125

Valentino, Rudolph, 1
VanDeMark, Brian, 70, 217

Venezuela, 96
Vietnam, 1, 3, 11, 13, 14, 26, 64,
      139, 149, 156, 191, 207–8,
      213
   Bush, George and, 161, 164–9,
      171–9, 190, 218
   Carter, Jimmy and, 125–34,
      148, 189, 217
   Clinton, Bill and, 101, 182–7,
      202, 204–5, 217, 219
   cold-war meta-narrative and,
      188–90
   Eisenhower, Dwight D. and, 51,
      56, 57
   Ford, Gerald and, 115–24, 132,
      189, 217
   Forrest Gump (film) and, 201–
      2
   Gulf War and, 168–9 170, 174
   impact upon presidency, 220–3
   Johnson, Lyndon and, 9, 59–61,
      67–8, 71–7, 80–6, 102, 103,
      109, 111–12, 117, 126, 156,
      176, 217, 220
   Kennedy, John F. and, 5, 8, 10,
      49, 50–4, 57–61, 63, 68, 72–3,
      78, 81, 102, 111, 147, 211,
      216–18, 220
   nation-building, 55–6
   Nixon, Richard and, 9, 51,
      97–8, 100, 101–3, 109, 111–
      12, 124, 126, 132, 152, 176,
      217
   Reagan, Ronald and, 12, 126,
      138, 140–8, 150–3, 172, 178,
      217
   Watergate and, 97, 100, 109,
      111, 119–21, 124–5, 127, 130,
      132, 138, 142, 152, 219
Vietnam: A History (Karnow), 51,
      144, 145
'Vietnam and the Revival of an
      Anti-Imperial Mood?'
      (Williams), 188–9
'Vietnam Syndrome', 12, 142–3,
      148–50, 152–4, 170–97

Bush, George, and, 161, 166, 169, 172–3, 174–5, 177–80, 217, 221
Carter, Jimmy, and, 116, 131
defined, 131
Gulf War and, 162, 166, 171, 172–3, 175, 177
Vietnam: The 10, 000 Day War (Maclear), 51
Virgin Land (Smith), 30
Vital Center, The (Schlesinger), 16
Vlastos, Stephen, 143, 169

Wag the Dog (film), 208, 210
Wallerstein, Immanuel, 152
War and Politics (Brodie), 72
Warner, David, 55
Warren Commission, 117
Washington, George, 1, 123, 218, 220
Washington Post, The, 173, 212
Washington Times, The, 173
Watergate, 112, 116, 154, 159, 203, 210, 211
Carter, Jimmy, and, 124–7, 130, 132, 217
Ford, Gerald, and, 112, 117, 119–21, 123–4, 221
Nixon, Richard, and, 11, 97–8, 100, 104–5, 107–9, 111–12, 115–16, 119, 124, 126, 152, 161, 176, 217, 218
Vietnam and, 97, 100, 109, 111, 119–21, 124–5, 127, 130, 132, 138, 142, 152, 219

Watergate: The Corruption and Fall of Richard Nixon (Emery), 108
Wattenberg, Ben, 170
Weber, Max, 98, 99
Webster, Daniel, 45
West, Nathanael, 140
Westmoreland, William, 150, 170
White, Theodore, 70, 111, 129, 130, 223
White Jacket (Melville), 9
'White Negro, The' (Mailer), 215–16, 222–3
Whitman, Walt, 13, 42, 62, 67, 117, 126, 151, 188
Why are We in Vietnam? (Mailer), 80, 83–4
Why We Were in Vietnam (Podhoretz), 147–8
Wicker, Tom, 107
Williams, William Appleman, 48, 188, 189
Wills, Garry, 92, 93, 95, 136, 137
Wilson, Gilbert, 9
Wilson, Woodrow, 19, 76, 187
Winthrop, John, 36, 141, 142
Witcover, Jules, 159
With Nixon (Price), 107
Wolfe, Tom, 49, 68
Woodward, Bob, 108, 212

Yugoslavia, 163, 167

Zapruder, Abraham, 209